Being Indian in Hueyapan

D1411590

Contents

LIST OF ILLUSTRATIONS

Figures

Tables

Songs

Photos

(Unless otherwise indicated, the photos were taken in 1969–1970)
Cover image: Corner of Calle Morelos and the San Miguel
plaza on market day in Hueyapan

PREFACE TO REVISED EDITION

When Palgrave Macmillan invited me to prepare a new edition of *Being Indian in Hueyapan*, I welcomed the chance to return to the arguments I had made several decades before. A great deal had happened over the intervening years: in the lives of the inhabitants of Hueyapan, in Mexico more generally, and in the discipline of Anthropology. Yet despite all the changes, my earlier concerns remained sadly contemporary.

When I first came to Mexico in the late 1960s, Indians, as Indians (as opposed to Indians as peasants), were major tourist attractions, and had been for decades, contributing significantly to the national economy, while remaining desperately poor themselves. Featured as living artifacts in an archeological garden, Indians drew visitors to Mexico every year who wanted to see something old and authentic. What appealed to foreigners appealed to Mexicans as well, inspiring members of the nation's elite to celebrate their country's indigenous heritage, by assigning to present-day Indians the task of representing the people who were living in Mexico at the time of the Spanish conquest.

Now, in the early years of the new millennium, tourists see Indians performing the same economic and cultural services that they did before, while continuing to live in terrible poverty. But some things are different. Today, members of indigenous communities are demanding their political and cultural rights and are doing so in impressive numbers. Rejecting negative stereotypes of themselves, they proudly embrace their identity as Indians, defining a dynamic new role for themselves in the unfolding drama of Mexico's "transition to democracy." Since 1994 and the Zapatista uprising in

Chiapas, thousands of Indians have been claiming their place as indigenous citizens of their country.

Many see this recent turn of events as a positive development, but I remain a little skeptical, for reasons discussed in a new final chapter prepared for this edition of the book. Suffice it to say here that given the history of Indians in Mexico, I worry about using identity politics as a strategy for organizing indigenous people to combat the particular forms of oppression that have plagued their communities for centuries. In the short term, however, the strategy has generated a great deal of support, largely thanks to the popularity of the EZLN (Ejército Zapatista de Liberación Nacional) and to Subcomandante Marcos, a non-Indian intellectual who has played an important role in building this indigenous movement. The EZLN has captured the imagination of people around the world and given the Indians of Mexico a voice in national debates about multiculturalism and citizenship.

With their extensive international network, the EZLN helped expose human rights abuses in Mexico, embarrassing the government to make modest changes in the way the state "managed" diversity. The movement contributed as well to the success in 2000 of a nation-wide effort to topple the PRI (Partido Institutional Revolucionario), the party that had been ruling Mexico for over 70 years. In the process, Zapatistas unintentionally strengthened the hand of Vicente Fox—the candidate for the conservative party PAN (Partido de Acción Nacional)—who eventually won the presidential elections.

In his first year in office, President Fox made indigenous affairs a high priority and got controversial legislation on the matter through congress. Carefully crafted, the new law gives Indians the right to develop their languages and cultures in unobtrusive ways that will not jeopardize the authority of the state. In its present form, the *ley indígena* seriously weakens a set of proposals presented to the government several years before as the San Andrés Accords by members of the EZLN. Responding angrily to the way the new law has been formulated, indigenous rights activists accuse the legislation of circumventing the aims of the original accords, which specifically called for political, economic, and cultural autonomy for Indians in Mexico.

This is not the place to review in detail the complex history of indigenous rights in Mexico, or to analyze the role the EZLN has played within a wider political movement. Volumes have already been written on the subject and excellent work will appear in the near future.[1] In chapter nine, however, I have updated the argument I made years ago about the influence anthropologists have had, since the days of the Mexican Revolution, in both defining the Indian problem and offering solutions to it. In that context, I discuss the ways anthropologists have supported the indigenous rights movement in recent years and the impact the movement has had on Hueyapan.

Otherwise, the book remains essentially the same.[2] With the passage of time, I continue to agree with the analysis I made of the Indian question in Mexico, but not with the advice I offered to North American and European anthropologists in chapter eight (the concluding chapter of the first edition), where I recommended that we stop doing fieldwork among peoples living in the Third World. At first, I thought about eliminating those remarks, but in the end I decided against it.

This, then, is the work of a young anthropologist who went into the field in 1969, a year after students staged major demonstrations in Poland, Japan, France, the United States, Czechoslovakia and, of course, Mexico, where hundreds of protesters were massacred by police during an infamous confrontation in the nation's capital.[3] As a graduate student in the United States, I identified with those in my generation who were fighting for change on university campuses and, more ambitiously, in society at large. While participating actively in efforts to reform higher education, I marched for civil rights and women's liberation and against U.S. involvement in the Vietnam War. My political commitments strongly influenced the conclusions I reached in my research, convincing me to proclaim, along with other anthropologists who shared my convictions, that people like me, with my background and privilege, should avoid doing fieldwork among Indians in Mexico or among other victims of North American and European colonialism, even when we championed their cause.

With the benefit of hindsight, I now question that injunction, but I took it very seriously in the mid-1970s. I, therefore, abandoned the idea of doing more fieldwork in Mexico and went off to Europe to study the Jewish question in France and the ways Jewish intellectuals of the generation of 1968 responded to their identity as Jews. Despite a major shift in my area of research, I still remained tied to Mexico and continued to participate now and again in debates about indigenous politics. More important, I never lost touch with Zeferina Barreto and her family, the people I lived with when I first came to Hueyapan to work in this indigenous village. Thanks to these personal attachments, I have continued to visit Hueyapan regularly and keep up with the changes taking place in the *pueblo* and in the lives of the people I met there many years ago.

In 1969, Doña Zeferina was 64 years old. A commanding presence, nobody questioned her position as head of her family's large household. To quote Rafael Vargas, her schoolteacher son, Doña Zeferina was "*la mera jefa*," the one really in charge. In 1991, Maestro Rafael passed away, but Doña Zeferina lived on, holding the family together with authority, intelligence, and charm. Although most of her children, grandchildren, great grandchildren, and great great grandchildren were living elsewhere by then, they all visited Hueyapan regularly to see the old woman, rejoicing in the fact that she remained full of life and extremely good company to the very end. On Doña Zeferina's ninety-fourth birthday, the husband of her granddaughter Lilia made a video of her dancing the polka at a vigorous pace with her grandson Arturo.

I last saw Doña Zeferina in June 2001. During that visit, we talked about the fiesta she was planning to have on her hundredth birthday. For the occasion, the family would ask the local priest to celebrate Mass in her honor. We spoke again on August 26 to mark her ninety-sixth birthday, and still again on Christmas Eve, at which time she said she was not feeling very well, that her time, she thought, had finally come. Having heard Doña Zeferina complain before, I dismissed her premonition and urged her on. We were all looking forward to the big event in 2005 and expected her to be there, as strong and indomitable as ever. Well, Doña Zeferina did not make it. The day after Christmas, the family took her to Cuernavaca to see a doctor and spend a few days in the home of her daughter

Angelina. There, on the 30th of December, Doña Zeferina's heart gave out.

A few days after I completed the first edition of *Being Indian in Hueyapan*, my father died of lung cancer, losing a long and painful battle with the disease. Twenty-seven years later, as I began the research for the second edition, Doña Zeferina passed away. Having dedicated the first to the memory of my father, I dedicate the second to Doña Zeferina:

May you rest in peace, Doña Zefe, up there beyond the sun— "*cachi ompa den tonal*"—and may this book keep your memory alive, down here on earth.

New York, August 2005

Zeferina Barreto and author at SUNY, Purchase. The photo, taken by Wilbur Funches, was published in *The Journal News* (The Gannett Westchester Newspapers), May 3, 1990, 8.

Acknowledgments

I want to thank once again all those I acknowledged in the first edition of this book, many of whom I mention on the pages of this edition as well: members of my immediate family; curators and other researchers at the American Museum of Natural History; my professors at the University of Chicago; funding agencies that supported my research (U.S. Government grants awarded to me through the University of Chicago and the Wenner-Gren Foundation for Anthropological Research); friends and colleagues in the United States, Mexico, and France; and, of course, Zeferina Barreto and her family, who gave me a home in the fullest sense of the term, during the many months I lived in Hueyapan.

I would also like to reiterate what I said about the villagers themselves and about our collective decision to use the real name of the *pueblo*. Having done fieldwork in Mexico in the late 1960s and early 1970s, during a period of political unrest in the country, I knew I would not be able to "protect" the anonymity of the people I met by adopting the convention, widely used in Anthropology, of changing the name of the *pueblo* and of the villagers I interviewed. We all agreed in Hueyapan that I stuck out like a sore thumb. Everyone knew about the *"gringa"*—from government officials in the region to the inhabitants of neighboring towns. Had I changed all the names, I would not have fooled anybody, unless I had taken the ultimate step and changed my name as well. Short of hiding my identity, the only thing I could do was to watch what I wrote and make sure I avoided sensitive issues that might get certain villagers in trouble with the law. Finally, many people liked the idea that I was writing about them and urged me to do so.

Here, in a slightly edited form, is what I said in 1975:

Let me express my warmest thanks to the people of Hueyapan, who generously accepted me into their community and encouraged me to write about them. I want to point out that the villagers know of the publication of this book. At a town meeting held on August 4, 1973 [during the fiesta celebrating the *pueblo*'s saint's day], those in attendance unanimously voted in favor of using the real name of the *pueblo* and of identifying correctly the people I referred to in the text. I have followed the request of the villagers and have been careful to represent them as honestly and respectfully as I could. I hope that my friends will not be disappointed.

A year before the book came out in Spanish, I returned to Hueyapan with the translated manuscript to review with villagers who figured prominently in the text what I had written about them. I then returned again on November 20, 1977, to take part in the national celebration of the Mexican Revolution, and to present *Ser Indio en Hueyapan* officially to the community.

As I worked on the revisions, I received additional help from a number of people. I would like to thank Jorge Capetillo, Marithelma Costa, Julia Cumming, Johannes Fabian, Kate Heidemann, Agnes Heller, John Heuston, Richard Kaye, Marnia Lazreg, Claudio Lomnitz, Angela Luna, Elzbieta Matynia, Marcelino Montero, Guillermo de la Peña, Francesca Sautman, Maribel Vargas, Saúl Velasco, Evelyn Birge Vitz, John Womack, and my editors at Palgrave Macmillan, Farideh Koohi-Kamali and Erin Ivy. I also want to express my appreciation to Jennifer Raab, President of Hunter College for giving me the time I needed to finish the book while I was serving as dean of arts and sciences. Finally, I am deeply grateful to my husband, Erwin Fleissner, who encouraged me enthusiastically through multiple drafts of the manuscript.

Introduction

In the years following the Mexican Revolution (1910–1920), government leaders called on artists and intellectuals to celebrate their country's triumph and traditions. Painters, architects, historians, philosophers, writers, anthropologists, and others embraced the task with enthusiasm, joining forces with politicians to create a new image of Mexico. Together they produced the proud portrait of a people: the descendants of a union that mixed blood and tradition. Neither Indian nor Spanish, Mexicans, they proclaimed, were a single people with a double heritage.[1]

To pay tribute to Mexico's hybrid or Mestizo man, the government built monuments throughout the country. In Mexico City, for example, we find the Plaza of the Three Cultures, also known as Tlatelolco. The square symbolizes the blend of Aztec and colonial Spanish traditions with three imposing structures: an Aztec pyramid, a sixteenth-century Catholic church, and a mid-twentieth-century office building. Near the church a simple stone plaque commemorates the historic significance of the site: "On August 13, 1521, heroically defended by Cuauhtémoc [the last Aztec emperor], Tlatelolco fell into the hands of Hernán Cortés. Neither a victory nor a defeat, this was the painful birth of the Mestizo people, the people of Mexico today."[2]

Despite the eloquent sentiments expressed on the plaque, the monuments in the Plaza tell a different story: one of Spanish victory and Indian defeat, of how the Spaniards destroyed Aztec culture and substituted their own. The Catholic church, built nearly 500 years ago, was constructed out of the very stones of the Aztec pyramid. In excellent repair, it serves a large congregation today, performing rituals introduced during colonial times. The Aztec pyramid, on the other hand, is in ruins. It bears witness to a great, but dead civilization.

In the Plaza of the Three Cultures, like everywhere else in Mexico, colonial Spanish and modern Mexican traditions live on in well-maintained buildings and institutions dedicated to practicing the religious and secular customs of the country. As for Indian cultures, they rest quietly nearby, in the graveyard of history, respectfully displayed in archeological gardens, on the faces of statues of long dead heroes and in museums that collect artifacts of a "primitive" way of life.

To find evidence of Spanish culture in contemporary Mexico was easy; to find evidence of the Indian, more difficult. With great dedication, archeologists and historians organized expeditions and conducted archival research to learn about the nation's prehispanic past. Cultural anthropologists participated as well, settling down in rural communities in remote parts of the country to record the customs of people still identified as Indians. Salvation projects for the most part, scholars and amateurs did what they could to give modern Mexicans an understanding of their noble indigenous heritage. In the process, certain groups were selected to serve as living links to a world that existed in Mexico before the Spanish arrived.

This book examines the reality of being Indian in Mexico in 1969–1970 and compares it to the idealized image of the Indian, constructed to represent the nation's prehispanic past. Specifically, I discuss what it meant at that time to be Indian to the inhabitants of the rural community Hueyapan, a village of 4,000 people situated in the highlands of the state of Morelos. Drawing on historical and ethnographic evidence, I make the case that indigenous culture in Hueyapan was in ruins and had been for centuries, just like the Aztec pyramid in the Plaza of the Three Cultures. The villagers, however, were painfully aware of still being Indians.

As I analyze Hueyapan's indigenous identity, I take a hard look at traditions found there that were associated with Mexico's prehispanic past. Through this painstaking exercise, I try to show how colonial Mexico invented the Indian—custom by custom, ritual by ritual—and how this old social category has continued to serve the present-day needs of a modern nation. Since the sixteenth century, the people of Hueyapan[3] have participated as Indians in the cultural and economic life of a non-Indian state. As they worked the colonizers' lands, their blood was diluted and their indigenous traditions dramatically altered.

By the time I arrived in Hueyapan in 1969, the villagers were practicing very few customs that had roots going back to prehispanic times. What traces I saw of this earlier period had been carefully "baptized" many centuries ago to conform to European sensibilities and the evolving needs of the new colonial order. From the perspective of "culture," therefore, the villagers were virtually indistinguishable from non-Indian Mexicans.[4] Where they differed significantly was socially and economically.

It was actually quite by accident that I ended up studying the problem of being Indian in Hueyapan. When I first came to Mexico in July 1969, I expected to work with members of a political group based in Mexico City who were trying to revive Aztec culture. Known as El Movimiento Restaurador de Anauak, I believed at the time that the group had something in common with Black Power and Native American Red Power in the United States. Interested in examining the possible similarities, I wanted to compare what the Movimiento was doing with what minority rights groups were doing back home. I also wanted to see how the Movimiento's interpretation of Aztec culture might differ from that of scholars in the academy.

After spending a few months with the group and interviewing its leaders, I became disillusioned. Although people had told me that the Movimiento had between 400 and 800 members in Mexico City alone, I soon learned that the number was closer to 30. They also assured me that the Movimiento had a large Indian constituency, but I only met Mestizos, middle-class urban professionals, for the most part—primarily schoolteachers—who simply visited among themselves in one another's homes.[5] In sum, I was disappointed, confused, and angered by the group. As far as I was concerned, they had let me down—a curious formulation, I agree, but there it was. Not until much later did I realize that my feelings of hostility were a defensive response to the similarities that existed between them and me. Had I been more honest with myself, I would have recognized the fact that this group was an accurate, albeit embarrassing, caricature of my own romanticized view of the Indian.

Finding it difficult to relate sympathetically to the subjects of my research, I decided to change my project. Instead of focusing on the Movimiento, I would try to understand what it meant to be Indian to individuals living in a rural community that both fit the popular stereotype of an indigenous *pueblo* and met the criteria of anthropologists as well. In other words, I would look for a village where the inhabitants spoke one of the many languages still used in the country today that existed in Mexico before the Spanish conquest. The inhabitants would hopefully practice other customs as well that dated back to the nation's prehispanic past.[6] After visiting a number of *pueblos* in Central Mexico, I settled down in Santo Domingo de Hueyapan, a community located in the northeast corner of the state of Morelos, on the border with Puebla. The villagers spoke Nahuatl, the language of the Aztecs, and Spanish, and the women wove textiles the ancient way, on the backstrap loom. If I succeeded in earning their trust, I would try to get people to talk about what it meant to be Indian in Hueyapan. I would also try to find out if the villagers had any contact with Indian Power groups of the kind I expected to find throughout indigenous Mexico. Had they heard, in particular, about the Movimiento or other urban-based efforts to revive indigenous cultures? If so, how did members of the community respond to this city-inspired enthusiasm?

After spending a year (1969–1970) in Hueyapan, I have remained in close contact with my friends in the village and have continued to visit the *pueblo*.[7] Over the years, I found answers to many of my questions. I discovered as well that the work I had done with the Movimiento had not been a waste of time, but crucial to interpreting what I saw in the village. In Hueyapan, I also learned, in direct and personal terms, what it meant to be oppressed and how confusing it was to be discriminated against for being Indian, while admired at the same time for representing the indigenous soul of the nation. The experience, finally, led me to see parallels between the villagers and other oppressed ethnic and racial groups who had similarly been serving the romantic longings of members of an alienated middle class.

There are several ways to approach a study such as this, each one offering a different level of analysis. I suggest we begin, as I did in

Hueyapan, by meeting some of the villagers and observing how they live. Let me start, therefore, with a description of life in the home of Zeferina Barreto and her family. These are the people I lived with while I was doing research in Hueyapan. As Doña Zeferina and I got to know each other better, she began to talk about her past. Much of what she told me I have recorded here, partially in her words, but mostly in mine. The more abstract ideas that follow will have more meaning, I believe, after looking at what life was really like in Hueyapan in 1969–1970, at least from the perspective of one family.

Next, we will jump to a higher level of analysis. After looking at Doña Zeferina's family, I turn to the village as a whole, summarizing the history of Hueyapan from the time of the Spanish Conquest to the early 1970s. I then talk about how the villagers themselves define their Indian identity. While I lived in Hueyapan, I had the opportunity to discuss the matter formally and informally with several hundred people. Finally, I describe the roles non-Indian groups have played, over a period of nearly 500 years, in preserving the villagers' socioeconomic position as Indian, while eliminating or transforming their indigenous traditions—Catholic priests, Protestant missionaries, representatives of the government (schoolteachers and social workers), members of Aztec renaissance movements, and anthropologists.

The chapters on Doña Zeferina may seem to have little to do with the question of being Indian. That, however, is just the point. Doña Zeferina, like everyone else in Hueyapan, was first and foremost a poor Mexican peasant who happened to live in a rural community where cultural vestiges of the prehispanic past lingered on. Evocations of an earlier time, these vestiges represented a tenuous tie to a culture destroyed long ago. They had little to do with the daily concerns of a rural woman struggling to support her big family with very few resources at her disposal. As we shall see later on, what was significant was the meaning outsiders attributed to these links with the past, no matter how tenuous they might be. For the time being, then, I want to focus on the rhythm and chores of everyday life in the home of one particular family.

In choosing to write about Doña Zeferina, I do not mean to imply that she was typical of the people I met in Hueyapan—whatever that means. On the contrary, she was quite exceptional. I tell her story, because through her experiences I gained a deeper understanding of what I saw and heard in the company of others. Doña Zeferina taught me many things over the year I lived in Hueyapan; about her need, for example, to be constantly vigilant, to be one step ahead of the people she met, some of whom, she knew, would use every trick in the book to try to take advantage of her. For Doña Zeferina, almost every action was in reaction. Looking back over the years, she described her life as an endless series of dangerous encounters that forced her to use creativity and wit to protect her family and give them enough to eat, while preserving her own reputation as an honorable woman. Although I wish she had had the luxury to devote her talents to more positive pursuits, that was not in the cards. And so she spent her life inventing ingenious ways to outsmart her enemies, relying on one of her favorite sayings to give her the strength to carry on: "A person must know how to defend herself."

CHAPTER ONE

ZEFERINA BARRETO AND
HER FAMILY (1969–1970)

The House

In comparison with others in Hueyapan, Zeferina Barreto's family lives reasonably well, in a comfortable house just off the square, near the center of town. They do not, however, rank among the wealthier members of the community. Like other homes near the plaza, Doña Zeferina's house conforms to a familiar Spanish architectural design, carefully conceived to maximize privacy (figure 1). On the south side, facing Calle Morelos, an *adobe* (mud) brick wall, plastered over and painted light blue, extends the full length of the property, closing out the street entirely. This imposing barricade also serves as the exterior wall of the two main bedrooms. To separate the compound from the properties of their next door neighbors, the family also built walls on the east and west sides. Protected in this way, it is possible to spend much of the day out of doors in the courtyard, feeding chickens, washing dishes, or just sitting in the shade of a tree, securely out of view of the busybodies in town. Visitors announce themselves by knocking on one of the bedroom windows or against the big wooden gate, located on the east end of the south wall.[1]

Doña Zeferina does not produce enough food to feed the entire family, but she does contribute a significant amount, providing about half of what they eat. Having inherited two plots of land from her mother (75 by 25 meters each), she presides over the planting of corn, beans, calabash squash, and *chile* peppers that is carried out by other members of the family. She also has a small orchard on the land, which in a good year produces several bushels of walnuts, pears,

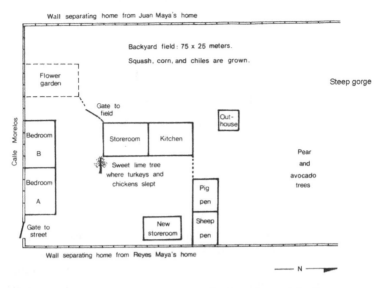

Figure 1 Schematic drawing of the home of Zeferina Barreto's family.

and other fruit to sell in local markets. One of these plots is part of the property that came with the house; the other is about a mile away.

Doña Zeferina also has 15 sheep, 10 chickens, 4 turkeys, 2 sows and their piglets, 1 horse, 3 dogs, and 2 cats. The sheep provide wool for weaving, while the chickens and turkeys supplement the family's diet on very special occasions. As for the little pigs, they are fattened up and then sold to the village butcher.

Members of the Household

Zeferina Barreto—The head of the house. A strong, authoritative woman, Doña Zeferina learned how to survive and watch out for her family early in life, first as a child during the Mexican Revolution, then as a young widowed mother. At 64,[2] she still plays a significant role in supporting the household financially, by selling an eclectic array of merchandise in the weekly market—plastic toys, of the five and dime-store variety, inexpensive porcelain plates and tin utensils, dried *chiles*, and garlic. When in season, she also sells fruit from her own orchard. In addition, Doña Zeferina serves as one of the local healers (*curanderas*) in town.

José Flores—Doña Zeferina's third husband. Don José is a quiet man about the same age as his wife. He spends his days farming his own family's fields and those of Doña Zeferina. He also cares for his wife's herd of sheep, chops firewood, and performs other household chores. Don José, unfortunately, drinks too much, a vice that led to his death in the fall of 1970.

Rafael Vargas—Doña Zeferina's oldest son.[3] Maestro Rafael is 42 years old and works as a schoolteacher in the local primary school in the mornings and in a secondary school in nearby Temoac on several afternoons a week. The *maestro* also plays an important political role in the *pueblo*. As a young boy, Rafael attended school irregularly, because he had to help his widowed mother support the family. He was, however, a good student. With Doña Zeferina's encouragement, Rafael returned to school when he was 28 and eventually earned his teaching certification. Presently, he is taking courses on weekends in Cuernavaca at the Instituto Federal de Capacitación Maesterios to make himself eligible for promotion to the post of regional school inspector. Having endured such a difficult childhood, Maestro Rafael is understandably proud that he has done so well and enjoys the fact that his friends admire his achievements. In the late 1940s, Maestro Rafael was married by the Church and State to a woman from Hueyapan. The couple remained childless for six years; then, soon after their son Arturo was born, the marriage fell apart and they separated. A few months later, Maestro Rafael settled down again with a distant cousin of his first wife, with whom he has since had six children.[4]

Juana Espinosa—Maestro Rafael's common-law wife. Doña Juana is 32 years old and mother of six of the eight children living in the house. She is presently pregnant with her seventh. Doña Juana is always working, taking care of her children, and doing most of the cooking and housework for the entire family. To accomplish all that she has to do, she rises earlier than everybody else and goes to sleep only after the others have retired. A quiet woman, Doña Juana hardly ever initiates a conversation, except with her children.[5]

Arturo Vargas—Maestro Rafael's son by his first marriage. Arturo is 14 years old. When his parents separated, he stayed with his father and was looked after by Doña Zeferina. In June 1969, the boy finished secondary school. He had been studying in Yecapistla, a nearby *pueblo*, and living with schoolteacher friends of his father. A few months later, Arturo took and failed the qualifying exam for continuing his studies in a preparatory school. He now has to wait another year before taking the test again. In the meantime, Arturo is living at home, helping Don José plant the corn, graze the sheep, and attend to other chores around the house.[6]

Rosa Vargas—Doña Juana and Maestro Rafael's oldest child. Rosa is 12 years old and is in her last year of primary school. She is a good-natured, quiet girl who already assumes many responsibilities in the house. Her mother relies heavily on her to help out.[7]

Raúl Vargas—The second child of Doña Juana and Maestro Rafael. An aloof boy, Raúl is ten years old and in fifth grade.[8]

Héctor Vargas—The third child of Doña Juana and Maestro Rafael. Héctor is eight years old and slightly darker in complexion than the other members of the household. The butt of many jokes, people tease the little boy because of the color of his skin. Although nobody seems to make the connection, Héctor is a disciplinary problem both at home and at school. This year, he is repeating first grade for the second time.[9]

Maribel Vargas—The fourth child of Doña Juana and Maestro Rafael. Often called by her nickname Maruca, Maribel turned six in December and is very eager to begin school. Loud, a bit bossy, and clearly very bright, people say she resembles her grandmother, Doña Zeferina.[10]

Reyna Vargas—The fifth child of Doña Juana and Maestro Rafael. A very affectionate little girl, Reyna, at four, is her father's favorite. When the *maestro* is home, she routinely climbs into his lap and cuddles. When he goes to town, Reyna tags along.[11]

Angel Vargas—The sixth child of Doña Juana and Maestro Rafael. Better known by his nickname Quico, Angel is a temperamental two-year old who demands a lot of attention. Still, over the year, he has grown up very quickly, allowing himself to be weaned from his mother's breast without a whimper.[12]

Angelina Hernández—Doña Zeferina's only daughter and the youngest of her three surviving children. Maestra Angelina is 28 years old and the mother of Lilia, the eighth child living in the house. In the early 1960s, she married a man, in a civil ceremony, against her mother's wishes. The couple settled down in the lowlands. After a few months, she moved back to Hueyapan pregnant. As Doña Zeferina had predicted, the man treated her badly. Maestra Angelina had the baby in her mother's home. Once the infant was weaned, she returned to school to get certified as a teacher. During the week, she lives in Hueyapan with her daughter, her mother, and her brother Rafael's family. On weekends, she goes to Cuernavaca to study at the Instituto Federal de Capacitación Maesterios. Leaving her daughter with Doña Zeferina, she spends the night in Cuernavaca in the home of her brother Ernestino, together with his wife and their child.[13]

Lilia Pérez—Maestra Angelina's daughter. Lilia is five years old. Like Arturo, she is Doña Zeferina's ward and as such receives more attention from her grandmother than do the other children in the house. Although she is pampered and indulged, Lilia remains gentle and sweet.[14]

A Day with the Family[15]

Doña Juana is the first to rise. It is about 6:30 AM and still dark outside. Having gone to sleep in a slip and underclothes, she silently puts on the cotton dress she was wearing the day before, ties an apron around her waist, and slips into her plastic shoes. Wrapping herself up in a cotton *rebozo* (shawl), she hurries out into the brisk morning air to try to beat the long lines that will soon be forming at Reyes Maya's corn mill, which (conveniently) is located next door. Before starting the arduous task of making *tortillas*, she must grind a bucket of corn. Having stewed several quart-size measures (*maquilas*) of dried corn kernels the previous afternoon, all Doña Juana has to do now is fill the bucket with the moist *nixtamal*, as the cooked corn is called, and have Don Reyes grind it for her at the mill. As far as she is concerned, it is well worth the 20 *centavos*[16] to avoid grinding the *nixtamal* by hand. Doña Juana vividly remembers how every morning her "poor mother" spent hours on her knees, grinding the softened

Photo 1   Three of Doña Zeferina's grandchildren (Lilia, Maribel, and Angel).

corn into dough on a slab of volcanic rock (*metate*), crushing the kernels with a heavy roller (*mano*) made out of the same stone. When she compares their lives, Doña Juana agrees that she has it much easier—at least she does not have to rise at 4:30 AM the way her mother used to do.

When she returns from the corn mill, Doña Juana rekindles the fires in the kitchen and puts up two cans of water, one for coffee, the other for Maestro Rafael, who insists on performing his morning ablutions with warm water. Next, she heats the beans she had prepared the day before and washes down the flat griddle (*comal*) used for making *tortillas* with water and lime (*cal*)—a chalk-like substance.[17] Once everything is under control in the kitchen, Doña Juana goes out to the backyard to cut a few *chiles* for the *salsa* she will serve with the beans.

Don José rises a little after Doña Juana. He slips on his shirt and a pair of pants over the long underwear he slept in, puts on his well-worn sandals (*huaraches*),[18] then grabs his weather-beaten straw hat and woolen *poncho* (*gabán*). Silently, the old man leaves the bedroom and goes off to perform his early morning chore—providing the family with drinking water from the stream at the bottom of the Barranca de Amatzinac, one of the several deep gorges surrounding the village. Placing a wooden yoke on his shoulders, Don José is able to balance two large cans of water in a single trip. It takes two or three trips to fill the earthenware jugs kept in the storeroom off the kitchen. Almost every morning, Doña Zeferina tries to get Arturo out of bed to help Don José carry water, but the sleepy teenager refuses to budge.

A few minutes later, Raúl and Héctor make their appearance. They have the job of sweeping the front yard with two homemade brooms that are always falling apart. Next, Rosa folds back the covers and reluctantly rises, waking Maribel in the process, who then joins Reyna and Quico in their parents' bed, and starts a pillow fight. Before long, even the little ones want to get up and they call for Rosa, who is still not ready to face the day, to take charge of Quico.

Like her younger sisters, the 12-year old girl has slept in her dress, a torn sweater and a pair of pants. She takes off the pants, puts on her plastic shoes, and straightens out the wrinkles in her dress. She then picks up Quico, wrapping him and herself in her mother's black wool *rebozo*. By this time, the little boy has begun to cry, tearfully demanding his morning piece of bread. Rosa takes Quico to the kitchen, where Doña Juana quiets his insistent plea for *pan*, by giving him a 20-*centavo* coin. With the money tightly clenched in his little fist, the cranky child orders Rosa to carry him down to the corner store so that he can purchase a freshly baked sweet roll.

By this time, Maestra Angelina is up and has gone to the kitchen to heat Lilia's bottle. Although Doña Zeferina and Maestra Angelina have tried to discourage the habit, Lilia insists on drinking milk from a bottle and will not get out of bed until she has had her way. Reyna also drinks milk from a bottle, but she has to wait until her mother finds time to prepare one for her.

With the exception of Lilia and Arturo, Doña Zeferina is the last to rise. She has been awake, however, for a long time, ever since Don José got up to fetch water, but it was too cold, she explained, to leave her bed any earlier. Since today is Tuesday, market day in Hueyapan, she will honor the occasion with a freshly ironed dress and apron, but not until after she has had breakfast and washed up. For the time being, she gets back into the clothes she had been wearing for the past few days. Before leaving the bedroom, she puts on her agave-fiber sandals (*ixcactles*), grabs her favorite coral-colored sweater and a cotton *rebozo*.

As she crosses the yard from the bedroom to the kitchen, Doña Zeferina orders everyone about: "Raúl! Héctor! Why aren't you sweeping? If you've finished, then go help Don José carry water . . . Arturo! Get out of bed—that child is lazy as can be when it comes to working, but quick as anything for being fresh . . . Angelina! Lilia is crying. . . . Dog! Get out of the kitchen."

Doña Zeferina finds her short-legged chair and sits down by the fire, where the coffee is heating in a tin can. "Juana," she asks, "is there any *chimis* (sugar brandy or *aguardiente* in Spanish)?" Nothing remains from what they bought the night before, so Doña Zeferina gives Rosa a *peso*, 20 *centavos* and tells her granddaughter to take the family's half-pint bottle over to the house of their *comadre*[19] Epifania Alonso, who lives across the street, and ask her to fill it up. Not only do Doña Epifania and her husband Adelaido Amaro sell a local sugar brandy, distilled in the nearby village Zacualpan, they also prepare a delicious cocktail called *cuatecomate*, a mixture of *aguardiente* and a powder extracted from a gourd-like fruit.

After Lilia finishes her bottle, Maestra Angelina helps the child get dressed. They then cross the yard and enter the kitchen. Lilia sees her grandmother and runs over to be cuddled by her *mamacita*, freeing her mother to grind up a handful of cooked corn kernels for the chickens and turkeys. Kneeling down before the *metate*, Maestra Angelina lifts the heavy *mano* and grinds the *nixtamal* into mush. She then gives the coarse gruel to her mother, who takes the mixture out to the barnyard and calls the birds over in a high-pitched voice, crying "*pío, pío, pío*" to the chickens and "*cuny, cuny, cuny*" to the turkeys. Doña Zeferina is surrounded in no time by a hungry, peeping flock. How the old woman loves these noisy creatures! She never stops talking about how beautiful they are, particularly her rooster.

While Doña Zeferina is feeding her chickens and turkeys, Maestra Angelina helps Doña Juana in the kitchen, taking over the preparation of the *salsa* and frying up a few eggs—a special treat for the older members of the household. Now Doña Juana can devote herself entirely to the endless task of "throwing" *tortillas*: in a single meal, her family can eat up to 40 or 50.

All of a sudden, the children hear the 8:00 bus groaning in the distance, as it makes its final ascent to the plaza. Héctor bolts out of the house and dashes down to the square, to be there to watch his father get off the lumbering vehicle. Maestro Rafael had spent the night away from home to take care of a business matter in Cuautla.[20] A few minutes later, the child returns and casually announces that *papá* has arrived. Maestro Rafael will make his appearance after stopping first at Don Timoteo's store to have a quick drink with some friends.

Finally, Maestro Rafael opens the heavy gate and enters the front yard. Raúl, Héctor, Maribel, Reyna, Lilia, and even little Quico run over to greet him. Competing for attention, several of them hang on to their father/uncle at the same time. In whining voices, the children plead, "*Papi, papi, ¡dame un 20!*" (*Papi, papi*, give me 20 *centavos!*). Rosa and Arturo look on from a distance, within view of their father so that he will not forget them, but too self-conscious to carry on like the younger children. Raising his voice slightly, producing a tone of authority and irritation that everyone knows well, Maestro Rafael calls Rosa over, hands her ten *pesos*, and tells her to go to the corner store to get him some change. Since today is market day, the *maestro* has decided to give the younger children 50 *centavos* each and the older ones a *peso*. Everybody is delighted.

Maestro Rafael crosses the yard to the kitchen. As he walks through the doorway, he asks for his mother: "*Y la jefa*" (And the boss lady)? By this time, Doña Zeferina has returned to her little seat next to the fire. She smiles proudly at her son and offers him a drink. After catching up on the latest news, Maestro Rafael turns to Doña

Juana, whom he entirely ignored when he first came in, and asks her to give him some warm water. The woman silently leaves her cooking, fetches a pail, and mixes boiling water with cold water until it reaches the right temperature. Without another word, Maestro Rafael takes the bucket and goes outside. Disregarding the chilly morning air, he takes off his shirt, meticulously washes himself, and shaves. He then goes to the bedroom to find a clean shirt—every day the *maestro* wears a different one. Now properly dressed for school, he returns to the kitchen to have some breakfast, calling out to Doña Juana in a commanding voice to give him something to eat: "¡*Dame de comer!*"

While Maestro Rafael eats his breakfast, Doña Juana continues to make *tortillas*, placing them in a straw basket (*tenate*) and covering them with a white embroidered cloth to keep them warm. Don José and some of the children join the schoolteacher at the table. Little Reyna, of course, grabs the seat right next to her beloved *papi*. As for Doña Zeferina, she remains by the fire and, using a little bench for a table, eats her breakfast there. Mother and son dominate the conversation.

In Cuautla, Maestro Rafael tells her, he heard that a group of *campesinos* (peasants) from Tlacotepec[21] had been in a terrible car crash on their way to Cuernavaca to participate in a political rally to suppport the PRI's candidate for governor of the state of Morelos. Several people had been severely injured. Describing the accident in gruesome detail, the *maestro* muses philosophically about how fate intervenes: some people travel all the time, and nothing happens to them, while others leave home only once and the poor slobs get hit by a car.

Maestro Rafael looks at the watch he just bought for 1,500 *pesos*. It will soon be 9:00, he announces, showing off his expensive acquisition; time to leave for the plaza to round up the children for the morning flag exercises and announcements. As he rises from the table, Doña Zeferina asks him to give her some money to purchase a kilo of freshly butchered beef in the market for lunch, the main meal of the day. He ignores the request and leaves the kitchen without saying another word, but she calls after him, warning that if this was the way he was going to respond, then the family would do without meat. Shaking her head, she complains, unfairly, that her son never helps with expenses. Later that morning, Doña Zeferina will break down and use her own money to buy the kilo of beef from her *compadre* Don Lauro, the local butcher, who has a post in the market right next to hers.

Doña Zeferina leaves the kitchen to wash up and get dressed. With the place to themselves, Maestra Angelina and Doña Juana can finally sit down and eat breakfast. Close in age, they enjoy each other's company very much. It makes little difference to either one of them that Maestra Angelina has almost completed her studies and will soon begin teaching school while Doña Juana has never learned to read or write.[22] One of their most affectionate habits is to call one another, "Patricia," a name they both think is pretty.

Doña Zeferina slowly washes herself, combs, and braids her hair and puts on a clean dress and apron. In the meantime, Don José, Arturo, Rosa, Raúl, and Héctor make several trips to the plaza to carry the many boxes containing the merchandise that Doña Zeferina will try to sell in the market. When the school bell rings at 9:00, Rosa, Raúl, and Héctor run off to join their classmates, leaving Don José, Arturo, and the preschool grandchildren to complete the task and wait for Doña Zeferina.

As the teachers and pupils file into the school house, Doña Zeferina comes down Calle Morelos and turns the corner onto the plaza, making her way slowly up the main street of the village toward her selling post in the market. Over her left arm, she carries a straw basket where she keeps the coins she needs for making change. In her right hand, she holds a small scale used to weigh the dried *chiles* she hopes to sell. Along the way, she stops to greet the other vendors and to see what they have today.

Finally, Doña Zeferina reaches her assigned post, making it possible for Don José to excuse himself and get on with the daily chore of taking the sheep out to pasture. Arturo remains behind to help Doña Zeferina unpack the merchandise and arrange everything systematically—first the *chiles* and garlic, then the kitchenware and toys, following a specific order that never varies from week to week. When they have finished, Doña Zeferina attaches sheets of plastic to the wooden posts planted firmly in the ground on either side of her selling area, protecting herself with this makeshift awning from the burning sun. By 9:30, she is ready and the long day formally begins.

Doña Zeferina is in her element in the market. Every Tuesday, she catches up with friends and acquaintances whom she rarely gets to see on other days of the week. *Compadres* who live in the outlying *barrios*[23] and in neighboring *pueblos* are sure to come down to the main plaza on Tuesdays. Everybody stops to say hello. Some purchase toys for their children or grandchildren, or perhaps a new plate for the house. Others take five *pesos* worth of *pasilla chiles* and a bulb of garlic. No matter what the day brings, the old woman sits patiently on her *petate* (straw mat), her feet delicately tucked under her dress. Surrounded by colorful merchandise, she flashes a warm smile at potential customers, appealing to them to stop and not simply walk by.

Doña Zeferina has a reputation for striking a hard bargain and rarely coming down on the price she first gives. But people know she is honest—it goes without saying that she would never cheat her *paisanos* (her neighbors and friends)—and they are usually willing to pay what she asks. Doña Zeferina is confident as well that her fellow villagers would never take advantage of her.

When she leaves town, however, things are different. Everybody is suspicious of everybody else. Many years of experience have taught the old woman to beware of dealing with people she does not know. More often than not they will try to cheat her. Some will attempt to rob her straight out, while others will charge exorbitant prices for inferior goods. Doña Zeferina is therefore always on guard, but she still falls victim now and again to unscrupulous sharks.

For example, in February 1970, Doña Zeferina went to the annual fair in Tepalcingo, a village in lowland Morelos, to purchase red bowls made out of dried gourds, which she then planned to sell in Hueyapan. Even though she was careful, in the end she lost out. Under the punishing sun, she dragged herself from stall to stall, looking for a good bargain. Every time she approached a vendor, she went through the same routine:

DOÑA ZEFERINA:	What do you sell these for, Marchante?
VENDOR:	Three *pesos* apiece, Marchante.
DOÑA ZEFERINA:	Why so much?
VENDOR:	I should charge even more!
DOÑA ZEFERINA:	And in lots of a hundred?
VENDOR:	I don't sell by the hundreds.

DOÑA ZEFERINA: Well, then, by the dozen?
VENDOR: 2.80 a bowl, if you buy by the dozen.
DOÑA ZEFERINA: Did you say 2.60? [Her "poor hearing" always interpreted things in her favor.]
VENDOR: No, 2.80!
DOÑA ZEFERINA: I am purchasing these in order to sell them again myself. If I pay what you are asking, how will I ever make a profit, Marchante?

Then, Doña Zeferina walked away, hoping the vendors would lower their price. They never did. Hours later, she found somebody selling bowls on the edge of the fairgrounds for a real bargain—if you bought in bulk—at 2.50 *pesos* apiece. Feeling triumphant, she purchased 50 of them, only to discover, when she finally got home, that the thieves had given her several cracked bowls.

Photo 2 Doña Zeferina making a sale in the Hueyapan market.

Back in the Hueyapan market, a woman Doña Zeferina knows from the San Felipe Barrio stops by to settle a bill. She owes the old woman a *peso* for the injection Doña Zeferina gave her son the week before. Pleased to hear that her patient has recovered from his illness, Doña Zeferina accepts the payment and pulls out a small notebook where she keeps a record of all those who still owe her money. Slowly, she goes through the list, methodically reading each name out loud in a quiet voice, until she comes to the woman in question. Picking up her pencil, she draws a line through her name and acknowledges with a smile that the debt has been cleared. While waiting for Doña Zeferina, the woman examines the toys. How much does the water gun cost, she wants to know. 1.50 *pesos*? That sounds a little high, but since Doña Zeferina refuses to come down to 1. 25, the mother gives in and buys the toy for her son.

A man from Santa Cruz, Puebla also stops by, bringing sad news from his village. One of Doña Zeferina's *compadres* died there the week before, in a brush fire that he and his two sons had tried to put out, in the hills on the outskirts of the pueblo. As they made a last desperate attempt, the *compadre* tripped and hurt his foot. Unable to keep up, he called out to his sons to run for their lives and the boys dutifully obeyed, leaving their father to burn to death. Doña Zeferina shakes her head, "How terrible . . . the poor man . . . and his wife!" She presses the man for more details. Her *compadre* used to come to Hueyapan regularly on market days. She is going to miss him.

The recess bell rings at 11:30 and children pour out of their class-rooms into the market area. First, they go over to the vendors selling candy and snow cones; then, to Doña Zeferina to see the toys. Fortunately, Arturo is there to help keep an eye on everyone, for some of the rowdy boys are capable of stealing. Together, they manage to control the children and to make a few sales—miniature purses for dolls that cost 20 *centavos* to the girls; pistols and trucks for a *peso* or two to the boys. Most of the children simply look on. They are saving what little money they have to buy another snack.

During the half-hour recess, Maestro Rafael and some of the other schoolteachers chat among themselves. The district school inspector will be holding a meeting later this week in Tetela[24] and the *maestros* agree to cancel their classes in order to attend. The subject then turns to lighter matters and one of the teachers entertains the others with an election-year joke, this one chosen for the benefit of the North American anthropologist: "In the United States you Americans think that you have a more efficient system of voting in national elections than we do, because thanks to modern technology citizens in your country hear the results of the elections almost immediately, within minutes after the polls close. But you're wrong. In Mexico, things are even more efficient. We know the results six months before the elections have even taken place!"[25]

By 12:00, Doña Juana has finished all the morning chores. With the help of Maestra Angelina, she has made the beds, swept the floors of the bedrooms and kitchen, washed all the breakfast dishes, and fed the dogs and pigs. Now it is time to think about the main meal of the day.

Maestra Angelina goes down to the plaza to pick up the kilo of beef that Doña Zeferina has purchased and to get instructions from her mother about how to prepare it. For lunch, Doña Zeferina would like beef soup, flavored with green tomatoes,[26] *chiles*, onions, cloves, pepper, and fresh peppermint. The main dish, of course, will be accompanied by *tortillas* and followed by the usual serving of boiled beans.

Doña Juana goes into the kitchen to add fuel to the fires. She wants to put the soup up immediately to give the meat plenty of time to stew and get tender. Fortunately, there are still enough beans left over from breakfast so that she will only have to reheat them at the last minute.

Quico follows his mother into the kitchen and asks as forcefully as a two-year old can ask that she give him some more bread. Responding to his plea, Doña Juana hands him the remainder of the sweet roll he had purchased earlier that morning. She then tells the boy to leave the kitchen and to take the dogs with him. Quico scampers off enthusiastically, only to return a few minutes later without any pants on. Doña Juana admonishes the child gently, warning him playfully that if he continues to run around naked like this, the dogs will bite off the "little bird" (*pajarito*) he has dangling there between his legs. Quico giggles shyly and allows his mother to dress him again.

By the time school lets out at 2:00, the beef soup is ready and Doña Juana is back at the hearth, making *tortillas*. The children drift home one by one and ask to be fed, each brusquely demanding, "¡*Mamá, dame de comer!*" Doña Juana complies silently, giving the youngest ones tiny portions of beans and a morsel of meat. Since small children have little tolerance for hot peppers, she does not serve them any soup. Maestra Angelina joins the youngsters at the table, eating earlier than the other adults, so that she might take Doña Zeferina's place at the market and give her mother a break.

Don José returns home with the sheep at about the same time as Doña Zeferina and Maestro Rafael do. While they eat, Doña Zeferina shares the tragic news about their Santa Cruz *compadre*. A little self-conscious about describing the incident in great detail, she confesses that Maestra Angelina has criticized her for being so interested in gory subjects. But that is the way she is. Some people even say that this capacity of hers to tolerate blood has made her a good healer—for example, the nurses who came to Hueyapan in 1945 to train *curanderas* like her to give injections and to use other medical techniques preferred by modern doctors.

Maestro Rafael reports that soon the family will have running water. On his way home for lunch today, he ran into their neighbor Juan Maya who announced that everything was about ready. Twenty-five families in the Centro have agreed to combine resources to dig a well at the site of a deep pool of water that several villagers found, about five kilometers away, in the hills surrounding Hueyapan. Each family will have to contribute 350 *pesos* and seven days of labor. In addition to digging the well, they will have to lay down rubber hoses to connect the houses of participating families to the source of the water. Everyone is delighted. How nice to think that soon they will not have to carry water to the house twice a day from the bottom of the *barranca*.

Doña Zeferina gets up to return to the market. As she leaves, she tells her daughter-in-law to prepare the *adobe* brick steam bath (*temascal*) for the evening so that she can heal her aching head. She traces the cause of her malaise to what happened to her over the weekend on a bumpy bus ride back to the village, when a melon fell off the rack above her seat and hit her on the head. Before the bathing begins, Doña Juana has to change the hay on the floor of the steam chamber and make a fire in the attached smaller chamber (figure 2).

When the *maestro* finishes eating, he joins some men in the plaza to discuss a local political matter that concerns him directly. It seems that the *ayudante* (top village officer), who belongs to the opposing conservative faction, has mounted a public campaign against Maestro Rafael and another native schoolteacher, Regino Lavana. The *ayudante* accuses the teachers of not performing their jobs adequately in the classroom, infuriating the *maestros* and other members of the progressive faction. This man, they claim, is in no position to judge others, for he has been negligent in his own duties. What is more, they continue, the *ayudante* lacks "culture" and cannot possibly evaluate the work of "educated" schoolteachers. To respond to this outrage, leading citizens in town have decided to write to the

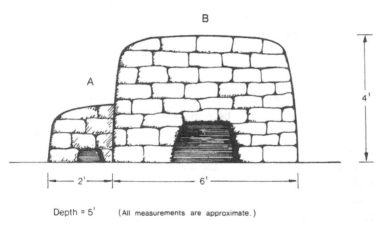

Depth = 5'   (All measurements are approximate.)

Figure 2   The *temascal* or steam bath in Doña Zeferina's kitchen (A) Chamber where fire is built (B) Bathing chamber.

governor of Morelos to ask him to remove the man from office and replace him with the second in command (the *suplente*), someone whose allegiance to the progressive faction is well known. Today, the villagers will write the letter and Maestro Rafael has volunteered to help draft the formal complaint.

Back at the house, Rosa helps her mother and aunt wash the luncheon dishes. When they are done, Doña Juana puts up the beans for supper, making enough to feed the family for the next day. She also prepares the *nixtamal* for tomorrow's *tortillas*. Leaving Rosa to take care of Quico, Doña Juana then goes off to a nearby stream to do the laundry. There, she joins a few women she knows well and enjoys a rare moment of gossiping with her friends, out of earshot of her commanding husband and mother-in-law. Kneeling down at the edge of the stream, the women scrub their families' soiled clothing, on rocks placed in the water for that purpose, and lay the clean laundry out to dry on the sloping banks behind them.

At 3:30, the red and blue bus of the Estrella-Roja line departs in the direction of Tlacotepec, providing transportation to visitors who live along the Hueyapan–Cuautla bus route. Neighbors who live in *pueblos* within walking distance of the village gather their wares and take off as well, abandoning the plaza to the resident vendors, who slowly pack up their merchandise and make their way home. Doña Zeferina is always one of the last to leave, because it takes her and Arturo a very long time to put everything back in the right boxes. By 5:00, they too are ready to go and Don José, Arturo, and a few other children drag the boxes home and tuck them away for another week in Doña Zeferina's bedroom and in the storeroom off the kitchen.

Before night falls, Doña Zeferina has to make a house call to an elderly couple, both of whom are ailing. Maribel pleads with her grandmother to take her along. Once she has packed her medicine kit, Doña Zeferina nods to the child and the resident anthropologist and the three of us leave for the San Andrés Barrio, walking east up Calle Morelos, away from the plaza. On the streets of Hueyapan, we pass several people Doña Zeferina knows and exchange friendly greetings. Usually, a simple "*madiotzin*" (good-bye)[27] suffices, but sometimes a villager is nosey: "Good afternoon, Doña Zefe, where are you going?" "Over there," she replies with a vague gesture of the hand, refusing to give anything away. Although it is nobody's business, we are on our way to the home of Maestro Regino's old uncle and aunt who have been ill all week with the flu. Doña Zeferina visited the couple yesterday and offered to give them injections, but only the husband accepted the proposed treatment. Today, she will give her cooperative patient a second shot.

The couple lives in two small *adobe* brick rooms, a bedroom and a kitchen, both of which are in serious need of repair. The man reports that he is feeling better today than yesterday, but he is still in bed, stretched out on a raised wooden platform, cushioned by a thin *petate*. Chilled to the bone, he wears nothing more than a soiled pair of *calzones*,[28] and tries to warm himself as best he can under an old blanket and several burlap bags. The old man explains that he feels hungry today, but his wife tells him that they have nothing to eat. As for the woman, although her condition is not much better than his, she is up and about, dressed in a ragged *xincueite*.[29]

Doña Zeferina sterilizes the hypodermic needle with rubbing alcohol, but does not submerge it into a flaming container the way the government nurses taught her to do. Next, she fills the needle with *clorhidrato de tetracaina*, instructs her patient to roll over, and gives the man an injection on his buttocks. Using a single teaspoon, she offers the couple a little cough medicine and promises to check in on them again tomorrow. In the meantime, they should keep warm and drink tea.

By the time Doña Zeferina returns home, it is about 6:30. The fire is burning in the *temascal* and the bathing will begin in about an hour. Doña Juana and Maestra Angelina have already made two trips to the bottom of the *barranca* to fetch water. Don José has come back from the communal lands with extra wood to keep the fires going throughout the evening. He carried the logs home on the back of the family's horse Norteño, skillfully tying the wood to the animal's saddle.

Doña Zeferina must now prepare the medicine that she will use to cure her aching head. First, she instructs the youngest children in the house to urinate into a chamber pot. Although they complain that they "don't have to go," Doña Zeferina insists that they try. Reluctantly, Lilia, Maribel, and Raúl comply, taking turns, using a

Photo 3 Doña Zeferina holding a book of medicinal cures, given to her by a schoolteacher (photo by Brian Weiss).

metal receptacle.[30] Doña Zeferina pours the urine into a smaller pot and adds tobacco leaves. She then heats the mixture over the fire until it begins to boil, at which point she removes it from the hearth and adds a little rubbing alcohol. Returning to her bedroom with the receptacle, Doña Zeferina places it on her night table and, using the boiled tobacco as a sponge, she applies a small quantity of this *medicina* to her head, saving the rest for the other bathers, who will rub down their bodies with the mixture, before steaming themselves in the *temascal*. Finally, Doña Zeferina ties a scarf tightly around her head to protect her from the cold; she will keep the scarf on for 24 hours.

When their grandmother finishes, Maribel and Lilia ask Doña Zeferina whether they might perform the nightly ritual of lighting the holy candle kept on the table below a large picture of the Virgin of Guadalupe. Every evening, the old lady lights the candle and waves smoking embers of *copal* incense before the family's sacred shrine. Doña Zeferina monitors their actions carefully and teaches the girls to recite a little prayer. For occasions like this, the prayers are informal, she explains, and should come from the heart: "My mother of Guadalupe, Queen of the Heavens, take care of me. Mother of mine, Thou who art all-powerful, cover us with Thy robe and do not foresake us, merciful Mother."

The family goes into the kitchen to have a light supper of beans, reheated *tortillas*, and coffee. Although it has been a long day, everybody is in lively spirits. The adults all share a half-pint bottle of sugar brandy that Doña Zeferina bought in the late afternoon. As Don José takes his turn and accepts the communal glass, Maestro Rafael eggs him on, "Come on, Don José, down with it." Having had quite a bit to drink already, Don José chuckles and lifts the glass, making a toast to the assembled: *"Para el frío"* (To protect us from cold weather). Even Doña Juana, in her own quiet way, enjoys the moment. As she takes the glass and swallows some brandy, she adds, smiling, *"¡Qué carambas entonces!"* (Goodness gracious).

Joining the fun, Maribel starts horsing around with her older brother Héctor. Delighted by the playfulness of her spunky granddaughter, Doña Zeferina grabs Maribel by the arm and breaks into song, teasing the child with a popular ballad that dates back to the Mexican Revolution. Substituting the little girl's nickname Maruca, for the original "Marieta," she offers a rousing rendition of: "Maruca don't be a coquette, for, men are very bad. They promise many gifts, but when the time comes, they beat you instead." Freeing herself from Doña Zeferina's grip, Maribel screams and runs out of the kitchen.

Maestra Angelina eats a quick supper before putting Lilia to bed. The child must have company until she falls asleep, or else she will cry. By this time, Quico has dozed off in a small wooden cradle that is hanging in the storeroom off the kitchen and Reyna has curled up in her father's lap. Once the little girl has fallen asleep, Maestro Rafael carries her back to the bedroom, lays her down on the bed, and covers her affectionately with several blankets.

As soon as Lilia drifts off to sleep, Maestra Angelina slips out of bed, takes off her clothes, wraps herself up in a blanket, and returns to the kitchen. Doña Zeferina has also changed out of her clothes and is waiting patiently to enter the bathing chamber, seated on a *petate* in front of the door of the *temascal*. The old woman and her daughter then take turns backing into the *temascal*, closing off the entrance behind them with the *petate*. Now the steam bath officially begins.[31]

Maestro Rafael is the only adult member of the house who does not participate in the ritual steam bath. And he refuses defiantly, repeating the story everybody knows about the time he got sick when he was still a small boy and his mother decided to "cure" him in the *temascal*: No sooner did she begin beating the child with the leafy branches of the *cebolleja* bush,[32] than he bolted out of the bath and ran into the yard, naked. Never again would he allow himself to be subjected to such torture. Listening to him reminisce, Doña Zeferina laughs loudly from inside the *temascal* and teases her 42-year-old son about his fear of the traditional bath.

Talking about this childhood experience brings back other frightening memories. Calling out to his mother, Maestro Rafael asks whether she remembers the time when a man in Zacualpan wanted to buy him. Without waiting for her to answer, he gives his version of the story: One Sunday, when he was about 14 years old, Rafael and his mother went to Zacualpan to sell *pulque* in the weekly market. While serving people glasses of the fermented juice of the *agave* plant, they met a man who had no son of his own. Regretting his sad lot, he suggested to Doña Zeferina that she sell him Rafael. Doña Zeferina replied that she would think it over and let him know what she had decided when she returned the following week. Fearing that his mother had found the offer attractive, Rafael refused to accompany her to Zacualpan, when Sunday rolled around again.

Calling out from the bathing chamber of the *temascal*, Doña Zeferina tells her son that she thought his reaction was ridiculous then and she still thinks so today. How could he have ever imagined that she would sell him to a stranger? He was her son after all, not a donkey.

One by one, the remaining children leave the kitchen to go to sleep. Rosa is the last of the young people to retire, because she has to wash the supper dishes and put them away. By 10:00, everyone has turned in for the night, except Doña Juana who has stayed behind in the kitchen to switch off the lights,[33] fetch Quico from the cradle, and secure the door of the kitchen storeroom with a wooden bar, to make sure it stays closed while Raúl and Héctor are sleeping.

Back in her bedroom, Doña Zeferina lights a cigarette and turns on the radio, worrying little about those who may already have fallen asleep. Her favorite soap opera, "Chucho el Roto," ended hours ago, but she finds something else to listen to. Maestro Rafael, who is not yet asleep, calls out to his mother from the other room, again unconcerned about waking the family, to repeat the punch line from a joke they had both enjoyed earlier that evening. Finally, it is quiet, as everyone drifts off to sleep.

Chapter Two
The History of Doña Zeferina and Her Family

Although kinship rules and residence patterns favor the paternal side of the family, Doña Zeferina's story is one in which mothers, not fathers, figure prominently. For three generations, her family relied on women who, for a variety of reasons, never lived very long with the fathers of their children. First, her grandmother, then her mother, and finally, Doña Zeferina herself supported their families essentially alone. Of the three women, only her grandmother followed tradition and settled down in her husband's house. But even she ended up having to raise her children without the help of a man. In the following two generations, the women stayed home with their mothers, in the house where they themselves had grown up.

Under the circumstances, it is hardly surprising that Doña Zeferina talked more about her mother and her mother's side of the family than she did about her father, José Ocampo, with whom she lived only for the first two years of her life. In 1907, her father moved to Tlacotepec, 11 kilometers away. Closing his store in Hueyapan, he left Doña Zeferina's mother for another woman and for the opportunity to make a better living in the lowland community.

Despite his decision to abandon her mother, Doña Zeferina never lost touch with Don José. When she was old enough to travel alone, she visited him in Tlacotepec. In later years, even after he had died, she continued to see her paternal half-siblings. Her sense of connection, however, was not very strong and she expressed little interest in her father's side of the family. On her mother's side, she had stories to tell that dated back to the mid-nineteenth century, to the days when her great grandparents were young.

Photo 4 Reproduction of a composite photographic portrait, which hangs in Doña Zeferina's bedroom, of Doña Zeferina (center) and her children by three different unions. Starting with the photo on the top left and going counterclockwise: Rafael and Raúl Vargas, Ernestino Noceda, and Angelina Hernández (photo by Brian Weiss).

Doña Zeferina got to know one of her great grandmothers (her grandmother's mother) before the old lady died. Her name was Francisca Pérez and she lived until Zeferina was about 11 years old. Their visits, however, were not very frequent because Doña Francisca was frail and lived far away in an outlying *barrio*. When Doña Zeferina described Hueyapan as it was in the days her great grandmother was young, she repeated stories she had heard from her mother and grandmother, who clearly had lively imaginations. Doña Zeferina learned, for example, that people back then were considerably larger than they are today, including her own great grandfather Rafael Crisantos, who was so enormous, they said, that he could eat half a sheep and a dozen eggs in one sitting. To make enough *tortillas* to satisfy the appetite of a man his size was a major undertaking, demanding the collective efforts of his wife and their daughters—he could polish off an entire basketful (*tenate*) in a single meal!

In the 1850s, most of the villagers were monolingual speakers of Nahuatl. The language, however, had long been mixed with Spanish, in both its grammatical structure and vocabulary. The names parents gave to their children, for example, were those of Catholic saints, or Greek mythological figures, reflecting the impact of European culture, even back then, in the daily lives of indigenous families.

When Doña Zeferina's great grandparents were young, a priest lived in Hueyapan and encouraged the villagers to take their religious obligations seriously. Guided by the priest, Catholic ritual was more elaborate then than it was in 1969–1970, in particular, on major holidays like Easter. On Good Friday, men reenacted the agony of Christ by carrying prickly pear cactus on their bare backs. To increase the pain further, they wore chains around their ankles that induced bleeding and made walking in the processions more difficult than it already was.

In the mid-nineteenth century, most women wore *xincueites*, the traditional black wool skirts of the region that were woven on backstrap looms, using a technique that dated back to prehispanic times. Men dressed in white linen *calzones*, the costume identified with peasants (*campesinos*) throughout Mexico. The pants were fashioned out of one piece of store-bought cloth. For shirts, men used wool *ponchos (gabanes)*, locally woven on the backstrap loom and sewn up on the sides. Neither men nor women wore sandals or other kinds of footwear.

Among the many stories Doña Zeferina heard about the olden days, one of her favorites was about a mountain on the edge of Hueyapan that had special powers. Known as the "Enchantment" (El Encanto), one side of this mountain opened up every year on New Year's Eve, giving passage into a huge cavern. At the appointed hour, the villagers rushed into the mountain to gather up kernels of corn that were scattered on the floor of the cave. Every kernel they touched turned into a silver coin.

Since the mountain stayed open only for a short period of time, people knew that they had to work fast. One year, however, a man lost track of the hour and was left behind. Twelve months later, his fellow villagers found him still alive and in perfectly good health, totally unaware of what had happened.[1]

Thanks to the Encanto, people in Hueyapan used to be very rich and, Doña Zeferina added, they enjoyed doing things on a grand scale. If a man borrowed money, for example, he did so by the basketful. In her own family, Doña Zeferina's great grandfather Manuel Sardinias had a bull's skin filled to the brim with silver.

Using his considerable wealth, Don Manuel bought some land on what we now call Calle Morelos.[2] Three generations later, Doña Zeferina inherited part of this original purchase. In Don Manuel's time, however, the family had enough land that he did not have to divide this particular plot among his heirs. Instead, he passed down the entire property to Doña Zeferina's grandfather, Dionisio Sardinias, his eldest son.

Doña Zeferina's grandparents Don Dionisio and Doña María had three children. Soon after their third child was born, Don Dionisio was convicted of murder and sentenced to 20 years in the Cuautla prison. This terrible event forced Doña María to find ways to support their children by herself, dramatically changing the way the family lived.

Don Dionisio committed the crime while serving on the local police force in Hueyapan. One day, he heard that somebody had stolen livestock from a female cousin. When he went to see her to find out what had happened, his cousin gave him the name of the person she thought was the guilty party. Don Dionisio then took the law into his own hands, hunted down the alleged thief, and shot him, killing him on the spot, in the thickly forested Amatzinac gorge, about a kilometer away from the town's plaza. Although he must have thought that he was alone, a local woman witnessed the murder and reported the incident to others in the village, who in turn alerted members of the federal army. A few days later, a company of soldiers arrived in Hueyapan, arrested Don Dionisio, and brought him to Cuautla, where he was tried and sent to prison.

To make sure that they never forgot their father, Doña María took the children to Cuautla as often as she could to visit Don Dionisio. Then, in 1909, three years before the end of his term, Don Dionisio was released from jail. According to Doña Zeferina, he gained his freedom as part of a general declaration of amnesty for all prisoners by the new governor of Morelos, Pablo Escandón, who took office that year, after winning a notoriously scandalous election.[3] For Don Dionisio, however, it was too late. By the time he got out, he was a broken man. Even though he held on for another five years, he never regained his strength.

Doña Zeferina was only nine when her grandfather died and she did not remember him well. What she knew about him and the time in which he lived she learned, once again, from her grandmother, who passed away many years later, in 1932, when Doña Zeferina was a woman of 27. In reminiscing about Doña María, Doña Zeferina always began by saying how much she adored her grandmother. Nobody influenced her more as a child than she did, not even her own mother.

According to Doña Zeferina, Doña María belonged to a distinct race of people who had dark skin and beautiful light hair. She did not look like others in the village. When Doña María settled down with Don Dionisio, he made her stand out even more than she already did by forbidding her to dress like an "Indian." As a result, Doña María never wore a *xincueite*, but she held on to the local tradition of going barefoot, even after others in Hueyapan began wearing sandals. Doña Zeferina remembers that once she gave her grandmother a pair of *ixcactles* (*agave*-fiber sandals) and the old woman put them away, solemnly proclaiming that she would save them to wear on the day of her funeral, when she went to meet her Maker. Until then, she preferred to walk around without anything on her feet, carrying as many as 25 liters of corn on her back over rough country roads. Today, Doña Zeferina noted with scorn, people cannot even manage ten, with or without shoes!

With Don Dionisio in jail, Doña María supported the family by selling *pulque* in nearby villages. In later years, even after she had grown quite old, she continued the weekly routine, traveling long distances by herself. Attracted to the life of a market woman, Zeferina asked her grandmother, when she was still very young, to let her come along, but Doña María made the child wait until she was ten and was old enough to help.

On the days they sold *pulque*, Doña Zeferina remembers that her grandmother rose at 3:00 in the morning and went out alone into the fields to collect the juice of the *agave* plant (*agua miel*). When people heard about what she had done, they asked how come she was not afraid. "Why should I be scared?" she replied. "I have my dogs and my *machete*. If someone threatens me, my dogs are there to protect me; if an animal attacks them, I can use my *machete*."

In the early 1900s, Doña Zeferina's mother, Doña Jacoba, settled down with José Ocampo, a man from Hueyapan who owned a small store. Following local custom, Doña Jacoba moved into his home, and on August 26, 1905, she gave birth to Zeferina. Two years later, Don José abandoned his family and moved to Tlacotepec, at which point Doña Jacoba returned to her parents' home with their little girl.

When Zeferina was still very small, Doña Jacoba began seeing Lucio Barreto, who came from the lowland community of Jantetelco. A decent and responsible man, Don Lucio asked Doña Jacoba to settle down with him in his village, but she refused. She wanted to stay in Hueyapan with her mother. Although the couple never lived together, they saw each other frequently, as often as Don Lucio could leave his fields and come up for a visit. When they started having children, Don Lucio adopted Zeferina and gave her his name so that she would not be different from the others in the family. Over the years, Doña Jacoba and Don Lucio had five children, three of whom died in infancy. Don Lucio himself died in 1922, just after Doña Zeferina was married.

Like Doña María, Doña Jacoba supported her children essentially alone, without the help of a man. She made ends meet by working as a seamstress, sewing on a pedal-operated Singer machine that she bought for herself, the first one ever owned by anyone for miles around. As her reputation grew, people came from neighboring villages to commission her considerable skills. In later years, Doña Jacoba tried to convince her daughter to become a seamstress as well, but Doña Zeferina preferred the life of an itinerant merchant. When the time came for her to make a decision, she followed in her grandmother's footsteps and chose to travel from village to village, selling meat, eggs, fruit, and *pulque*.

The Mexican Revolution broke out in 1910, when Zeferina was only five years old, and it lasted for ten chaotic years, making it virtually impossible for children in the countryside to go to school. Despite the difficulties, Doña Zeferina recalled having one excellent teacher—Eligio Pérez, the son of the man who founded the first school in Hueyapan in the 1870s. Thanks to her teacher, Doña Zeferina learned a great deal of history, much of which she could still remember. What children learned in secondary school today, she received, she said, in three years of primary school. Proud of her achievements, Doña Zeferina also acknowledged her weaknesses, admitting freely that she was poor in math. Not until she became a merchant and needed to make numerical calculations did she learn how to add, subtract, and multiply with ease; she never really mastered division.

Given the dangers of living in war-torn Morelos, Doña Zeferina spent most of her childhood at home, within the walls of the family compound. To keep her daughter busy, Doña Jacoba bought the child a book of prayers and the young girl spent hours committing sacred verses to memory. She also borrowed a collection of fairy tales from Maestro Eligio and gave them to her restless child. Eager to have something interesting to do, Zeferina adored reading the stories and did so over and over again until she had learned them by heart. In later years, she enjoyed the reputation of being a wonderful storyteller and she frequently put her talents to use to entertain her grandchildren, great grandchildren, and the resident anthropologist, regaling us with the adventures of kings and princesses from foreign lands.[4]

In 1914, when Zeferina was nine, Doña Jacoba sent the little girl to Tlacotepec to live with an aunt for a year, where she hoped things would be a little safer than they were in Hueyapan. As an adult, Doña Zeferina often wondered what life would have been like had she been a little older at the time, met a man, and settled down in this Mestizo village. Three years later, in 1917, Doña Jacoba sent her daughter away once again, this time to live in Mexico City in the home of her godmother, a woman who used to teach primary school in Hueyapan.

After giving birth to Zeferina, Doña Jacoba followed local custom and looked for a godparent who might help her daughter rise above her social class. She, therefore, asked a young schoolteacher working in Hueyapan to do her family the honor of holding her baby during the baptismal ceremony and becoming Zeferina's godmother. Shortly thereafter, the *maestra* left the village and returned home to Mexico City, where she subsequently married and settled down. Doña Jacoba, however, never lost touch with her *comadre*, and when she needed help during the Mexican Revolution, she asked the woman to take care of her godchild for a few months.

Doña Zeferina enjoyed her stay in Mexico City very much and said that her godmother treated her like a member of the family. Although the woman may have been very kind, Doña Zeferina's descriptions suggest that she was one of the servants. In later years, when she was a grown woman, she worked as a maid—no nuances here—in the home of her godmother's sister, something she would probably never have done had she really been treated like a member of the family.

Even though Doña Jacoba tried to protect her daughter from the dangers of war by sending the child away for months at a time, Doña Zeferina spent most of the Revolution in Hueyapan, where she lived through some terrifying moments. Here, in her own words, is one of her most dramatic memories:

Maestra[5], I am going to tell you about what happened to me during the time of Zapata's war. Well, we were children then. I was about thirteen years old. In those days, everybody used to run. The bells would ring to announce that soldiers were coming and everybody would run. People ran because if government troops came, they killed the villagers and if the Zapatistas—you know, the rebels—came, they killed villagers too. So we would not wait for either side. It was better to run. Finally, to try to bring an end to the war, a lot of government troops came to Hueyapan. One general came via Tetela. Another came from the hills we call El Monte. Another came from Tochimilco, Puebla. And still another came from this other place in Puebla called San Marcos. In this way, government troops closed off the five exits of the *pueblo*, to keep the villagers from escaping.

Well, here in the house lived an uncle of mine and he killed a pig. And this pig was big and fat. I had my brothers. We were four, no more, and then my mother . . . the poor thing, since she was pregnant, she couldn't run. She also had to dismantle the sewing machine, the one that I still have. Well, I carried my youngest brother. And since it upset me to leave the meat, I grabbed a few pieces of pork, *xales, chicharrón,*[6] and a bag of *tortillas*. And in this way, I took off, carrying the child on my back. I was carrying my little brother who was Quico's age, about two or three. The government soldiers were right behind me, and the rebels in front. Then, the rebels took a path like this [pointing left] and disappeared. And I took one toward the gorge [right] and the government troops followed me. They thought that I was the rebels' woman, or who knows what they thought. They used foul language with me, Maestra. "Stop, you daughter of a so-and-so!" And bullets whizzed by and more bullets. And then, a bullet came close to my brother's head and made a hole in his hat. But we weren't hurt. And when I got to the bottom of the gorge, I took this little path so I could hide myself, my brother, and the food.

In this path, I left everything: meat, *tortillas, xales, chicharrónes*—I left everything there. And I waited until that "baldy"[7] who had been following me passed by. Finally, I heard that all the soldiers had left the gorge and gone over to the other side. Since it was very quiet, you could hear everything. Over there, they were breaking windows and well . . . it was ugly. I stayed hidden, but I heard that now they were gone. So I said to my brother, "You'd better not cry, because if you cry, they'll come back and kill us. Don't cry."

I picked him up again and traveled around the entire gorge. Who knows where we ended up, Maestra. Soon, I didn't even recognize the place. And I didn't want to go down into the gorge again. I said, "Now where can I go? There is nothing but gorges and more gorges. I just won't go." So I stayed there. And as I waited, I couldn't keep from crying, because I was scared. But then, two men I knew passed by. One was Francisco Bautista and the other, who is still alive, was Esteban Maya. I saw them and since I knew them, I spoke to them.

"Where are you going?"

"We're going over there now, back to the *pueblo*. Why are you crying?"

"Because I don't know how to return."

"Let's go. Don't cry now, child. Let's go." So they took me back and as we were walking, they said, "The government troops have gone now. The bastards have gone."

We came to the spot where we were hiding before and I said, "I'll go see if the meat is still there." I went down the gorge again and took the same little path. And there it was! There was the meat, the *xales*, everything. So I picked up the food and returned to the *pueblo* to look for my mother who, people said, was at Don Miguel's house. There, I found her and she was crying, because they told her that they had killed us, that who knows what. I said to her, "But who could have told you that they killed us when nobody saw us? No, here we are. And you, how did you defend yourself?"

"Well, I never left," she said. "The government troops caught me." They put my mother in the house of a certain man by the name of Pedro Escobar. That is where they put everyone they caught, people said. But they did nothing, *absolutely* nothing, to my mother. We then went home.

And that was what happened to me when I was a girl. It was like that, all of it true; I saw it. We suffered many things during that time, Maestra.

In 1922, when she was 17 years old, Doña Zeferina married Felipe Vargas. She was the first in her family to have an official wedding, blessed by the Church and the State. Most people in Hueyapan simply moved in together without going through the expense of having a formal ceremony. Then, as now, a religious wedding was costly, but it brought honor and prestige to the family.

Doña Zeferina's mother tried to discourage the marriage, warning her daughter that being a wife meant doing a lot of hard work. Ignoring the advice, she went ahead with the wedding, but before long she regretted it. Every few days, Doña Zeferina had to rise at 4:00 in the morning to grind corn and make enough *tortillas* to feed her husband for two or three days, while he worked in distant fields and stayed away from home. When he returned, Doña Zeferina had to start all over again and spend long hours in the kitchen.

After five years of marriage, Doña Zeferina went on strike. She had infants by then and refused to subject herself any longer to this arduous routine. Forced to find someone else to do the cooking for him, Don Felipe asked his sister to feed him, promising her many gifts in return. For years, this dutiful sister kept her side of the bargain, but, Doña Zeferina noted dryly, she received nothing from Don Felipe.

Doña Zeferina and Don Felipe had four children: Zeferino, Rosalía, Rafael, and Raúl. The oldest, Zeferino, was born with three testicles and died by the age of seven. People said that the boy was a direct descendant of Rafael Crisantos. Had he lived, he would have grown to the size of one and a half men. Their second child, Rosalía died as well when she was five. Then, in 1931, a few months after their fourth child was born, Don Felipe passed away, leaving Doña Zeferina widowed at the age of 26.

Soon after her husband died, Doña Zeferina left her surviving two sons in the care of her mother and went to Cuernavaca for a year to work as a maid in the home of her godmother's sister. She then spent another two years in Mexico City, where she served in three different households, but finally she returned home, fed up with having other people boss her around. "I wasn't an orphan," she said, adding defiantly, "and had no reason to put up with such treatment."

Although her time as a maid in Mexico City was not a happy period of her life, in later years, she enjoyed reminiscing about her experiences in the home of one particularly horrible mistress, who was married to a very rich man. Doña Zeferina had observed for herself the extent of the man's wealth when she saw him one day open a chest that was filled to the brim with money. Every time she began the story, Doña Zeferina chuckled in her characteristic way, shook her head, and said, "I'm a sly one, Maestra" (*Soy bien canija*, Maestra).

The mistress had a reputation for being very "mean." No maid lasted for more than a month. Doña Zeferina, however, held on for six. One of the mistress' irritating habits was to get up very late in the morning. As her maid, Doña Zeferina was expected to wait for her to rise and finish breakfast before having anything to eat herself. But she ignored the house rules and made breakfast for herself as early as she felt like eating. Having the same tastes as her mistress, she enjoyed drinking warm milk in the morning. And so, every day, she poured milk into a large saucepan, boiled it up, added sugar, and helped herself generously, making sure that she had enough to satisfy her healthy appetite. To hide the "sneak serving," Doña Zeferina added water to the pot equivalent to the amount of milk she had taken for herself. While the woman slept on, Doña Zeferina finished the routine tasks and waited calmly to see what other chores her mistress would come up with when she finally made her appearance.

Having had breakfast, Doña Zeferina would no longer be hungry. This used to puzzle her mistress who often asked how she managed to stay nice and plump when she never seemed to eat. Smiling to herself, Doña Zeferina explained that she had breakfast in the market, when she went out to do the family's shopping.

This "mean" mistress used to wait until the very last minute before asking Doña Zeferina to buy food for lunch. On very short notice, she expected her maid to rush out, do all the shopping, and still get back in time to prepare the afternoon meal. The pressure was unbearable, so Doña Zeferina stopped waiting to be told what to do. Taking matters into her own hands, she went to the market, when she had finished her other chores, making all the necessary decisions by herself and laying out the money for the groceries. Following her own schedule, she usually had finished all the shopping before her mistress had even begun to think about lunch. Pleased with the way Doña Zeferina managed the household, the mistress always reimbursed her immediately.

In 1935, about a year after returning from Mexico City, Doña Zeferina left her children with her mother again, this time to join her maternal half-brothers, Falconériz and Benjamín, in San Juan Ahuehueyo, a small hamlet (*rancho*) in the lowlands, south of Hueyapan, near Tepalcingo, where the two men were working as peons. Doña Zeferina went there to keep house for her brothers, who were still bachelors at the time.

From the very beginning, Doña Zeferina knew that she would not remain in the lowlands, so far from Hueyapan. While she was there, however, she wanted to earn a little money and offered to wash the clothes of peons who were living alone, without female companionship. Working together with a few other women, she took loads of dirty laundry every day to a little stream, located at some distance from where they were living.

One day, Doña Zeferina made the mistake of going to the stream by herself. A man stopped her on the road and said that he wanted to make her his wife. If she refused his polite offer, he would take her by force. Although everyone knew that Doña Zeferina was no longer a *señorita* and had children back home, several admirers had already proposed to her, including this man who had grown increasingly insistent in recent weeks. Now faced with a serious threat, Doña Zeferina told her suitor that she would be happy to marry him, but she wanted to do it right. She therefore requested that he go to Hueyapan and ask Doña Jacoba for her daughter's hand. The man agreed, although, he added, people said that Doña Zeferina could not be trusted. He warned her that she had better keep her word. Doña Zeferina solemnly promised and he left without compromising her.

When she told her brothers what had happened, Don Falconériz and Don Benjamín got very angry with their sister and said that she would have to marry the man and remain in San Juan Ahuehueyo. Doña Zeferina refused and ordered her younger brothers to find a way to get her out of there. First, they thought about putting her on a train—the Salitre station, after all, was not far away—but a ticket cost too much money. The only other option was to accompany her on foot all the way back to Hueyapan.

To complicate matters further, Doña Zeferina had caught malaria in San Juan Ahuehueyo and was suffering regularly from bouts of fever. Anxious about leaving, she got sicker and sicker. At least, her illness served as an alibi for not attending a dance scheduled to take place a few days before she was planning to escape. Had she made an appearance, she would surely have been abducted.

Finally, the big day arrived. Doña Zeferina remembered that it was August 14. Her brothers told her to sell what corn they had, so that they would have a little cash, and to say absolutely nothing about their plans. When people asked her why she was selling the corn, Doña Zeferina replied that she was too sick to make *tortillas*.

Later that evening, Don Falconériz checked to make sure that the coast was clear and the three of them left. Although they had taken every precaution, when they reached the main road and heard horses galloping toward them, they panicked. Hiding Doña Zeferina in the bushes, they let the riders pass and disappear into the night before they continued on their way. By 1:00 AM, they had reached Jalostoc, where a woman they knew lived. In need of a break and a little refreshment, they went to her house to rest for a while. When they said good-bye to their friend, they asked her to keep their secret: if anyone stopped by looking for Doña Zeferina, she should say she had not come that way. Six hours later, they arrived in Tlacotepec. Too exhausted to travel the final 11 kilometers to Hueyapan, Doña Zeferina remained in the village for the day and took part in the fiesta that was already in full swing, to celebrate the Feast of the Assumption of the Blessed Virgin Mary. Her brothers, however, went on to alert their mother and to bring back a donkey for Doña Zeferina. Finally, the next day, Don Falconériz and Don Benjamín returned to Tlacotepec and accompanied their sister home.

On the morning of the 15th, some men came looking for Doña Zeferina and her brothers in San Juan Ahuehueyo, but it was too late. As for the amorous admirer, nothing ever came of the "romance." If the man had been worth anything, Doña Zeferina added, something she had doubted from the very beginning, he would have come after her, all the way up to Hueyapan.

In 1936, Doña Zeferina began living with Rosalío Noceda, a local man from Hueyapan. They settled down in Doña Zeferina's home and she bore him a son whom they named Ernestino. A year later, Don Rosalío died, leaving Doña Zeferina widowed for the second time.

By now, her two surviving children from her first union were old enough to accompany her on extended trips and this made it possible for her to take up the life of an itinerant merchant—the work her grandmother had prepared her for. Doña Zeferina depended, in particular, on her older son Rafael to help her sell *pulque*, eggs, fruit, and meat. From the time Rafael was nine, Doña Zeferina took the boy out of school so that he could keep her company over the rugged mountain roads that separated one community from the next. Then, when he was about 14, Rafael began carrying loads as well, sharing the burden with his mother and the family's *burros*. During the late 1930s and early 1940s, Doña Zeferina organized her week around the schedule of market days in the neighboring *pueblos*: On Sunday, she took 60–80 liters of *pulque* to Zacualpan, where she sold a cupful for 15 *centavos*. Then, on Monday, she went to Atlixco (a small city in Puebla), where she sold eggs, fruit, and meat. She claimed she could carry 300 eggs on her back and Rafael 200. Mother and son used to leave Hueyapan for Atlixco at 5:00 AM and arrive there around 2:00 or 3:00 PM. She purchased the eggs for five *centavos* each and sold them for ten. They then spent the night in Atlixco, sold eggs in the market on Tuesday morning, and left for home in the early afternoon. On Wednesday, around noon, they left Hueyapan again for Yecapistla, arriving in the early evening. There, they spent the night and were ready early on Thursday to sell pears, peaches, and avocados in the local market. On Saturday, Doña Zeferina and Rafael—or sometimes only Rafael and his younger brother Raúl—walked for four hours to Ocuituco to buy meat that their grandmother, Doña Jacoba, sold locally in Hueyapan over the week in the five *barrios* of the village.

Although Doña Zeferina kept Rafael out of school, she always saw to it that he did his homework. When mother and son returned to Hueyapan after a long and exhausting trip, Rafael sat down and did the week's lessons. Since he was very bright, he almost always did well on his exams.

Doña Zeferina continued to support the family as a traveling merchant until Hueyapan opened its own weekly market in the early 1960s. Ready to slow down by this time, she decided to sell plastic toys, kitchenware, dried *chiles*, and other condiments in the village's market on Tuesdays and from her house on the other days of the week. Several times a year, she replenished her stock at the Mercardo Manzanares, a vast open market in Mexico City. Although he was a schoolteacher by then and the father of a large family, Rafael accompanied his mother on these big shopping expeditions.

In addition to working as a market woman, Doña Zeferina made a living as a healer (*curandera*) in Hueyapan. According to local tradition, only people who "return from the dead" have the gift of healing. Doña Zeferina came back to life on two separate occasions. This is why, she explained, she "knew how to heal." The first time it happened, she was still an infant, too young to remember the incident, but her mother told her about it.

When little Zeferina was about a year old, she suffered from a severe case of whooping cough. As the illness progressed, her breathing grew weaker and weaker. One day, her mother decided that she had stopped breathing entirely. Reluctantly, she lit a candle and quietly resigned herself to the idea that her daughter had died. Later that day, one of Zeferina's aunts stopped by to look in on the sick infant. Alarmed by Doña Jacoba's assessment of the situation, she refused to accept that Zeferina had died. Picking up the baby, she began rubbing her niece's body vigorously and succeeded in bringing her "back to life."

Doña Zeferina "returned from the dead" a second time just after the birth of one of her children. Following tradition, she took a steam bath in the *temascal*, but she fainted and was out, she thought, for about an hour. During that time, she dreamed that she was entering a large church. As the doors opened wide to receive her, she looked down at her feet and saw that she had forgotten her sandals. This bothered her, she said, because she knew she had reached the gates of heaven and would have the embarrassment of meeting her Maker in bare feet. At this point in the dream, she woke up.

For years, Doña Zeferina cured people exclusively with herbs and eggs, using what was known as the "rustic" technique. Then, in 1945, a team of government-sponsored nurses came to Hueyapan to train local healers as part of a social work program known as the Cultural Missions. Recruited by the nurses, Doña Zeferina attended classes in the village to learn how to give injections. The government nurses were very impressed by the fact that Doña Zeferina was not afraid of blood or of catching other people's diseases. Offering her the opportunity to get more advanced training, they invited her to go back with them to Mexico City. Although she wanted to accept, in the end she declined because she had to stay home and take care of the family; her mother was old and sick by this time and could no longer look after the grandchildren. Whatever training she got would have to take place in the village itself. Over the years, she relied more and more on her newly acquired skills, giving her patients intramuscular and intravenous injections, and bandaging wounds the modern way. At the same time, she continued to prescribe traditional herbal remedies and to deliver babies by the "rustic" method.

But we are getting ahead of the story. Doña Zeferina lived through some difficult times during the 1930s and 1940s that made a deep impression on her. Over these years, the villagers had to contend with pillaging soldiers. As a single mother, she was particularly vulnerable. Although the Mexican Revolution had technically ended in 1920, agrarian rebels in Morelos carried on their struggle against the government well into the 1940s and recruited people from Hueyapan to join them. One latter-day Zapatista in the highlands of Morelos was Enrique Rodriguez, nicknamed Tallarín, or Noodle.[8] Between 1936 and 1940, Tallarín and his men swooped down on rural villages in the area and killed local officials such as tax collectors and schoolteachers. Since Tallarín had many sympathizers in Hueyapan, the villagers were drawn into conflicts reminiscent of the "real" Revolution (*la mera revolución*).

Doña Zeferina had vivid memories of the period and enjoyed telling her grandchildren and the resident anthropologist about the many dangers she faced. Her favorite story involved a particular general and his men who came to Hueyapan looking for Tallarín:

Maestra, I am going to tell you a story that took place during the time of Tallarín. Well, at home, Rafael—who is now a schoolteacher—was still only a child, about 14 years old. In those days, I used to sell *pulque* in Zacualpan. Every week, Maestra, I went to Zacualpan. Since I didn't know how to load up a *burro*, I went to the house of my neighbor Refugio Barrios to find somebody to help me. He's still alive, by the way. One day, I went to see him and I said, "Listen, come help me with the *burros* and accompany me, because I'm going to Zacualpan." He said, "Sure, let's go." Well, he lived just over there, nearby, so he came over and loaded up the animals.

While we were still getting ready, they were ringing and ringing the bells in the plaza, calling people together. And I said to my neighbor, "What's going on? It must be a robbery."

"Who knows," he replied. "There are a lot of people in the plaza."

Since we live right off the plaza, you could see the people there. But, Maestra, I didn't get scared, or think things like that. I thought it was just a robbery and that people were chasing after the animals that had been robbed from them. Around here, that's how it's done. When there's a robbery in a *pueblo*, people get help from the surrounding *pueblos*. They ring the bells, people come down to the center of town to receive instructions, and then go out in search of the thieves. Around here, we call them thieves [*ladrones*]. Elsewhere, they call them crooks [*rateros*], or whatever.

So, Maestra, I left. And I passed a lot of people, really a lot. However, I didn't pay any attention to them. I was going to sell in Zacualpan.

Well, this fellow Tallarín had gone to Ocuituco. He and his men went there to get none other than the tax collector; because at that time, they were pursuing all those who worked for the government—for example, school-teachers, and tax collectors. Tallarín used to kill all types of government people. In Hueyapan, he did not kill even one schoolteacher, but elsewhere, he killed them. Well, in Ocuituco, they surprised the tax collector who was dressed in nothing more than his underwear. They wouldn't even let the poor man put on his pants. Dressed like that, they brought him to Hueyapan. But since I was gone by then, I didn't see him.

When I got to a place in the road we call Las Mesas, I met some people, including a brother-in-law of mine.

He said, "Are you going to Zacualpan?"

I said, "Yes."

He said, "They say Tallarín is up there in Hueyapan."

I said, "Really?"

He said, "Well, it's true. There are a lot of people there and it's Tallarín. They have the tax collector also. What do you think is going to happen?"

I said, "Well, we're going to Zacualpan anyway. We'll wait to see what happens in the *pueblo*." And we continued on our way. I wanted to go to Zacualpan to get some snacks to give out on Christmas Eve. I wasn't scared.

After we got to Zacualpan, others from Hueyapan arrived. You see, people came every few minutes; for in those days, there was no bus service. We had to walk and some people left early, others late. We came and went. Soon, some villagers, who had left after we had, came over to tell me that they had killed the tax collector in the village.

"What, they were going to kill him?"

"Yes," they said.

They did it right near the plaza in a place called Tecaxtila. And that was that. My friends from the village said, "Now who knows what's going to happen to us in the *pueblo*, now that they came and did this; now that they came and implicated us."

Since they were looking for Tallarín, a little while later, a lot of government troops arrived in Zacualpan—and I mean a lot, Maestra. It was about 2:00 in the afternoon. And there . . . well . . . since I sell *pulque*, they came over to buy a drink from me.

"Where did you come from with this *pulque*?"

I said, "Hueyapan."

"Is it true that Tallarín is up there?"

"It's true. He's there."

"And are there a lot of men with him?"

"Well, they say he has at least 500."

The government soldier then said, "Mother of God, we'd better not go!" And with that, they didn't go, Maestra. Instead, they took the road leading to Ocuituco and Yecapistla. I told them that they should go to Hueyapan.

I said, "Come on. You have a lot of men too. Get it over with once and for all." But no; they didn't go, Maestra.

We decided not to go back either. We said to ourselves: "All right, now. If we leave and meet Tallarín on the road, he can hurt us; or, if we meet up with government troops—since they are furious because the tax collector was killed—well, something might happen to us on the road. We'd better not go; we'd better stay here in Zacualpan."

This took place on the 22nd of December [1940]. We didn't get back to Hueyapan until the 23rd. And as we made our way up to the *pueblo*, we met more people. They said, "Well, it's true. It took place. They've carried away the dead man. People from Ocuituco came and took him away." After we got home, nothing more happened. Neither government nor rebel troops came.

It took the government two weeks to send soldiers to Hueyapan. But then, a lot of them came. First, they arrested the village *ayudante*. At the time, Vicente Hernández was *ayudante*. He was still a very young man then. Now he is dead. Well, the soldiers got him and a few other men and tied them up in the plaza. They were going to kill them, but the villagers made a circle around the prisoners and managed to delay the execution. Then, the soldiers took the men to Tetela, *Maestra*. They took them there to shoot them.

But God was looking out for them and this Vicente Hernández was a very clever man, very . . . how shall I say . . . well, he did not get scared. He was not like that. If they were going to kill him, so be it.

So he said to the general, "I, General, yes, I am going to die. But if you would permit me, first let me say good-bye to the governor of the state and also to this person I know in Mexico City who will inform the president of our country that the *ayudante* of Hueyapan is no longer living . . . that they are going to kill him."

After that, they didn't kill him, Maestra. He called and everything [communicating by telegraph] and they didn't do anything to him. So the prisoners returned to the *pueblo*. The soldiers let them go and the government troops left.

About a week later, government troops came back to the *pueblo*. They were still angry . . . well . . . because the tax collector had been killed. We received word in our homes that we should prepare food for the soldiers, so that they would have something to eat. Not for free. We would be paid: "Make *tortillas*, make beans, make *salsa*, make rice. Prepare large quantities of food so that when the soldiers come they can be fed." Soon, the soldiers arrived and about 15 of them came to eat at my house.

Then, one of our own police officers [*comandantes*] came to see me—the *ayudante* had sent him—to tell me to prepare food for ten big shots—you know, the most important ones: generals and majors and captains . . . those kinds of people. But since I was selling food to the regular soldiers, my kitchen was filled to capacity. And . . . well, I paid no attention to the *comandante*'s orders. I said to myself, "There are so many women selling. Let some of them take care of these men. I'm not going to do it." And so I did nothing.

A little later, two more people came to speak to me. The second one was the assistant to the general himself. He said that the general had sent him to tell me to make something for them to eat. I replied, "Tell the general that I can't do it because I already have so many to feed. I have so many and they are eating."

Then in no time at all, the general arrived. Since the plaza is so close, he was here in less than ten minutes—a big gray-haired man with a big pistol in his hand—and he called out; "Does Señora So-and-So live here?"

I went out and said to him, "Yes, my General, at your service."

"And why, Daughter of the Fucked One, don't you want to give us something to eat?"

"Oh, my General, it is not that I do not want to. Come in and see for yourself what is going on here. I __am__ feeding people."

When they saw their general enter the kitchen, the soldiers rose to attention. "You can go elsewhere to find something to eat," the general told them. And he looked at his watch. "I am coming back at such and such an hour. And mother . . . there better be something to eat!"

And I, Maestra, well, to be sure, I am not easily frightened. I am . . . well . . . brave or I don't know what you call it. So I followed him. "My General, and if I am to make this meal, where will I get the money to do so? You chased away those who were going to pay me. Now the soldiers won't pay me. How will I manage?"

Well, if that general didn't come back and take out money from his pocket and give me 100 *pesos*! "Let's see what you can do with this!" My God, for ten people, Maestra, can you believe it? And he pointed to his watch: "By such and such time!"

And so, since I am clever and also not afraid, I ran to the house of a man who had a lot of chickens—Esteban Robles . . . he's still alive. I went there and I said to him, "Give me, if you would, some 25 or 40 eggs, because I am going to make a meal for those who have come. And they are ferocious." So he gave me the eggs. Then, at Don Timoteo's place, they gave me more.

I brought back everything—lard, *salsa*, a huge pot and, well, what do you expect? There were so many people to feed.

But no *tortillas*! I went to see the *ayudante*. I said to him, "What about the *tortillas*? I can't prepare the meal and the *tortillas* too." Well, he sent some women over immediately and they helped me. Then everything was all right.

The general, however, was still angry with me for not having responded more quickly, for not having wanted to prepare a meal for him and the other officers.

"Now we ate," he said, "We'll return for supper later and we want a hen . . . or perhaps two. Let's see what you can do." And, Maestra, what could I say to him? I said nothing. So, I went to see a woman whose name was Luisa, but she was asking a high price for the hens. I said to myself, "No, it makes more sense to return home and use my own hens." My mother too said we should use our own. Then, afterwards, if they paid me fine. But if they didn't, I wouldn't lose anything . . . well I'd lose the hens, but I wouldn't have spent any money.

We prepared the meal and they returned to eat, now for the second time. And that was that. Then the general said, "Tomorrow we'll come for an early breakfast. Again you're going to cook for us and we want to eat sweetened *tejocotes* [the fruit of the Mexican hawthorn]."

Maestra, we worked all night long, my mother and I, and well, with such fear, a person keeps going like a donkey. That's how it was.

After breakfast, they came again to have lunch. And after the mid-day meal, . . . after they ate, . . . all the officers were very appreciative. Since they were finally leaving the *pueblo*, they came to notify me. They said, "Well, now we are leaving. We won't have supper here this evening. At least you took care of us. How much do we owe you?"

I replied, "Well, it's up to you. If you feel that things were good, that I served you nicely, then . . . but perhaps you feel I didn't . . . well, depending on how things seemed to you, give me whatever you wish."

Maestra, although they spoke harshly to me in the beginning, now they were generous. They treated me well . . . all of them. One gave me 100 *pesos*, another 80. Almost all of them gave me big bills. And the general himself left me a ten-kilo bag of cheese, a lot of bread, rolls, and five kilos of sausage. A lot of everything. And this was on top of all the money. I collected about 600—or at the very least 500—*pesos*. At this moment, I did all right.

But before this, I suffered, because they threatened me. If the general hadn't found those soldiers in my kitchen, he would have killed me. In the end, the officers gave me money. They then said good-bye and left. But I suffered, I did, Maestra, during that war.

In 1941, Doña Zeferina began seeing a man from Hueyapan by the name of Pedro Hernández. When she became pregnant, Don Pedro asked her to settle down with him in his home, but she refused. Her mother was not well and Doña Zeferina did not want to leave the old woman in the inadequate care of her bachelor half-brothers. As she herself put it, "I loved my mother more than this man." Don Pedro soon married another woman, but he and Doña Zeferina remained friends.

When her time came, Doña Zeferina gave birth to a little girl. She called her Angelina. This was her only daughter and she adored the child.

Soon after she had weaned Angelina, Doña Zeferina left the baby behind with her mother and went to the lowlands with Rafael and Raúl to look for work as migrant field hands. For the next five years, they spent June, July, August, and December away from Hueyapan, the boys laboring as peons while Doña Zeferina ground corn. She and her sons did not always work for the same people, forcing the family to live apart and take shelter in different caves provided by their landowners.

In the last years of her life, Doña Jacoba divided the Calle Morelos plot among her three surviving heirs. Until their mother died, however, the old lady kept the property together. But once she was gone, the two men sold their shares to the Maya Cortés brothers; Don Benjamín moved to Cuautla and Don Falconériz to Tetela. Several years later, they returned to Hueyapan to try to force Doña Zeferina at gunpoint to give up her part of the inheritance. By this time, Rafael was a grown man, and he defended his mother. From then on, Doña Zeferina had nothing more to do with her maternal half-brothers.

In 1948, when Angelina was six, a little girl by the name of Julia appeared at the door. She was five years old. Dressed in rags, she complained that she had had nothing to eat all day. Angelina asked her mother whether they could give Julia some food and Doña Zeferina invited the child in.

Julia's mother had run off with a man and abandoned her three children, leaving them to sleep in hay stacks and to beg for something to eat. Taking pity on the child, Doña Zeferina told Julia that she could live with them if she wanted to and that she would be treated like a daughter. But if she said yes, she would have to stop running about and behave like a good little girl. Julia accepted the offer and remained with the family until she grew up, at which time Doña Zeferina took her to Cuernavaca to help her find work.[9]

In 1952, when Angelina was ten years old, Doña Zeferina went to live with José Flores, a widower who had a house in the San Andrés Barrio.

Angelina and Julia stayed behind with Rafael and his first wife, in the Calle Morelos home. By that time, Raúl was dead, having been murdered in a drunken brawl in Hueyapan, and Ernestino was in boarding school, on scholarship, in the state of Puebla. Doña Zeferina returned to the family compound daily to make sure that everything was going well. Then a year later, she and Don José were married by the Church and the couple took up permanent residence in Doña Zeferina's home. As Doña Zeferina explained it, she could not stand living so far away from the plaza, way up in the hills. Her patients stopped coming to see her and, more to the point, she simply felt out of things. Agreeing to the move, Don José sold some of his land and livestock to have money to invest in Calle Morelos, but he never really liked the new arrangement. It remained his wife's home, he complained, not his own.

In November 1970, Don José fell off the roof of a bus that was parked in the plaza. He was trying to lower a basket of fruit from the rack, but the poor man was drunk, lost his balance, and fell, hitting his head on the ground. A few hours later, he died. A widow once again, Doña Zeferina remained living on Calle Morelos, together with her son Rafael and his large family, and, until she settled down again and moved to Cuernavaca, with her daughter Angelina and Lilia.[10]

CHAPTER THREE
THE HISTORY OF HUEYAPAN

The Village before 1900

The Spanish chronicler Fray Diego Durán[1] traces the history of Hueyapan back to 902 AD, when settlers from Xochimilco took up residence in the village and the surrounding area, introducing a higher level of civilization to the local population than the one that had previously existed in the region.[2] About 600 years later, the Aztecs arrived, probably in the early 1500s; then the Spaniards, sometime between 1522 and 1524.[3] As Fray Diego tells the story, a Spanish woman by the name of María de Estrada rode at the head of the conquering party and she quickly subdued the Indians.[4] Having participated earlier in a number of campaigns across the highlands of Central Mexico, María de Estrada wanted to lead one herself. Cortés responded generously to her request and gave her the honor of taking Hueyapan. Offering the reader a swashbuckling account, Durán describes María de Estrada racing off into battle on horseback, brandishing a sword in one hand and a shield in the other. Uneasy at first about following a woman, Cortés's soldiers held back, but when they heard her cry out to Saint James for protection, a few gallant souls fell into line and accompanied the lady warrior into combat. Startled by the sight of a woman on horseback galloping toward them, the Indians of Hueyapan panicked and fled, hurling themselves blindly into the gorges that surrounded the village. Encountering little resistance, the Spaniards took Hueyapan with ease, together with the neighboring settlement of Tetela.[5]

The historian Carlos Martínez-Marín dismisses Fray Diego's account as more fanciful than true, but he confirms the accuracy of the dates. According to Martínez-Marín, Hueyapan was conquered between the years 1522 and 1524.[6] By 1526, the Crown had assigned the people and lands of Hueyapan and Tetela to one *encomienda* (land grant), awarding the two villages to María de Estrada's husband, Pedro Sánchez Farfán. In 1536, Pedro Sánchez Farfán died and the *encomienda* reverted to his wife—until she remarried in 1548, at which time the property was transferred to her second husband, Alonso Martín Partidor.[7]

In 1558, after the death of Martín Partidor, interested parties disagreed about who had the rights to these *encomienda* lands and to the Indians living on them. To resolve the dispute, the case appeared before the Council of the Indies, where the judges decided to turn the *encomienda* over to the royal government and incorporate it into a nearby *corregimiento*.[8] By 1643, the *corregimiento* to which Hueyapan belonged came under the jurisdiction of the Cuautla Corregimiento, first informally, then officially. By 1784, the village had lost its independent status entirely.[9]

With each administrative consolidation, the fate of the villagers fell into the hands of another colonial institution. And with every change, things probably got a little worse. In the early years, for example, although the Indians were forced to work for *encomenderos* on fields they used to consider their own, they still remained in Hueyapan and had land on which to grow food for their families. Over the years, the situation deteriorated to such an extent that subsistence farmers were forced to become migrant laborers. Men abandoned their wives and children for several months at a time to work in the lowlands for starvation wages. The *haciendas* employed the villagers to cut sugarcane on fields that had once belonged to indigenous *pueblos*.

During my stay in Hueyapan, several people told me the story of how the *pueblo* lost its land to the Santa Clara Hacienda.[10] Although they never gave me a date, I assume, the incident took place after the Cuautla Corregimiento had annexed Hueyapan–Tetela and government officials stopped coming to the village regularly—probably as late as the nineteenth century, after the War of Independence. With no outside authority based in the area, the villagers had even less protection than they had before from the land-hungry owners of *haciendas* (*hacendados*).[11]

According to the version of the story I heard in Hueyapan, the owners of the Santa Clara Hacienda proposed establishing a firm boundary between the *hacienda's* lands and those of the *pueblo*: On the appointed day, representatives from Hueyapan would depart from the main plaza of the *pueblo* in the direction of the *hacienda* and the *hacendados* would leave from the lowlands and make their way up to the village. The place where they met would become the official line of demarcation.

In agreeing to the plan, the villagers believed that they had nothing to worry about. Since the *hacendados* were rich, and rich people were lazy, the villagers assumed that the landowners would get off to a late start. As the villagers saw it, the *hacendados* would only reach the area surrounding Hueyapan in the afternoon. Given the distances involved, there was no need to rush. On the appointed day, however, the *hacendados* defied all stereotypes and left the lowlands exceedingly early, long before dawn. By the time the villagers had organized themselves, the *hacendados* had succeeded in getting within a kilometer of the village plaza. As a result, the inhabitants of Hueyapan lost most of their land and they did not regain it until after the Mexican Revolution.[12]

In addition to members of the landholding classes, the Indians of Hueyapan had to deal with representatives of the Catholic Church. Since I describe the "spiritual conquest" of the village at some length in chapter five, at this point I will note only briefly that the Augustinian brothers arrived in the village in 1534, eight years after Hueyapan had been assigned to an *encomienda*.[13] Serious efforts to convert the Indians to Catholicism did not begin, however, until the *pueblo* became part of a *corregimiento*, by which time Dominican friars had settled down in the community. According to Martínez-Marín, the Dominicans arrived sometime between 1561 and 1563.[14] Ten years later, they had built a church and a monastery, the finishing touches of which would not be completed until 1784.[15] The Dominicans left Hueyapan in 1751, when the Mexican Church decided to "secularize" the village.[16]

We still know very little about the history of Hueyapan during the 1800s.[17] Aside from the rather fanciful stories reported by Doña Zeferina about the days when her great grandparents were young, we can confirm that a local villager by the name of Francisco Pérez opened a school in 1870, after having learned how to read from the resident priest. As we see in chapter six, despite these early efforts, the village did not have a federally recognized school until after the Mexican Revolution.

The Early 1900s and the Mexican Revolution

According to Facundo Navarro, an old farmer in Hueyapan,[18] before the Mexican Revolution, many villagers went down to the lowlands to work on the *haciendas*. When Don Facundo was still a teenager, he cut sugarcane on the Casasano and Calderón *haciendas*, located near Cuautla. Peons earned 62 *centavos* a day, he explained, and took shelter in abandoned caves near the *haciendas*. To feed themselves, they purchased *tortillas* twice a week from itinerant vendors who came to the *haciendas* to sell food to the peons. The *tortillas* were very large, Don Facundo said, and five or six carried a man over from Sunday until the following Wednesday, when once again the *tortilla* vendor returned. Even if we dismiss Don Facundo's account as a little exaggerated, migrant workers, we know, survived on very little food.

One day, while he was cutting cane on the Casasano Hacienda, Don Facundo saw a band of Zapatistas ride by on their way to Cuautla, where they clearly intended to cause trouble. Eager to find out what they were going do, he followed the horsemen into town and arrived just in time to witness a shootout. When the fighting was over, a few rebels approached Don Facundo and asked him to help carry away the dead and the wounded. Instead of lending a hand, Don Facundo quickly fled.

In 1912, when he was 18 years old, a Zapatista accosted Don Facundo in the village of Tochimilco, Puebla, and stole his straw bag (*morral*) and a few other possessions. Furious and humiliated, Don Facundo concluded that if he wanted to avoid being robbed again, he would have to join the army and fight for his dignity. At first, he explained, he did not understand what the war was about, but he preferred the Zapatistas to the Federales, because, as he put it, the Zapatistas looked more like his kind of people.[19] Among his many adventures, Don Facundo enjoyed recalling the time he entered

Mexico City in 1914 with a triumphant Zapata and helped occupy the capital. In all, he spent six years in the rebel's army.[20]

From what I was able to ascertain, very few villagers from Hueyapan volunteered to fight in the Revolution. Of those who did, even fewer were still alive in 1969–1970 to share their experiences with me. In addition to Don Facundo, I had the opportunity to talk to another villager who had been a soldier in the war, but Timoteo Hernández did not join the army willingly. In the early days of the Revolution, when he was still a teenage boy, his family decided to leave Hueyapan and wait the war out in the state of Guerrero. They did not, however, get very far before they crossed paths with some of Huerta's men, who drafted Timoteo on the spot and sent the boy north to fight against Pancho Villa.[21] At that time, Timoteo was 16 years old. In recalling some of the more memorable moments he had while serving as a soldier in the federal army, Don Timoteo described the day he saw the great revolutionary from Chihuahua enter Guadalajara.[22]

The village itself played a minor role in the Mexican Revolution. In his book on the subject, John Womack describes the experiences of people in *pueblos* throughout Morelos, recording moments of local involvement both modest and great, but he never mentions Hueyapan.[23] Even if most of the action was taking place elsewhere, the villagers clearly suffered a great deal. On the verge of starvation, they had to stretch what little corn they had by making *tortillas* out of a mixture of ground corn, corn spikes, acorns, and *tejocotes*. According to Doña Zeferina, the final product looked like donkey excrement. After the war, she refused to eat *tortillas* made with red corn because they reminded her of the tasteless ones she was forced to consume during the Revolution. Instead of beans, the villagers substituted the red flower of the scarlet runner.

Several residents of the *pueblo* told me about a terrible epidemic that had ravaged Hueyapan in the final months of the war. As they remembered it, villagers turned yellow and dropped dead on the street. The numbers overwhelmed the community, making it difficult for families to organize individual funerals. The only way to address the problem was to bury neighbors and relatives together in communal graves. The epidemic lasted about two months, killing hundreds of people.

Like countless others in the state of Morelos, the villagers had fallen victim to the Spanish influenza, which hit the state in the autumn of 1918. Having endured many hardships over eight years of war, they were particularly vulnerable to this formidable disease that had devastated populations around the world. If we compare Womack's description of the epidemic with what I heard in Hueyapan, we see that the villagers were not exaggerating:

> As winter came on, a new and profoundly anxious tone sounded in Zapata's correspondence. He had local worries galore now. The Spanish influenza, rampant throughout the world in these months, appeared in Mexico City in early October 1918 and spread immediately into the south. There were the perfect grounds for an epidemic—prolonged fatigue, starvation diets, bad winter, continuing moving. In the mountains where the poorest villages were [e.g., Hueyapan] and where many chiefs had their camps, the biting cold broke the health of thousands. In towns bodies accumulated faster than they could be buried. By December Cuautla sheltered only 150–200 civilians. Cuernavaca was a refuge of less than 5000. As for the open countryside, a family might as well have tried to inhabit Gehenna. In makeshift huts men, women, and children lay in shivering chills for days, without food or care, until one by one they all died. Wise survivors deserted their dead and fled into Guerrero, to safer climes, south of the Balsas River. National patrols discovered whole villages abandoned literally to "the peace of the graveyard."[24]

Throughout the Revolution, villagers stood watch around the clock, strategically posted in the hills on all sides of Hueyapan and in the bell tower of the church. When a watchman saw soldiers approaching, he set off a firecracker, alerting the villager who was waiting in the church to start ringing the bells. Upon hearing the signal, the villagers gathered what little food they had and fled to the hills, abandoning their homes and meager possessions to the pillaging soldiers. In Hueyapan, it mattered little whether the soldiers were Zapatistas or Federales. When the bells rang, people ran for their lives.

Doña Zeferina described the following incident as an example of why the villagers feared the Zapatistas—if not Zapata himself—as much as they feared the Federales. The story involved a Zapatista general by the name of Fortino Ayaquica.[25] As she remembered it, the general had one of his soldiers deliver what looked like an official ultimatum to Hueyapan, ordering the villagers to carry safe-conduct passes with them at all times. If they disobeyed, they would be killed on the spot. Frightened and outraged, the *ayudante* of Hueyapan sent word to Ayaquica that the village needed time to prepare the passes and asked that he wait a few days before sending his soldiers. Then, instead of doing what he promised to do, the *ayudante* went to see Zapata who was camped in Tlaltizapan at the time.[26] Accompanied by the secretary of the village, the *ayudante* presented Zapata with the threatening ultimatum and a petition from the village that asked him to intervene on the *pueblo*'s behalf. Responding immediately to their request, Zapata sent a message to Ayaquica, informing him that he had no right to demand safe-conduct passes from the villagers. After that, neither Ayaquica nor his soldiers ever came to Hueyapan.

In the final months of the war, the bells rang incessantly, almost every day, making it difficult for children to go to school. No sooner did they settle down in class, than they had to flee. They never had more than a couple of days of school a week, and they frequently went as long as two months without having a single class.

Hueyapan since the Mexican Revolution

One of the greatest achievements of the Mexican Revolution was its agrarian reform. After confiscating properties from the huge *haciendas*, the federal government gave the land back to impoverished communities. Procedures for implementing the agrarian reform were spelled out in careful detail in Article 27 of the 1917 Constitution. But the general principles guiding the program came from the Plan de Ayala, Zapata's famous proposal of 1911, a document that bears the signatures of peasants from many communities in the state of Morelos, including two men from Hueyapan.[27]

The agrarian reform returned land to the villagers in two major grants, each of which included communal lands, for the use of all members of the *pueblo*, and individual plots, often of considerable size, known as *ejidos*. Hueyapan received one of these grants soon after the war ended and another a few years later.[28] Not everyone, however, benefited equally from these *ejido* lands. Don Facundo, for example, told me that although he had risked his life for "*tierra y libertad*," nobody at home saved any land for him. Another old farmer, who had remained in the village during the war, commented bitterly that he did not thank the Revolution for anything, not even for one cigarette, let alone a field on which to plant corn.

There are, no doubt, many explanations for the uneven distribution of *ejido* lands. When new fields became available, for example, nobody considered the land that the village received as being worth very much. Since the law stipulated that a family could take only as much land as they were prepared to cultivate, many people refused to commit themselves to farming sterile soil. Others, however, knew about chemical fertilizers and the success they were having in the lowlands. Planning for the future, they assumed responsibility for large tracts of land, anticipating the day when the same modern fertilizers would reach the village as well and turn their badly eroded soil into cultivable fields. Of course everyone knew about natural fertilizers, but it was difficult to transport manure to the *ejido* lands, which were located, for the most part, several kilometers away from the center of town.

Until chemical fertilizers became popular in Hueyapan in the late 1940s, the villagers were unable to support themselves by farming their own land. The poor quality of the soil, in addition to other economic realities, forced many families, including Doña Zeferina and her sons, to spend several months a year working as peons in the lowlands. During the 1930s, 1940s, and even into the 1950s, a handful of villagers, who had sufficient funds, rented large fields from lowlanders and hired people from Hueyapan to work for them, housing them, the way the big *hacendados* had done, in abandoned caves. Instead of growing sugarcane or other cash crops, these entrepreneurs grew corn, beans, and calabash squash.

Villagers had opportunities to work for lowlanders as well, but since the terms were essentially the same, they preferred, by and large, to remain with members of their own community. Instead of earning a real salary, peons received six-liter measures of corn kernels and access to land on which to plant them. In a good year, a man could harvest 12 large sacks or *cargas*.[29] This was enough to feed a family of six or seven comfortably for a year. Peons also received a weekly allowance of one *peso*.

Leaving their wives and young children back home in Hueyapan, peons frequently took their older sons and daughters with them and hired them out. If all the children were grown, they might take their wives as well. Widowed or abandoned women also went down to the lowlands, leaving their younger children behind in the care of grand-parents and taking the older ones with them. While boys joined the men in the fields, women and girls worked as corn grinders and cooks.

As compensation for their work, women received 25 *pesos* at the beginning of the season to buy cotton cloth to make themselves lightweight clothing—they would never have survived the heat of the lowlands in their wool *xincueites* and *rebozos*. Then at the end of the season, women received as many liters of unground corn as they managed to grind for their employer. They also earned a weekly allowance of 25 *centavos*.

Villagers spent June, July, and August in the lowlands, planting and caring for their crops. They then returned to Hueyapan and remained there until December, at which time they went down again for the harvest. When chemical fertilizers came to Hueyapan, this old routine changed.

Thanks to the fertilizers, men could make a better living cultivat-ing their own land at home than they could by going down to the lowlands and tilling other people's soil. Women, however, continued to make more money outside the village. By the late 1950s, there-fore, many more women than men were working elsewhere. As mechanized mills replaced their labor as corn grinders, women sought employment as maids, in greater numbers than they had done before, in Cuernavaca and Mexico City. Over the years, a hand-ful of men migrated as well to take factory jobs, like Doña Zeferina's son Ernestino who worked in Cuernavaca for the Burlington Textile Mills. By 1969–1970, when the village had a population of nearly 4,000 people, about 100 women held jobs in Mexico City alone.[30]

Villagers who left Hueyapan in the late 1960s/early 1970s to look for work elsewhere, differed significantly from those who used to go to the lowlands for several months a year a generation earlier. First of all, the new migrants went to urban centers primarily and settled down permanently in the cities. Absorbed into the ever-growing ghettos of the poor, they returned to the village only occasionally to visit their families. They no longer saw Hueyapan as their primary residence.

Second, the newly urbanized migrants began influencing the standard of living in Hueyapan in ways that their parents could never have done. On their visits to the *pueblo*, they left behind money and luxury items associated with the city. As a result, they played an influential role in incorporating Hueyapan into the consumer-oriented economy of Mexico. Although peons and corn grinders saw city life in Cuautla, they purchased very little, for they did not work for money the way the more recent migrants did, but for the right to grow a little food for their families on land that was more fertile than what they had back home.

By 1969–1970, villagers were no longer relying solely on their migrant-worker children for cash, but were earning money themselves. Thanks to chemical fertilizers, they abandoned subsistence farming and developed a number of cash crops, in particular fruit. Although people in Hueyapan had been growing fruit for hundreds of years before chemical fertilzers became available, their harvests had been meager. Now, the yields increased considerably, making it possible for the villagers to produce enough fruit to export to Mexico City. Their most lucrative harvests were sickle pears and a small variety of peaches; they also sold walnuts, apples, custard apples, pomegranates, and *tejocotes*.[31]

In 1953, the government of Morelos gave the villagers the dynamite they needed to build a dirt road, 11 kilometers long, between Tlacotepec and Hueyapan, so that trucks and buses might be able to get through to the *pueblo*. From Tlacotepec, the villagers could easily drive their produce over an excellent network of highways to major markets in Central Mexico, located in the cities of Cuautla, Cuernavaca, Mexico City, and Puebla. Since the villagers depended largely on volunteer help, it took the better part of five years to finish building the road and the final result was an uneven, amateur job that was often treacherous during the harsh rainy season. In the mid-1960s, the villagers built a second road, 12 kilometers long, to connect the village to its municipal seat in Tetela.

In 1963, the Morelos Estrella–Roja bus line extended its second-class Cuautla–Tlacotepec service to Hueyapan. Ten years later, it provided Hueyapan with a second line, connecting the village to Tetela. Soon, cargo trucks also started coming to Hueyapan—some from as far away as Mexico City, others from markets near by—to purchase fruit in the *pueblo*. Then in the late 1960s, several villagers acquired trucks of their own, and took over a role that had previously been played by outsiders. From that time on, more and more of the village's fruit went to Mexico City's Manzanares Market in vehicles owned by local people. As of 1971, seven families in Hueyapan had already purchased trucks.[32]

Once they had a new road, the villagers installed electricity, something they could only do after government workers had easy access to the village and could maintain the electrical lines. They also opened a weekly market. Although it was modest by lowland standards, the Hueyapan market provided a real service to the villagers and to the people living in communities even more remote than Hueyapan, located on the other side of the hills surrounding the village, in the state of Puebla.

In the early spring, when the weather was warm and the rains had still not made the roads hazardous, the Hueyapan market was at its peak. One Tuesday in June (1970) there were 55 different vendors in the plaza, most of whom were selling vegetables and fruit—peanuts, green peas, roasted ears of corn (*elotes*), green tomatoes (*tomates*), red tomatoes (*jitomates*), potatoes, kidney beans, onions, garlic, fresh and dried *chile* peppers, mangoes, limes, oranges, pineapples, and watermelons. Available as well were insect-derived foods, for example, *jumiles* (small edible insects, the size of ticks) and honey. Finally, vendors also sold candies, snow cones, bread, meat (beef and pork), and prepared food—beans, *tortillas*, *tamales*, and *mole colorado*—as well as cotton cloth, ribbons and thread, men's pants, plastic toys, dime-store variety kitchenware, *comales*, and earthenware pots.[33]

Even though they now had a market in town, many members of the community continued to travel from village to village on market days, with the hope of selling small quantities of fruit, bunches of flowers, and *pulque*. Making a living this way had become the fate of those who did not have the money to invest in *ejido* lands, or to buy enough merchandise to set up a little business in Hueyapan—single mothers abandoned by the fathers of their children, widows, and old couples whose children did not have the means to look after them. At least, they could now take the bus, as they traveled from village to

Photo 5 Market day in Hueyapan.

village, and spare themselves the burden of carrying heavy loads on their backs or on the backs of their stubborn donkeys—that is, of course, if they could afford the fare.

Other changes made life easier in Hueyapan, in particular for women. In the late 1940s, corn mills were introduced to the village, freeing women from the arduous chore of grinding corn meal by hand—if, once again, they had the money to pay for the service. By 1970, there were 11 mills in the village. The other improvement was running water. In the year I first visited Hueyapan, only a few villagers in the San Jacinto Barrio had this convenience. By 1971, perhaps half the villagers living in the two *barrios* near the main plaza had running water as well,[34] relieving families from the tedious task of fetching water from streams located at the bottom of the deep gorges that surrounded Hueyapan.

The inspiration for many of the changes taking place in the village came from government officials who were sent to Hueyapan to help the villagers acculturate. Schoolteachers played a major role, but others contributed as well, in particular social workers, known as cultural missionaries, who visited the *pueblo* in 1945, and again in the 1960s. As representatives of modern Mexico, government workers showed the villagers how to improve their standard of living. They also taught them to practice the traditions of the country's new "religion"—introducing them to the "sacred texts" of the Mexican Revolution and giving them a sense of national belonging.

In sum, by the time I reached the village in 1969, the history of Hueyapan had come full circle. During the early colonial period, Cortés made a gift of the villagers and their land to secular and religious representatives of the Crown. Spanish priests responded quickly and settled down in the *pueblo*, dramatically changing the customs of the villagers and integrating the Indians into the economy and religion of New Spain. Forced to work on *encomienda* and *corregimiento* lands, the villagers became Christians and assumed their place at the bottom of the social hierarchy. The situation grew even worse during the late colonial period when the villagers had no other option than to become migrant laborers and work several months a year on *haciendas* in the lowlands near Cuautla. And so they remained until after the Mexican Revolution, when the nation's leaders embraced the ideas of Emiliano Zapata's agrarian reform and provided the villagers with the land they needed to farm at home. But no sooner did they settle down to a new life in the village, than missionaries arrived once again, this time sent by the federal government, to incorporate the Indians into postrevolutionary Mexico. Given this history, how could people maintain, as so many did in 1969–1970, that the villagers still lived in cultural isolation and that they had, as a result, preserved their indigenous way of life?

CHAPTER FOUR

WHAT IT MEANS TO BE INDIAN IN
HUEYAPAN (1969–1970)

Although embarrassed to admit it, most villagers acknowledged that they were Indians.[1] What this meant, however, was elusive. Calling themselves Indians did little to explain who the villagers were. It identified instead who the villagers were not. To make matters worse, the criteria used to determine the "who" in who the villagers were not, were constantly shifting.

Since colonial times, the villagers have faced the formidable task of filling in the void of their Indianness, something, it seemed, they could never do. Every time they tried to overcome their condition by adopting traditions associated with members of the non-Indian elite, the ruling classes introduced new cultural markers to keep the two groups apart, demoting their old outmoded practices to the lowly status of Indian. As a result, the villagers stayed Indian by virtue of the fact that they continued to lack what Mexico's elite continued to acquire.

People saw their Indian identity in a static, ahistorical way, which accurately reflected their social status in Mexico, but ignored the historical processes involved in keeping the villagers marginalized and poor. Having internalized a deeply negative understanding of what it meant to be Indian, the villagers overlooked the differences that existed between their so-called indigenous culture, which over the centuries had continued to change, and their class position in Mexican society, which had remained essentially the same.

This negative image had roots dating back to the sixteenth century, when the conquering Spaniards turned the native peoples of Mexico into Indians and incorporated them into the new colonial order. Although major differences existed between the cultures of Europe and those of the New World, indigenous customs quickly disappeared—or were significantly transformed—and Spanish traditions replaced them. After defeating the Aztecs in 1521, Cortés and his soldiers proceeded systematically to destroy indigenous societies. Performing acts of terrible violence, they justified these abuses as a necessary part of their sacred mission to save pagan souls. Backed by the authority of the Catholic Church, the conquerors forced Indians to follow the teachings of Jesus and to work for the king of Spain.

Scholars have written extensively about "the devastation" of indigenous Mexico, describing the hardships that Indians endured during colonial times. In 1580, after nearly 60 years of Spanish rule, the indigenous population had dropped to less than a quarter the size it had been at the time of the conquest. And as time went on, things only got worse. Victims of Spanish cruelty and European diseases, by 1650, the indigenous population had dropped to one-seventh the size it had been in 1521.[2] Given this long and terrible history, I did not expect to find in Hueyapan much evidence of the village's indigenous heritage. And I did not. What I found instead, in 1969–1970, was a profound sense of Indian inferiority.

As I settled down in Hueyapan and began meeting the villagers, I saw how humiliated people felt every time I identified them as Indians. To call somebody *indio* in 1969 was just as degrading as it was to call an African American "nigger." The official euphemism *indígena* (indigenous person), although more polite, was hardly more flattering. When I saw how people responded to the question, I stopped asking them directly about their indigenous identity or about what they thought it meant to call somebody Indian. I tried instead to approach the subject obliquely, making vague references, hoping that my "discretion" would give them the confidence to open up. It rarely did.

When I returned to the *pueblo* in December 1971, I knew the villagers better and felt I could take the risk of asking them to talk about this difficult subject, without beating around the bush and without having them think that I was prying. What I learned from these later conversations only confirmed what I had concluded on my own, after many months of observation. What follows, then, is a summary of the various contexts in which I heard villagers use the term *indio* or *indígena* among themselves and of the answers people gave when I asked them point blank to give me an explanation. In the end, I interviewed formally and informally several hundred members of the community.

In Hueyapan, people saw their Indian identity in comparative terms: they were more or less Indian than somebody else. Given my social standing in the *pueblo*, almost everyone was Indian in relation to me. From the moment we met, villagers indicated that they felt inferior to me by saying they were Indians. When, for example, I visited a family for the first time, the head of the household invariably apologized, as he welcomed me in, repeating a phrase I heard almost everywhere I went: "Please excuse us; we are only poor little Indians (*inditos*) here." It mattered little whether the family lived well or modestly by the standards of the village. In my presence, they were all poor and uneducated Indians. They wanted to warn me of this painful fact so that I would forgive them for any social blunder they might commit. According to custom, by admitting to me that they were "poor little Indians," I could not hold them responsible for doing anything wrong. Nobody, they knew, expected an Indian to have the manners or means to treat an honored guest properly.

The image of the Indian was so negative in Hueyapan that one woman used the term *indio* as a synonym for "bad person." In defending the *pueblo* against a recent accusation, Gregoria Lozada observed that outsiders considered the villagers to be *indios*, when, in fact, they were "very good people." After pressing her a little harder to help me understand, she said that Hueyapan used to be more Indian than it was today, but thanks to the schoolteachers and government social workers, the *pueblo* had become more "civilized."

When I first asked villagers to explain what it meant to be Indian, they often responded that they did not know. Trying again, I offered examples of the ways I had heard people use the term: "What did villagers mean," I asked, "when they said to me, 'Please excuse us, we are only poor little Indians'?" "They felt inferior to you," came the usual reply. "But why?" "Because the villagers were poor and uneducated, something anyone could tell right away upon hearing them speak Spanish." After this brief introduction, some discussed the matter in greater detail.

According to one farmer, Indians "don't know anything." Doña Zeferina's daughter-in-law Juana expanded on the point: "Indians don't know anything; they are foolish."[3] When I asked Doña Juana to tell me what she meant by "foolish," she said that we should take her as an example: she did not know how to read or write. A 73-year-old woman explained that being Indian meant that you ate ordinary food, nothing elaborate. Unlike city folk, who enjoyed tasty delicacies preserved in tin cans, Indians ate simply, limiting themselves to *tortillas*, beans, and *chiles*. Another old woman repeated that the villagers were Indians because they did not know how to speak Spanish well and this embarrassed them.

I discussed the matter of language with Elvira Hernández, a young woman from Hueyapan who had served as a Nahuatl informant for linguists in Mexico and the United States:[4]

> *J.F.:* You once told me, Elvira, that when people from Hueyapan go to Mexico City, they are afraid to speak Spanish. Why?
>
> *E.H.:* Because they know that their Spanish is bad, that they do not speak well, that they make lots of mistakes. They also know that city people speak Spanish perfectly and will have a negative opinion of the villagers for speaking badly.
>
> *J.F.:* What do city people say? If a villager is on a bus in Mexico City and he makes grammatical errors, what will people in the city say?
>
> *E.H.:* Something like, "Here is an Indian who doesn't know how to speak well."
>
> *J.F.:* And this makes the villager feel bad?
>
> *E.H.:* Yes, he feels bad because he knows himself that he doesn't speak well.
>
> *J.F.:* And does that mean he is an Indian?
>
> *E.H.:* Yes, because of the way he speaks, because of his lack of culture.

When asked about being Indian, the weaver Epifania Alonso added that indigenous people did not know any better. Under the circumstances, it was not their fault when they did something wrong. They should not be blamed for their mistakes. Only people with education could be held responsible for what they did. As an illiterate farmer put it, the villagers had "squashes" (*calabazas*) for heads; how could people expect them to amount to very much?

The vast majority of the people I interviewed in Hueyapan defined their Indianness in terms of what they did not have or could not do. Almost nobody singled out a particular custom or worldview that made him or her Indian. Only one person volunteered that the villagers spoke a different language; almost everyone else only noted that they did not speak Spanish in a grammatically acceptable way.[5] Another villager mentioned the traditional skirt that some women wore (*xincueite*), but that was about all.

It goes without saying that the people I interviewed knew perfectly well that their language and dress marked them as Indians. For the villagers, however, a far better way to describe their identity was to talk about what they did not have. More than anything else, being Indian, in their eyes, meant being poor and uneducated.

Virtually everyone gave the same answer, differing only in the degree of detail. Villagers with more schooling or experience with outsiders repeated the formulaic explanation used by government officials: In Hueyapan, the villagers were Indian because they did not have any "culture" (*falta de cultura*). People with culture, they continued, had education and money. They could read and write. They knew how to speak with "respect" (addressing one another with honorific titles—Engineer Juan, Architect José—and flowery phrases). People with culture had confidence in themselves. They could speak in public before large crowds and use a microphone. Dressed like urban Mexicans, they lived comfortably, in homes furnished with store-bought beds, tables, and chairs. Unlike Indians, people with culture owned televisions and trucks, to name but a couple of status symbols frequently mentioned.[6]

Almost everybody had negative feelings about being Indian. The elderly and illiterate were fatalistic: to be Indian was their unfortunate lot. Nothing could be done about it. Other villagers believed that although they were Indians, they could hide it. Doña Zeferina, for example, who had ambitious dreams for the family, taught her children and grandchildren to keep their modest home orderly and clean. As she liked to put it, she wanted them to look "a little less sad, a little less poor, a little less Indian." A native schoolteacher, born in Hueyapan, tried to cover up the *pueblo*'s Indian status by instructing the villagers to respond in the affirmative on the 1970 census when asked if they had bathroom facilities in their homes. With the exception of this particular *maestro*, nobody, in fact, had anything more than a *temascal*, one of the few prehispanic features still found in the village.

Another way people tried to hide their Indian identity was to "pass" in the wider world. Maestro Rafael, for example, liked to describe how schoolteachers reacted to him when he attended statewide functions. Recognized for his ability to speak eloquently in public, his colleagues had trouble believing that he came from Hueyapan. When he revealed his secret, they invariably asked, "But aren't they very Indian up there?"[7]

When villagers called one another Indian, they almost always did so to be insulting or self-deprecating. Once I asked a villager whether his neighbor, who was poor, would participate in a project aimed at modernizing the *pueblo*. The man responded in disbelief: "That guy? Hell no. He's too Indian." In another instance, a fourth-grade teacher, who was not born in the *pueblo*, asked her pupils to name the original inhabitants of Hueyapan. Instead of saying, "The people of Xochimilco," as they had learned in school,[8] one boy yelled out, to the embarrassed amusement of others, "the Chichimecas!"—a disparaging term used in Central Mexico at the time of the Spanish conquest for nomadic tribes of the North. As every Nahuatl-speaking child in the classroom knew, the name Chichimeca meant literally, "son of a bitch" (as in female dog). To use this degrading term to identify their own ancestors was a disrespectful thing to do.

Several villagers knew the names of indigenous peoples located in northern Mexico who lived in greater isolation from mainstream society than did the inhabitants of Hueyapan. Referring to them by their "tribal" designations, the villagers did not consider them Indians. These people lived in an entirely different universe, where they still practiced "barbarous" customs. Of particular interest to the residents of Hueyapan were the Yaquis who, they told me, could "smell men out of their hiding places," and the Apaches who "ate" people. The Yaquis earned their reputation by fighting with the federal troops against Zapata during the Mexican Revolution and demonstrating extraordinary skill in tracking down rebels in the hills of Morelos. As for the Apaches, Doña Zeferina had heard—from reliable sources, she assured us—that there was an Apache living in Cholula, Puebla, who wore no clothes and had a beard down to his waist. This horrible creature, she continued, was locked up in a cage to prevent him from running about and killing people for food. His keepers fed him raw meat.[9]

When I asked the villagers to define what it meant to be Indian in Hueyapan, nobody suggested that Indians were descended from a distinct race. Although some people, like Doña Zeferina, noted that their own particular ancestors came from another race—in her case from people with dark skin and light hair—the villagers did not see skin color, or any other physical characteristic as a significant feature of their Indian identity. There were a number of reasons for this, including the fact that the villagers knew they did not look very different from non-Indian peasants in the surrounding area. They also knew that official definitions focused on culture—whatever that meant—not on physical traits.[10]

Despite all the rhetoric, people in Hueyapan acknowledged the obvious: generally speaking, the poor in Mexico were darker than the rich. What is more, having internalized the tastes of the ruling classes, the villagers took it for granted that "White was beautiful" and openly expressed their preference for light skin, blue eyes, wavy and/or blond hair; for any feature, in other words, that looked European. In their own families, they invariably favored the child with the lightest complexion. When a baby was born, one of the first questions asked was about the color of the infant's skin. Then, as children grew older, their mothers constantly warned them to keep out of the sun, so that they would not turn any darker than they already were.

In colonial times, the villagers "learned" that white skin and other European features were more attractive than Amerindian ones. From that point on, they have measured good looks by Caucasian standards. Government propaganda may have made the Mestizo the idealized symbol of Mexico, but the media have sent a stronger message: it was still better to be blond. Occasionally, a newspaper or magazine reached the *pueblo* and it offered the villagers a glimpse at how the rich and beautiful lived. Invariably, the illustrations showed fairhaired people with pearly white skin. Almost every home I visited had a calendar, often several years old, pinned up on a wall, with an alluring picture of a beautiful blond. Finally, by 1969–1970, about four or five people in Hueyapan had purchased television sets and the programs they watched reinforced the stereotype even further. For a fee of 20 *centavos*, owners of TVs invited their neighbors over to watch soap operas that frequently touched on the question of race.[11]

"Angelitos Negros"

During the year I lived in Hueyapan, Doña Zeferina's neighbor, Hermenegilda Pérez, invited me to her brother's home to watch an episode of "Angelitos Negros" (Little Black Angels), the most popular soap opera of the season. I later learned that this melodrama was a perennial favorite, not only in Mexico, but throughout Latin America and the Spanish-speaking Caribbean. It appeared first as a movie in the late 1950s and then again in the 1960s. The TV version was an adaptation of the film and had already had several reruns, both in Mexico and on Puerto Rican television in the United States.

Briefly, "Angelitos Negros" tells the story of a Black maid, Merced, who has a daughter, María Luisa, by a White upper-class man, the widowed master of the house where Merced works. As luck would have it, the baby is born lily white, with blond hair, and blue eyes. Soon after he sees his beautiful child, the father becomes deathly ill and passes away—but not before extracting a cruel promise from Merced to sacrifice her maternal rights to their daughter and to serve as the child's nanny. And so, as María Luisa grows up, she is totally unaware of the fact that Merced is her mother. Blond and beautiful, she is racist to the core.

As a young woman, María Luisa falls in love with the famous pop singer, Juan Carlos, and the couple marries. In time, the young bride becomes pregnant and she gives birth to a little girl, at which point everything goes wrong. Much to her horror and understandable confusion, she has brought a Black baby into the world. Pushing the infant away from her breast, she refuses to accept it. Her violent reaction shocks Juan Carlos profoundly who, in spite of being a celebrity, has a heart of gold and a special warm spot for Black people.

Terribly shaken by the turn of events, Merced takes Juan Carlos into her confidence and asks him to tell María Luisa that he has Black blood on his side of the family. Juan Carlos agrees to protect Merced's secret. Assuming the "blame," he then helps Merced raise his little Black child, smothering the girl with love and affection. As time goes by, María Luisa remains uncaring and mean, totally uninterested in her adorable child. Then, during one of her many fits of anger, she pushes Merced down a long flight of stairs. The poor woman has not been well and this last act of violence is the final blow. As Merced lies dying, Juan Carlos reveals the painful truth. Seething with anger, he tells his wretched wife that she has killed her own mother. Transformed on the spot, María Luisa takes Merced into her arms, and, sobbing, asks for forgiveness.

In the episode I saw in Hueyapan, we find Merced talking to a young Black woman by the name of Isabel, who performs in the band that accompanies Juan Carlos. The scene takes place while Juan Carlos and María Luisa are away on their honeymoon. Merced tells Isabel to beware of men, for they always take advantage of nice young women. Isabel replies sadly that she has nothing to fear. Who would take advantage of her? She's so ugly and black. Isabel then asks Merced whether she has ever been in love. Merced turns away momentarily, staring off into space. "No," she says. "Who would love me? I'm so ugly and black."

While Merced and Isabel shared confidences, the villagers whispered among themselves. "Look how black they are! All you can see are their teeth!" The message was clear. Here were people even darker than they and, by the standards of the village, even uglier.

Political Factions and Indianness

Almost everyone conceded that the villagers lived in an indigenous *pueblo*, a designation that meant that they were "culturally backward" and disadvantaged economically.[12] But some members of the community were eager for change. Calling themselves progressives, they joined forces with representatives of the federal government who had come to Hueyapan to "acculturate" the Indians. Others opposed these initiatives.

The progressives in town wanted Hueyapan to become more Mestizo and criticized their opponents for being too Indian. What distinguished the two factions, however, was not language, dress, and income, as I had expected. Almost everybody in both factions spoke Nahuatl fluently. What is more, older women in families on both sides of the divide continued to wear *xincueites*. There was little to distinguish them economically either. Where the two groups clearly differed, however, was in the willingness of their members to contribute to village-wide projects whose supporters claimed would help modernize the *pueblo*.

Upon closer examination, we see that the majority of those belonging to the self-proclaimed progressives lived in the center of town, while the so-called conservatives lived in the outlying *barrios* of San Andrés, San Bartolo, and San Felipe. Geography, in other words, played a critical role in determining political loyalties.

For literally hundreds of years, the Centro—the *barrios* of San Miguel and San Jacinto—had seen itself as the cultural hub of the village. Probably, the site of Aztec rituals as well, we know that by the middle of the sixteenth century, the Centro had become the place for villagers to gather on important religious and secular occasions. As we have already seen, Dominican friars built their church and monastery in the Centro in the 1570s. Then, in the late 1800s, during the days of Porfirio Díaz, the Mexican government had the villagers erect a building in the Centro to provide an office for the village's *ayudante*. By the time I got to Hueyapan in 1969–1970, nothing much had changed. The Centro still dominated. It had, for example, the only primary school in town that offered a full program, in all six grades.[13] It was also the site of the weekly market in town and the bus depot.[14]

After the Mexican Revolution, when government representatives came to the village to encourage people to modernize the *pueblo*, a number of inhabitants living in the Centro accepted the invitation with enthusiasm. Taking control of new community projects, they continued to dominate older institutions as well, causing those in the outlying *barrios* to question whether the Centro was looking out for the interests of the entire *pueblo*, or for only themselves. In the end, the conservatives concluded that people in San Miguel and San Jacinto did more for the Centro than for their neighbors in San Andrés, San Bartolo, San Felipe, and the satellite *ranchos*.

People living in the Centro preferred to interpret the resistance as the response of uncultured Indians. Native schoolteachers in particular insisted on describing the opposition in this way, while presenting themselves as local representatives of the nation's elite. In suggesting that political differences in the village had to do with culture, progressives in the Centro obscured the real issues of conflict. But they were not alone. Both sides defended their interests—and described their points of disagreement—in terms that conformed to the rhetoric of wider political debates that were taking place at the time in rural Morelos and elsewhere in Mexico. While the Centro supported schoolteachers and their urban-based ideas about "culture," faithfully endorsing the platform of the Partido Revolucionario Institucional (PRI), the national party of Mexico, the *barrio* faction embraced the position of a regional peasant party called the Central Campesino Independiente (CCI), a group that had been gaining support in the area by mounting an active campaign against schoolteachers and other government employees. In the process, the factions talked past one another. The Centro criticized the "uncultured Indians" of the outlying *barrios* for refusing to cooperate with projects aimed at improving the *pueblo*; while the *barrio* faction responded as *campesinos* (peasants), not *indígenas*, and claimed that they were defending themselves against the corruption of urban-identified villagers. According to their leaders, members of the *barrio* faction were not opposed to progress per se, but to the political and personal motives of schoolteachers and the like who had designated themselves spokesmen for the villagers to the outside world, without having the authority to do so.

Turning now to look at a major political conflict that persisted for several years during the 1960s, we see that, despite the rhetoric of the progressives in town, the issues at hand had less to do with the Indian question than they did with local struggles for political control. Events leading up to this particular clash began in 1964, when Maestro Rafael was serving as director of the primary school in the Centro. At the time, the *maestro* and other members of the Centro faction had recently succeeded in getting electricity installed in the village. Against strong opposition, they convinced the majority of households in town to accept to pay a monthly tax to cover the costs associated with having electricity. A few years later, Maestro Rafael succeeded again in getting a second bill passed, this time to fix the roof and drainage system on the government building in the Centro.

The repairs, of course, had a price tag as well. In voting for the improvements, the villagers had accepted the burden of yet another tax. When the time came, however, people allied to the *barrio* faction refused to pay the mandatory 50 *pesos*. Infuriated by the resistance, members of the Centro faction threatened to call in the Cuautla police.

As tensions mounted, supporters of the *barrio* faction stopped paying their monthly tax for electricity, justifying this second act of defiance on the grounds that they had opposed the earlier initiative as well. They were sick and tired, they said, of being told what to do by a few men. Responding quickly to the opposition, the *ayudante* arrested a prominent man in the *barrio* faction and sent him off to Tetela to be disciplined. An official in the municipal seat offered to pay the villager's bill, but the man refused, explaining angrily that he had not paid his taxes out of principle, not poverty. While the man defended his position and insisted he was right, others claimed he had broken the law. In the end, the municipal officer in Tetela sent the defiant villager to Cuautla, where he was put in jail.

Before long, the CCI got wind of the case. Using political connections, they had the man from Hueyapan released and sent him back home, in the company of a party leader who came from Tepalcingo. When the two men reached the village, they called a town meeting.

People crowded into the plaza to hear what the CCI leader had to say. Schoolteachers, he proclaimed, were causing trouble in town. They made *campesinos* pay taxes and then pocketed the money for themselves. In Hueyapan, he continued, there was one teacher in particular who exploited the villagers. And what was his name? "Rafael Vargas!" the angry crowd yelled back. Had Maestro Rafael been in town that day, he might have been killed. Fortunately, he was not. In the heat of the moment, the villagers divided pretty evenly on the question of whether he was guilty. Violence was in the air. One man who supported the *maestro* began waving his pistol and shouting to the crowd that he was ready to shoot it out with anyone who questioned the schoolteacher's integrity. Another member of the Centro faction reported that things deteriorated so quickly that friends of the *maestro* rushed off to Cuernavaca to seek police protection for the *pueblo*.

Before departing, the CCI representative promised to return to prove his case against the *maestro*. But he never did. Doña Zeferina said that she was not surprised, because the man had been very drunk that day and did not know what he was saying or doing. He was apparently so confused that he signed a petition that friends of the *maestro* had drawn up on the spot to defend the schoolteacher's reputation.

A few days later the school inspector for the district came to Hueyapan to ask the villagers to decide whether Maestro Rafael should remain the director of the school. Calling for a vote, the inspector instructed those who supported the schoolteacher to move to one side of the plaza and those who did not to move to the other. At first, only women came to Maestro Rafael's defense, but soon their husbands followed. So did all his fellow teachers. In the end, the overwhelming majority of the villagers gave Maestro Rafael their vote of confidence.

Although gratified by the community's show of support, Maestro Rafael decided to step down. The honor of being director of the school was not worth the political anxiety or the risk of future threats to his personal safety. Some villagers, he knew, were still very angry and would challenge him again. Since schoolteachers did not earn anything extra for assuming the responsibility of being director, why should he put up with the strain?

Customs Identified as Indian

As we have already seen, people in Hueyapan in 1969–1970 defined their Indianness primarily in negative terms, describing themselves by who they were not and by what they did not have. There were, however, a number of customs that everyone recognized as Indian. More often than not, what they called indigenous was first introduced to the village during colonial and postcolonial times. But a few "authentic" customs survived as well, largely thanks to representatives of the ruling classes. No matter where these traditions came from, Indian customs in Hueyapan were unambiguous class markers, evidence of the villagers' lowly place in the social hierarchy of the country. People said that these practices persisted, because the inhabitants of the *pueblo* lacked the education and money to stop being Indians.

While the villagers focused on what they did not have, outsiders focused on what the villagers had that distinguished them from non-Indians. The rich wanted to find evidence of Mexico's prehispanic past. The less fortunate wanted to prove that poor Mestizos like them were different from those who occupied the absolute bottom of Mexico's socioeconomic scale.[15]

As we turn now to look at the traditions themselves, we find customs with roots going back to prehispanic times that Spanish priests and other members of colonial society transformed long ago and incorporated into the culture of non-Indian Mexico. It is, however, their clear link to the past that has given these traditions their special value. Paying little attention to the context in which the villagers practice them, outsiders describe these Indian customs in ways that ignore almost 500 years of Hueyapan's history. Since the sixteenth century, the villagers have been part of a European cultural, economic, and social system.

Although we still find traces in 1969–1970 of the community's prehispanic past, these vestiges bear witness to a process, many centuries old, of forced integration and cultural change. Known as "syncretism" in the literature, the customs evolved over many years of European domination, during which time Spanish priests and landowners creatively combined pre-Columbian and European traditions, incorporating practices that might smooth the transition of dislocated Indians into a new society. Many of these cultural innovations have fallen out of use over the years, but a few exotic traditions linger on, inviting visitors to single them out, in an anachronistic fashion, as "evidence" of the villagers' resistance to change and ongoing ties to their prehispanic ancestors.[16]

The Nahuatl Language

Although there were very few monolinguals left in Hueyapan in 1969–1970, almost every adult in the village still spoke the language fluently.[17] Recognized by everyone as prehispanic in origin, the villagers considered Nahuatl inferior to Spanish. It was a "dialect," they explained, not a "language," with "no grammar" or written literature. The idea that Nahuatl lacked a grammatical structure dates back to early colonial times, when missionary priests tried to learn this indigenous tongue and found it difficult to do so. Using Latin as their model, they assumed that languages, as opposed to dialects, had written rules of grammar that systematically described how one conjugated a verb and declined a noun. Nahuatl, of course, <u>had</u> grammatical rules, but no primers available to help the priests learn how to use the language properly.

In later years, when state schools finally reached Hueyapan, teachers told villagers that they spoke Spanish badly because they refused to abandon Nahuatl. As a result, parents stopped using their mother tongue with their children, hoping to give the next generation a better chance to succeed than they had had themselves. In Doña Zeferina's home, the old woman spoke Nahuatl to Don José and Doña Juana, but rarely to her children or grandchildren. Although they knew Spanish better than Nahuatl, Maestro Rafael and his sister Angelina spoke Nahuatl too, as did some of the older grandchildren, having learned it by listening to the language at home and in the streets of Hueyapan.

Since Spanish has coexisted with Nahuatl for centuries in Hueyapan, we can see the influence of the conquerors' idiom on this prehispanic language, both lexically and grammatically. Well aware of the fact that the Nahuatl they spoke borrowed heavily from Spanish, the villagers told me that this had always been the case, for as far back as they could remember, probably, they assumed, since long before the Mexican Revolution. Spanish, in fact, began influencing Hueyapan Nahuatl during the early colonial period, at a time when the villagers were still unfamiliar with Spanish phonemes. Unable to imitate the way the Spanish language sounded, they distorted the pronunciation of words introduced into their "dialect" to identify foreign objects and concepts. *Sombrero* (hat), for example, became *xonblelotle* in Nahuatl.

Over the years, Nahuatl became a virtual reservoir of terms from old Spanish that had dropped out of circulation in urban centers of modern Mexico. Today, a donkey, for instance, is *burro*. In colonial times, it was *asno* and has been preserved as *axnu* in Nahuatl. In Hueyapan Nahuatl we even find Arabic terms that have disappeared from contemporary Mexican Spanish—an unexpected place to find the influence of the Moors on the culture of Spain.[18] To give one example, in present-day Mexican Spanish, a fraction of a *peso* is a *centavo*, while in Hueyapan Nahuatl the word is *tomin*, derived from the old Arabic term *thumin*.[19]

Most Spanish words found in Hueyapan Nahuatl are currently in use in Mexican Spanish as well. When the Indians became part of colonial New Spain, they had to find words to identify a wide range of imported items, including different kinds of food, pieces of clothing, and medicine, as well as religious, political, and economic practices, new methods of farming and transportation, weights and measures, and so on. Even when the villagers had equivalents in Nahuatl, they often replaced them with loan words from Spanish, because the cultural context had changed so dramatically that their indigenous vocabulary lost its relevance. For example, Indians used the colonizers' kinship terminology when referring to members of their own families. Having been forced to adopt a new kinship system, it made little sense to hold on to Nahuatl expressions to describe bonds and obligations that had taken on entirely new meanings. As time went on, the villagers began doing numerical calculations in Spanish as well.

Borrowing vocabulary, of course, went both ways. Not only did Spanish words turn up in Nahuatl, but Nahuatl entered Spanish as well to identify, for example, Aztec delicacies that the conquerors brought home and introduced to European markets—*chocolate* (*xogolatl*), *tomate* (*tomatl*), and *aguacate* (*ahuagatl*),[20] to name just a few. During colonial times, as the Mexican dialect of Spanish evolved, it incorporated many words from Nahuatl, for local use only. Once adopted into Spanish, the term also survived in Hueyapan Nahuatl.[21]

Spanish language and culture became so dominant in Hueyapan that I could find only one activity in the daily life of the villagers where Nahuatl terminology and the accompanying technology survived "virtually intact," without entering into Mexican Spanish and the homes of Mexico's non-Indian elite—the prehispanic custom of weaving on the backstrap loom. But as we shall see, even here, in this exceptional case, the clothing produced by this ancient technology was made out of an imported fiber and conformed to colonial Spanish ideas of modesty and taste.

In addition to using Spanish vocabulary, Hueyapan Nahuatl has borrowed grammatical structures as well. For example, the Spanish prepositions *de* (of, from) and *para* (for) have replaced postpositional forms: "I am coming from school" is *nihuitz de escuela* (*vengo de escuela*). The villagers have even integrated Spanish-style contractions into Nahuatl, such as *den* (*de*+*in*), the equivalent of the Spanish *del* (*de*+*el*)—"of the" or "from the." We therefore get: *in ixcactle cah tlacpac den xonblelotle* (*la sandalia está debajo del sombrero*) for "the sandal is under the hat."

Given the political power of Spanish, why has Nahuatl survived at all? There are several reasons, I suggest, some of which reach back to early colonial times, to factional struggles within the Catholic Church and between the missionaries and the Crown. In the sixteenth century, priests belonging to the monastic orders defied a royal decree instructing colonists to teach the Indians Spanish, a point I will take up in greater detail in chapter five. By speaking to them in their native tongues, the priests kept their indigenous wards dependent on them and isolated from others in colonial New Spain. In recent years, villagers have used the language as a social boundary to close others out. As we have seen, Doña Zeferina took pride in the fact that she knew how to defend herself from a hostile world. So did other villagers I met. One way to do this was to speak a language that members of the dominant classes could not understand. However, since native speakers of Spanish had destroyed the traditions of native speakers of Nahuatl, the villagers could only use their indigenous tongue to talk about matters intimately tied to European culture and society. And in doing so, they necessarily relied on vocabulary and concepts that they had borrowed from the language of their conquerors.[22]

Spinning and Weaving

To spin thread with a spindle shaft and whorl and weave pieces of cloth on the backstrap loom are practices that go back to prehispanic times. Like the Nahuatl language, however, this indigenous technology adapted itself to the culture of non-Indian New Spain, providing garments for Indians that conformed to a sixteenth-century royal decree about how indigenous people should dress.[23] By 1969–1970, most villagers wore clothing made out of store-bought cotton cloth. Such garments were easier to sew and considerably less expensive than the woolen skirts and shawls that some of the older women still wore. Even if the local demand for woven clothing had decreased, older women in the village have continued to weave and spin their own thread, motivated, in part, by tourists, anthropologists, and textile aficionados.[24]

The loom itself has changed very little over the centuries, but the villagers use a fiber imported from Europe. Before the conquest, Mexicans made cloth out of cotton and *agave*. Cotton grew in the eastern lowlands of the Aztec Empire and was highly valued. Too

Photo 6 Epifania Alonso weaving a *gabán* on the backstrap loom.

expensive for commoners, only upper-class people wore cotton cloth-ing.[25] For their own consumption, the poor made garments out of *agave* fiber, but they frequently wove cloth in cotton as well, to pay tribute to Aztec lords. Given Hueyapan's social standing in prehis-panic Mexico, I assume that the villagers wore clothing made out of *agave*. Nevertheless, I did find a spindle whorl in Hueyapan that dates to prehispanic times and could only have been used to spin a fine fiber like cotton.[26] After the conquest, the villagers began spin-ning and weaving wool from sheep that came over to the New World from Spain.

In tables 1 and 2, I provide a list of Nahuatl terms for identifying the various implements used to spin and weave wool in Hueyapan. In contrast to other areas of cultural life, such as kinship, cooking, medicine, religion, and clothing, where we clearly see the influence of Spanish, the terms here are virtually untouched. When I asked vil-lagers to describe the technology, I discovered that they did not know the equivalent terms in Spanish for parts of the backstrap loom.

Clothing

In identifying Hueyapan as an Indian *pueblo*, people often men-tioned the clothing worn by older members of the community. As I have already noted, the *pueblo's* so-called indigenous costume dates to colonial times. Before the Spanish conquest, men wore a loin cloth (*maxtlatl*) and cape (*tilmatl*) in Central Mexico and women a long skirt (*cueitl*). Made out of one piece of cloth, women wrapped the skirt around their waist and kept it in place with a wide embroidered belt. Women also wore a sleeveless blouse called a *huipil*[27] and, like the men, they protected themselves from the cold with a cape. The clothing of lower-class men and women was usually white, while that of the privileged was colorful, even elaborately decorated on festive occasions. Finally, the lower classes went barefoot, while those with more status wore sandals (*cactli*) that had *agave*-fiber or animal-hide soles and *agave*-fiber lacings.[28]

In the years immediately following the conquest, King Carlos V proclaimed that the Indians of Mexico had to dress in ways that con-formed to Iberian standards of decency. Of the many restrictions

Table 1 Spinning and weaving terms[a]

English	Spanish	Hueyapan Nahuatl	Classical Nahuatl	Reference[b]
Wool	*Lana*	*Tomitil*[c]	*Tòmi-tl*	Swadesh and Sancho, 69
Teasel head	*Carda*	*Calon*[d]	*Tiapochin-altiloni*	Siméon, 578
Thread	*Hilo*	*Icpatl*	*Ic-pa-tl*	Swadesh and Sancho, 84
Spindle whorl	*Malacate*	*Malagatl*	*Malacatl*	Siméon, 222
Backstrap loom	*Telarcito*	*Iquiti*[e]	*Iqui-tia*	Swadesh and Sancho 50
Warp		*Nocpah*		
Weft		*Itlan calagueh*		
Woven piece	*Tejido*	*Cesotl*[f]	*Zo-tl*	Swadesh and Sancho, 77
Side selvage		*Iten*	*Ilpicayotl*	Siméon, 167

Notes

[a] I have used Spanish terms only when my informants knew them. Furthermore, I have included Classical Nahuatl words—the terms used at the time of the Spanish Conquest—when I was able to locate them in Classical Nahuatl texts.

[b] References cited are M. Swadesh and M. Sancho, *Los mil elementos del mexicano clásico* and R. Siméon, *Dictionnaire de la langue nahuatl.*

[c] This word actually means "hair," which by extension includes wool.

[d] The Hueyapan Nahuatl word for teasel head is clearly Spanish. This implement is used for combing out wool before spinning.

[e] The villagers did not have a noun for loom, only a verb describing the act of weaving. This is true, apparently, wherever the backstrap loom or its equivalent is used in America. The reason for this, according to Bird, "is simply that when the work of weaving is completed and the product removed, what remains are the separated sticks which serve as loom bars, heddles and shed rods" (Bird, pers. comm.).

[f] When I asked for the Nahuatl word meaning woven material, the reply was, "one piece of cloth"—*ce* meaning one, *sotl* meaning cloth.

placed on indigenous peoples in those terrible early years, the new dress code was probably one of the least onerous, especially for those living in the highlands where temperatures often dropped below freezing. In Hueyapan, the new clothing woven out of wool, was certainly warmer than what they had worn before.

In 1969–1970, almost every woolen garment seen in the village was woven locally on the backstrap loom. Cotton clothing, made out of store-bought material, was either purchased ready-to-wear, sewn by hand, or made with the help of a pedal-operated sewing machine. *Agave*-fiber products—small bags for men (*morrales*) and sandals for women (*ixcactles*)—were manufactured entirely outside the village.

Table 2 Terms for parts of the backstrap loom[a]

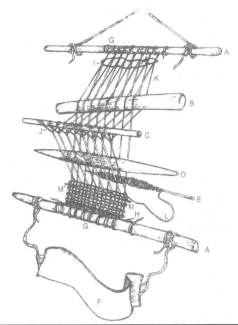

Label in diagram	English	Hueyapan Nahuatl
A	Loom bars	*Cuahtzomitl*
B	Shed rod	*Ohtlatl*
C	Heddle rod	*Xiotl*
D	Batten or sword	*Tzotzopastle*[b]
E	Bobbn	*Paguitl*
F	Backstrap	*Tlaixcuaitl*
G	Warp lashing[c]	
H	Heading string[c]	
	Lease cord	*Cuitlzcole*
J	Lease cord	*Icpatl bolita*[d]
K	Warp	*Nocpah*
L	Weft	*Itlan calagueh*
M	Tenter	*Octagatl*

Notes
[a] The diagram is a modified version of a drawing found in Wendel Bennett and Junius Bird, *Andean Culture History*, 266.
[b] There is a smaller batten used to help change sheds called an *oyastle*.
[c] I did not get information about the names for either warp lashing (G) or heading string (H).
[d] This is store-bought thread and the *bolita* refers to the fact that the thread comes on a spool.

At the time I was doing fieldwork, men who dressed traditionally wore white linen *calzones*, the symbol of the rural peasant throughout Mexico. The pants closed in front without a zipper or button-down fly but with a cloth belt, sewn on to the waist band of the pants that tied tightly around the man's middle. The shirt had long sleeves and a Chinese-style collar. It slipped over the head and had buttons on the upper half of the bodice and on the cuffs. Doña Zeferina still remembered the time when men did not wear linen shirts at all, but covered themselves with woolen *ponchos*, sewn closed on the sides. In 1969–1970, in the chilly hours of the morning and evening, men put on woolen *ponchos* over their shirts. Called a *gabán*, the *poncho* was woven locally on the backstrap loom and had a simple design— alternating stripes of either blue and white or brown and blue. When it was really cold, men wore woolen scarves as well. Called a *bufanda*, the garment was usually white, decorated with blue stripes. Men also wore commercially manufactured straw hats (*sombreros*) and cow-hide sandals with car-tire soles (*huaraches*).

When dressing traditionally, women wore long black wool skirts, made out of a huge piece of cloth. Pleated together at the waist, the *xincueite* stayed in place with the help of an elaborately woven red and black wool belt (*faja*) that wrapped several times around the waist. This was clearly a modified version of the prehispanic skirt. Women's blouses had short sleeves and were usually made at home out of store-bought cotton. Sometimes, the blouses had embroidered designs around a collarless neckline, but more often than not, they were plain. Women also wore black wool shawls (*rebozos*) and *agave*-fiber sandals (*ixcactles*).[29] Doña Zeferina could remember the time when some of the men and most of the women still went around barefoot.

In table 3, I list the names used locally for pieces of clothing considered to be indicators of Hueyapan's Indian identity. More often than not, the villagers did not have words in Nahuatl to identify these garments and borrowed instead from the Spanish. Having adopted the terms in the years immediately following the conquest, the villagers had not yet learned enough Spanish to imitate accurately the pronunciation of foreign words, hence the distortion of terms like *sombrero*. Even when villagers held on to Nahuatl terms, the articles of clothing bore little resemblance to what they had

Table 3 Traditional clothes in Hueyapan

English	Spanish	Hueyapan Nahuatl	Classical Nahuatl	Reference
Pajamas	*Calzones*	*Gazon*		
Men's sandals	*Huaraches*	*Cuitlaxcactila*[a]	*Cac-tli*	Swadesh and Sancho, 43
Hat	*Sombrero*	*Xonblelotle*		
Poncho	*Serape*	*Gabán*[b]		
Men's scarf	*Bufanda*	*Bufanda Quechquemelolle*		
Shawl	*Rebozo*	*Payo*[c]		
Skirt	*Falda*	*Xincueite*[d]	*Cue-yi-tl*	Swadesh and Sancho, 83
Belt	*Faja*	*Cenidor*	*Max-tli*	Swadesh and Sancho, 83
		Ilpigatl	*Ilpicayotl*	Siméon, 167
Blouse	*Blusa*	*Saco*	*Ulpi-l-li*	Swadesh and Sancho, 73
		Cotón		
Women's sandals		*Ixcactle*[e]	*Cac-tli*	Swadesh and Sancho, 43

Notes

[a] In this context *cuitlax* means leather, villagers told me, and *cactil* means shoe.

[b] *Gabán* is a Spanish word meaning overcoat.

[c] The Mexican *rebozo* is unquestionably of Spanish origin and in its original Iberian form was often more like a head cloth or *pañuelo* than a long shawl (Foster, 98). The Nahuatl word *payo* could very likely be a phonetic distortion of the old Spanish word *paño*, meaning cloth.

[d] *xi-n(i)* means unsewn or unspun (Swadesh and Sancho, 74). *Cue-yi-tl* mens skirt. Perhaps the first woolen skirt seen in the village were on Spaniards, and the villagers decided that this cloth was not spun or sewn.

[e] *ix(tle)* stands for the agave fiber out of which the sandals were fashioned.

previously signified. The white *agave*-fiber *cueitl*, for example, had become a black wool skirt. Although the *cactli* sandal might look more "authentic," we should still be cautious, at least in Hueyapan, for the sandal only made an appearance in the village relatively recently, during the lifetime of Doña Zeferina's grandmother.

Cooking Technology and Food

The villagers considered the "simple" food they ate and the way they prepared it to be Indian. Here, of course, they were right. Their basic diet of *tortillas*, beans, and *chile* peppers had deep roots going back into prehispanic times. After the conquest, these foods remained staples of the national cuisine, thereby ensuring their survival in Hueyapan. Today, we find many Nahuatl terms in Spanish to identify food items that the European conquerors had never seen before as well as utensils and pieces of technology used to prepare and serve

Photo 7 A woman preparing the corn meal for *tamales* at a fiesta in Hueyapan.

them. Thus, we find in Mexican Spanish today such words as *chocolate (xogolatl), tomate (tomatl)*, etc., and *metate (metlatl)*—grinding stone, *comal (comale)*—griddle for cooking *tortillas, chiquiguite (chigui-huitl)*—wicker basket, and *tenate (tenatl)*—special basket for serving cooked *tortillas*.

In addition to *tortillas*, beans, and *chiles*, Indian food, the villagers told me, included *tamales*, calabash squash, *pulque*, and certain fruits, such as *tejocotes*. All of these existed in Mexico before the Spanish conquest and continue to delight the palates of people of all classes and ethnicities throughout the country. Outsiders often mentioned *mole* as well as a typically Indian dish. When we look at the

Table 4   Ingredients used in *mole colorado* in Hueyapan

Ingredient	Origin of ingredient at time of conquest
Pasilla chile	Indigenous
Sesame seeds	East India
Turkey or chicken soup	Turkey: indigenous; chicken: Europe
Chocolate (bitter)	Indigenous, but from tropical Mexico
Peanuts	Indigenous
Cloves	Moluccas
Cumin	India
Garlic	Europe
Pepper	India
Cinnamon	Ceylon and China
Almonds	Morocco and Barbary
Anise	North Africa
Raisins	Mediterranean
Onions	Indigenous, with European equivalents
Salt bread	Europe
Tortillas	Indigenous

ingredients of *mole colorado*, the preparation preferred in Hueyapan (table 4), we see how Spanish colonial tastes influenced the cuisine of the Mexican Indians, turning a prehispanic *chile* stew, made with turkey,[30] into an exotic sauce of Asian spices, served ceremoniously over chicken or turkey on special religious holidays.

Under the careful supervision of colonial priests, *mole colorado* began to look more like an East Indian curry than an Aztec dish. When we keep in mind that the Spanish "discovered" America while they were trying to reach Asia by sailing west, this culinary curiosity begins to make sense. And since, as we know, colonial priests played a major role in incorporating Indians into the culture of non-Indian Mexico, it stands to reason that missionaries changed the eating habits of their wards and imposed their own very European preference for Asian spices on the local cuisine.[31] *Mole*, after all, is a fiesta food and feast days are tied to the Catholic Church.

Healing

In 1969–1970, Hueyapan had a number of healers who used "rustic" methods to help ailing villagers. To cure a villager in the traditional way, a healer lifted the disease from the patient's body by rubbing a

Table 5   Recipe for rustic cure of bronchitis

Ingredient	Origin of ingredient at time of conquest
Butter	Europe
White wine	Europe
Green tomato	Indigenous
Cumin	East India
Peppermint	Europe
Balsamon tranquilo	Unknown
Lilimento	Unknown
Fennel	Europe
Oregano	Europe

The herbs are crushed and then heated with the other ingredients in a small pot. The mixture is then applied to the chest and back of the patient once a day for three of four days.

raw egg over the sick person's head, trunk, and limbs. She then cracked the egg open into a glass. By studying the configuration of the yoke, she would be able to identify the precise nature of the malady. After making a diagnosis, the medicine prescribed invariably combined insights dating back to the traditions of sixteenth-century Europe and of prehispanic Mexico. In colonial times, the Spanish were very impressed by indigenous medicine and learned to use local remedies to cure their people. As we see in table 5—and in the description of bathing in the *temascal* given in chapter one—Indian remedies in Hueyapan offered a blend of the Old World and New, but relied more heavily on imports from Europe.[32]

Rustic healers in Hueyapan did not usually recite prayers while administering their medical cures. When they did, however, they called upon Catholic saints and other European symbols to help treat their patients: "Saint Bartholomew of Castile, come to us on your horse and take the shadow away from this place."[33] By the time I got to the village, people still sought the advice of local *curanderas*, but they considered their methods of healing to be Indian, meaning backward, and far less effective than the modern techniques that had recently reached the *pueblo*.

Religion

People identified a number of religious practices in Hueyapan as Indian. As we have already seen and as I discuss in greater detail in the next chapter, the village became Catholic soon after the conquest of New Spain. With few exceptions—several hundred evangelical Protestants and a handful of villagers influenced by an Aztec renaissance movement—almost everyone in the *pueblo* in 1969–1970 identified with the Catholic Church. Some of the villagers' religious practices, however, looked exotic to outsiders, for they incorporated indigenous customs from prehispanic Mexico.[34] Adopting strategies dating back to medieval times, Spanish priests converted the Indians to Catholicism, with methods first perfected by Roman missionaries working in Europe during the early Middle Ages. Applying these ancient techniques to the Indians of New Spain, colonial missionaries "baptized" indigenous customs, imitating the way their spiritual forefathers had taken traditions associated with the winter solstice and turned them into symbols of the birth of Jesus—the Christmas tree, for example.

Praying for rain was probably the most exotic example of a ritual conversion that I learned about in Hueyapan. Some villagers occasionally called on religious specialists to intervene and protect their crops from drought. These rainmakers ate hallucinogenic mushrooms and recited, supposedly, ancient incantations. Thanks to the efforts of a native schoolteacher, we have published versions of some of the prayers for rain, in both Nahuatl and Spanish, and they offer an excellent illustration of how the Spaniards "baptized" an indigenous tradition and turned it into a Catholic rite. Rainmakers in Hueyapan relied solely on Christian symbolism and sought the assistance of Catholic saints.[35]

More often than not, when people identified religious customs as indigenous, they referred to Spanish traditions of colonial origin instead. The elaborate processions, the *mayordomo* system,[36] special foods eaten during fiestas—virtually all of these traditions came to Mexico via Spain, or were significantly transformed by Spanish priests after 1521. The list is long and includes secular forms of entertainment as well—firecrackers, bull riding, pageant plays,

marching bands, and dances. People talked, for example, about performing traditional indigenous music on an Indian instrument called
the *chirimía*, the descendant, in fact, of a double-reeded wind instrument of the oboe family that was popular in Europe during the
Renaissance.[37] Then, as we see in the next chapter, every year the village celebrated the fiesta of the Virgin of Guadalupe—the holiday
commemorating the apparition of the Virgin Mary in 1531 to a
recently converted Indian—by performing a play that reenacted battles between Moors and Christians. Based on a medieval epic called
The Song of Fierabras, the original dates back to twelfth-century
France.

CHAPTER FIVE
RELIGION IN HUEYAPAN

The vast majority of the people living in Hueyapan in 1969–1970 were practicing Catholics. There were, however, some notable exceptions, the majority of whom came from Protestant families that had embraced evangelical sects in the early decades of the twentieth century. By the time I got to the *pueblo*, there were several hundred Protestants in Hueyapan and their numbers were growing.[1] A handful of villagers had rejected Christianity entirely and joined an Aztec renaissance movement, accepting the invitation of an urban-based group that had contacted Hueyapan in the 1950s with the hope of recruiting Nahuatl-speaking Indians to their cause. As we see in chapter seven, even though the movement never really caught on in the village, it captured the imagination of a few people in town, in particular the members of one family.

Catholics in Hueyapan shared strong cultural bonds with Mexicans across the nation, from Mestizos living in the surrounding communities to members of the ruling elite. Although outsiders often discriminated against the villagers and treated them like "poor little Indians," the inhabitants of Hueyapan had the satisfaction of knowing that they belonged to the same religious tradition as almost everyone else in Mexico. Rich or poor, non-Indian or Indian, as Catholics they worshipped the same Christian God and prayed to the same saints. Proud to belong to a wider religious community, Catholics identified themselves with local religious symbols associated with the faith to establish their superiority over others in the village. Those who lived in the Centro, for example, made sure visitors noticed that the only church and chapel in town were located in the San Miguel Barrio.

As we saw in chapter three, Augustinian missionaries reached Hueyapan in 1534, only 13 years after the Spanish conquest.[2] Systematic conversion of the villagers began nearly 30 years later, in 1561, when Dominican friars settled down in the village.[3] According to a pictographic map of Hueyapan, by 1570, the village and the surrounding area already had a big church and five chapels.[4] Finally, by 1581, the Dominicans baptized the village Santo Domingo de Hueyapan and divided it into three *estancias* (*barrios*), each of which bore the name of a different saint: San Miguel, Santo Bartolomé, and Santo Tomás.[5] From that point on, even the spatial organization of the town reinforced the villagers' ties to Catholic traditions.

In early colonial times, Dominican friars and members of other monastic orders (Augustinians, Franciscans, and Jesuits) played a critical role in converting the Indians of Mexico to Catholicism and incorporating them into the cultural system of New Spain.[6] To simplify their task, they petitioned Carlos V to let them organize indigenous settlements into villages modeled on Spanish towns. The king granted their request and Indian *pueblos* soon appeared across the land, all of them conforming to the same basic plan: every village had a central plaza, on one side of which stood an imposing church with a spacious courtyard (*atrio*).

In Hueyapan, missionaries probably used the same methods they had used in other communities in Central Mexico to convert the Indians. Trying not to scare the local population, friars arrived in small groups, barefoot and unarmed. Initially, in the early years, they needed interpreters, but the priests learned Nahuatl, and the other relevant languages, and were soon working directly in indigenous tongues. First, they converted the head of the community, convinced that if they recruited the leader his people would follow.

The religious orders used indigenous villages as centers of political power and did their best to keep other Europeans out. As they saw it, *encomenderos* controlled the Indians' land and labor, but missionaries had authority over their homes and souls. Assuming responsibility for the education of their wards, they managed local affairs in these newly established communities. In addition to teaching the liturgy, they arbitrated disputes, settled questions of succession and inheritance, looked after widows and orphans, and built hospitals to care for the ill. Their work, they argued, necessarily extended beyond the walls of the church, for they wanted to destroy pagan traditions, wherever they might be, in every social and cultural institution. Taking it upon themselves to teach the Indians to be good Christians in all aspects of their daily lives, the priests showed their new converts how to plant kitchen gardens and care for their fruit orchards. They also introduced the Indians to European-imported livestock, such as the chickens, sheep, and goats still raised in Hueyapan today.

The religious orders established themselves as intermediaries between their indigenous wards and the European colonists who were seeking their fortune in New Spain. They therefore discouraged the Indians from learning Spanish, preferring to be their interpreters. When, for example, Philip II proclaimed in 1550 that the colonists should teach Indians Spanish, many priests ignored the decree and continued working in indigenous tongues, requiring their missionaries to learn Nahuatl, or, if circumstances required, another language instead. As Robert Ricard explained it, the priests defended their policy of working in indigenous tongues on theological grounds:

> [T]o become a true Christian, the Mexican must break entirely with the past, except, and this is very important, with his language; because to become a true Christian, as everyone knows, it is not at all necessary to become Spanish. It is permitted, even recommended, that the Indian remain Mexican. The Church . . . does not ask her sons to betray their country, nor turn against their race.[7]

In *pueblos* like Hueyapan, where missionaries settled down and built monasteries for themselves, catechism took place every Sunday and holiday. This involved a form of oral instruction based on simple sets of questions and answers that summarized the principles of the Catholic faith. On prayer days, an indigenous *alcalde* (mayor) instructed the villagers to rise especially early. He then lined them up and led them to church in a long procession, behind a member of the community who was given the great honor of carrying a large cross. When they arrived at the entrance of the church, the *alcalde* herded the Indians into an outside courtyard (*atrio*) for prayer, separating the men from the women. At this point, if available, an attending priest took over. Before reciting catechism and performing Mass, the priest took attendance—and it was no small matter if a member of the community was absent.

Since they did not have enough priests to teach all the new converts, the missionaries identified Indians, including young children, whom they felt they could trust (*de confianza*), and trained them to help with the instruction. Indians, however, could never become priests. Instead of ordaining them, the missionaries rewarded the most deserving followers by inviting them to hold special offices. Although these honorific posts gave Indians status and a few coveted privileges, they burdened them as well with economic and ritual obligations that combined religious and secular duties. Known today as the *cargo* system or the civil-religious hierarchy, the institution evolved slowly in early colonial times, developing more fully in the eighteenth century.[8]

In keeping with traditions they brought over from Spain, the priests encouraged Indians to organize elaborate processions with crosses, images of saints, incense, flowers, and music, allowing their charges to improvise as well with indigenous melodies and dances. They even let them perform religious ceremonies on special occasions at the sites of prehispanic deities. "Baptizing" local traditions in this way eased the transition to Christianity by giving Indians the chance to hold on to a few "harmless" customs and associations and to integrate them into an entirely new cultural context.[9] Before incorporating these pagan traditions, however, the priests tore down indigenous temples, desecrated their images, prohibited human sacrifices, and severely punished native priests; they then built their own churches, with new images and traditions, on the ruins of the old, preserving in the process traces of the past.[10]

We frequently hear that Spanish priests succeeded in their efforts to make Indians Catholics because they were flexible in the way they interpreted dogma and incorporated customs of the people they converted into rituals blessed by the church. Flexible, perhaps, but strategic. The priests knew exactly what they were doing when they took certain rites dedicated to prehispanic deities and transformed them into ones for the Virgin Mary, Jesus Christ, or one of the many Catholic saints. The dances and chants in themselves were not dangerous, only the ideas behind them.

Some members of the clergy worried, it is true, that if the Indians continued to practice indigenous rituals, they would remain pagans—and indeed many idolatrous practices persisted—but many others endorsed the strategy of "baptizing" traditions, arguing that it would help the conversion process. The strategy made it easier as well to keep the Indians Indian while assimilating them into an entirely non-Indian world. A good illustration of the process is the way the Church recognized the apparition of the Virgin of Guadalupe and made it central to Mexican Catholicism.

The Virgin of Guadalupe Fiesta

The Virgin of Guadalupe was the first apparition of the Virgin Mary in the New World. As the story goes, she appeared several times to the converted Indian Juan Diego at Tepeyac, the desecrated site of Cihuacoatl (Serpent Woman), the Aztec goddess of fertility, who, later on, was also known as Tonantzin (Our Mother). The miracle took place in December 1531, ten years after the Spanish conquest, as Juan Diego was traveling to Mexico City to celebrate the fiesta of the Immaculate Conception, a day dedicated to the Virgin Mary. On the way, he passed by Tepeyac, and there, at the former shrine of the prehispanic deity, he saw the Virgin Mary.

When he arrived in Mexico City, Juan Diego asked to see the bishop, a Franciscan by the name of Juan de Zumárraga, to inform the head of the Mexican Church about the miracle he had witnessed. The bishop said that he needed concrete evidence and sent the Indian back to Tepeyac to ask the Virgin to give him a recognizable sign. This he did and when the Virgin reappeared, she told Juan Diego to gather all the flowers on top of the hill, wrap them up in his *agave*-fiber cape, and take them to the bishop. The converted Indian faithfully followed instructions and returned to Mexico City. When he opened his cape before the bishop, the flowers had disappeared. In their place was a painted image of the Virgin. Zumárraga acknowledged the miracle and placed the cape in the cathedral. Two years later, he had a small shrine built for the Virgin at Tepeyac and preserved the cape there. In 1566, Zumárraga's successor, the Dominican bishop Alonso Montúfar, added a silver statue of the Virgin to the sanctuary.

Nearly 100 years later, the Franciscan priest and chronicler, Sahagún, proclaimed that the goddess Tonantzin-Cihuacoatl demonstrated the universality of Christianity. As Jacques Lafaye tells the story, Sahagún reinterpreted the significance of Cihuacoatl for the Aztecs in order to "prove" that the Indians knew about "our mother Eve who was abused by the serpent."[11] It took only another small step to turn the Aztec serpent mother into the Mother of Christ, for the Virgin Mary was known as the New Eve.[12] Having made a connection between Cihuacoatl and Mary, Sahagún provided the theological justification necessary for converting the former site of Tonantzin into the hallowed shrine of the Virgin of Guadalupe.[13]

In celebrating the fiesta for the Virgin of Guadalupe, non-Indians in Mexico recognize their country's indigenous origins, while the Indians reaffirm their sense of identity with the nation's European heritage. Over the centuries, the Virgin of Guadalupe became known as the Dark Virgin and the Virgin of the Indians, a reminder to non-Indians of Mexico's indigenous past and of the nation's racial and cultural diversity. For villagers in Hueyapan, however, the apparition of the Virgin to a converted Indian symbolized their ties to the same cultural tradition as other people in Mexico, a tradition they have shared for hundreds of years.

On December 12, the actual day of the Virgin of Guadalupe, little children throughout Mexico have traditionally dressed up to look like "Indians" (de indito), in memory of Juan Diego. This practice occurs almost everywhere in the country, in Mexico City and in regional centers. Although everyone knew about the custom in Hueyapan, on the two occasions I observed the fiesta (1969 and 1971), very few children came to church dressed de indito. More popular in urban centers than it was in indigenous villages, the tradition caught on only superficially in the pueblo, for to dress de indito meant to dress like a child's grandparents, or in rare cases, even his or her parents. By the late 1960s, children did not wear xincueites or calzones anymore, but these articles of clothing were part of the landscape, constant reminders of the village's lowly status in contemporary Mexico.

The seven or eight children who dressed de indito came from the most assimilated homes in the village. For the occasion, girls wore black *xincueites*—or facsimiles thereof, fashioned out of their mothers' black wool *rebozos*—white embroidered blouses, *rebozos*, and *ixcactles*. The boys wore white *calzones*, *gabanes* on which they pinned little pictures of the Virgin of Guadalupe, *huaraches*, and straw hats. On their backs, both girls and boys wore miniature packs or *huacalitos*, imitations of what Indians used in colonial times to transport their meager possessions. To complete the costume, boys, but not girls, carried walking sticks as well.[14]

Much more popular in Hueyapan than dressing *de indito* was the tradition of performing a play known locally as "The Moors and the Christians" (Los Moros y Cristianos). The version of the drama reenacted in the village was based on the twelfth-century French epic *The Song of Fierabras*, one of several fanciful accounts of how Christianity defeated Islam in medieval Europe. Written a century later than the better known *Song of Roland*, the events described in *The Song of Fierabras* supposedly took place three years before the infamous eighth-century massacre of Charlemagne's nephew Roland in northern Spain (at Roncevaux). The text itself has many of the same characters as the Roland epic on the Christian side, but a different caste of Moors.[15]

As the villagers participate in this yearly spectacle, they find themselves on more stable ground than they usually do. Identifying with the Christians, they enjoy the same sense of cultural superiority as anybody else in Mexico and they delight in Charlemagne's triumph over the Moors. For once, they are on the winning side.

Different versions of Los Moros y Cristianos came to Mexico with the Spaniards during colonial times and they were first performed for the amusement of the conquerors. Before long, however, the play made its way into indigenous villages, introduced there by Catholic priests who entertained the Indians with a story about pagans who either died or converted to Christianity.[16] Indigenous people in Mexico may have seen similarities between the Moors and themselves in the years immediately following the Spanish conquest, as the friars no doubt intended, but they no longer did in 1969, at least not in Hueyapan, where villagers identified enthusiastically with the Christians.

In the eyes of the villagers, performing the play came as close as any other tradition I found in Hueyapan to representing the pueblo's cultural heritage. A major highlight of the Virgin of Guadalupe fiesta, the villagers have been reenacting Los Moros since long before the Mexican Revolution. Be they old and illiterate or little children in primary school, everyone knows about Charlemagne and the Moors.

Throughout the month of December, people enjoyed a variety of plays and dances throughout Central Mexico, all of which were billed as versions of Los Moros y Cristianos. At the shrine of the Virgin of Guadalupe in Mexico City, troupes of actors took turns performing their individual interpretations of Los Moros. Each group had a Maestro de los Moros, and he alone had a copy of the script, a handwritten document that had probably been in his family for generations. Although the details differed from version to version, the overall structure was essentially the same. Mixing dialogue and dance, the players staged a series of battles between Christians and Moors, ending, of course, with the triumph of those who defended the Cross. In some versions, Saint James, not Charlemagne, led the Christians into battle and Pilate led the Moors.[17]

In Hueyapan, the villagers traditionally invited Estanislao Rendón from the nearby village of San Juan Amecac (Puebla) to direct the local production and he recruited members of the village to perform all the principal roles. The year I saw the play in the village, the sponsors (*mayordomos*) decided to hire a troupe from Icacingo (Mexico). I, therefore, never saw a San Juan Amecac production, but I did get to study the script. Thanks to Juan Maya, I visited Don Estanislao in his *pueblo* and commissioned him to make me a handwritten copy of the manuscript that his family had acquired in 1845, in the days of his great grandfather.[18] I never learned how the Rendón family came into possession of the text, but Don Estanislao explained that with the passing of every generation, the Maestro de los Moros appointed one of his sons to carry on the tradition. As we shall see, over the years the script has clearly changed and anachronisms have crept in, making the text a rich reservoir for scholars doing research on the history of Spanish colonialism and the age-old conflicts in Europe between Christians and Moors. It is also a fascinating document for those interested in the history of popular literature and theater in Mexico.

Photo 8 The Moors and the Christians in Hueyapan during the Virgin of Guadalupe fiesta (1969).

According to villagers familiar with the versions from San Juan Amecac and Icacingo, the two interpretations of the play were essentially the same. Don Estanislao's text, however, had roles for only 16 players, while the Icacingo play had parts for 24. Don Juan and Doña Zeferina added that the San Juan Amecac production had better costumes—Maum (Mohammed), for example, was clearly depicted as the devil, with horns and a tail.

The costumes I saw in Hueyapan and Mexico City were quite similar. Symbolizing evil, the Moors wore bright red satin robes, decorated with sequins in the shape of half moons, solar discs, and flowers. The Christians wore baby-blue colored robes designed with crosses, clover leaves, and flowers. On their heads, the Moors wore crowns decorated with crescent moons that could easily be mistaken for the horns of the devil. The Christians wore crusade-style helmets and looked unmistakably like medieval knights. Some of the Moors sported fake beards and everyone, on both sides, brandished *machetes* with straight blades.

The Maestro de los Moros, in Hueyapan and Mexico City, wore billowing *calzones* and carried a well-worn copy of the script. Serving as the prompter, he ran around the plaza with the actors, reading the lines, instructing the players to repeat after him and to make the appropriate dramatic gestures. Every few minutes, a brass band broke in with the familiar marching tune, associated with the play all over Mexico, the signal for the actors to fall into line and parade up and down in strict military formation, before engaging one another in battle.

To add to the entertainment, Hueyapan preserved the custom of the Renaissance theater of interrupting a play with the antics of clowns. Known as *terrones*, bands of young men, dressed in ragged clothes and papier-mâché masks, ran about the plaza while the play was in progress, making a general nuisance of themselves. The real fun, however, took place during intermission, when the plaza became theirs and the *terrones* turned their mischief on the audience, "terrorizing" the young women.

In Hueyapan, the play extended over two full days, beginning on the evening of December 11 and ending late in the afternoon on December 13. Using the San Miguel plaza as their stage, the actors performed about 12 hours a day, breaking only for meals and a little rest. As we turn now to look at the text itself, I rely solely on the version I acquired from Estanislao Rendón.

The Moors and the Christians
(San Juan Amecac Version)[19]

The full title of the play is *The History of Charlemagne (Carlo Magno) and the Almirante Balán, as recorded by the twelve Vassals of France.*[20] In the San Juan Amecac version, much of the action takes place in

Turkey, not Spain.[21] This mythical Turkey is located somewhere between France and Africa.

Charlemagne, the king of France, wants to convert the Moors to Christianity. With this goal in mind, he sends a few vassals to Turkey to try to persuade the king of the Moors, to accept the Catholic faith. Outraged and insulted, Balán orders his men to sneak into France and to steal the statue of the Virgin Mary. The Moorish king believes that he will weaken Charlemagne and his soldiers if Almirante Balán separates the Christians from their "idol."

The Moors succeed in capturing the Virgin early on in the play and they keep it until the end. In the intervening scenes, we witness various attempts on the part of the Christians to liberate their Virgin and convert the king of the Moors to their faith. Every time a vassal crosses into Turkey, Balán's men catch him and throw him into jail. But thanks to Floripes, the Moorish king's daughter, the soldier escapes almost as quickly as he finds himself behind bars. Princess Floripes, it turns out, has fallen in love with Borgoña, the Duke of Burgandy, and is eager to help the Christians.

After much back and forth, during which time the Moors capture Christian soldiers, who then quickly break free, Charlemagne's vassals eventually get away—at least almost all of them—and they take a very willing Floripes with them. Only Oliveros is left behind.[22] Knowing that Charlemagne will send his men back to Turkey to liberate the one vassal who has failed to escape, Balán locks Oliveros away in his most god-forsaken prison, together with the Filipinos.[23] He then sets up border patrols to prevent the Christians from slipping back into his country. As a final precaution, Balán tells his soldiers to telephone him immediately, if, despite all their efforts, the Christians get through.[24]

Needless to say, the Christians are successful. Using a magical telescope and elaborate disguises, they cross the famous Mantible Bridge,[25] find Oliveros, and fly him out of Turkey by means of a hot-air balloon. After the vassals are safe once again, the priest converts Floripes to Christianity and unites the young woman with her beloved Borgoña in holy matrimony.

When he learns that the Christians have outsmarted his men, an angry Balán sends an emissary to France to announce his intention of declaring war on the Christians. Eager to retrieve their stolen

Virgin and still hoping to convert the Moors to the Cross, Charlemagne accepts the challenge to settle matters officially, according to the rules of chivalry. And so, on the appointed day, the battle begins, at a mutually agreed upon location, equidistant from the two kingdoms.

Although the Moors and the Christians are evenly matched, Charlemagne's knights win every duel. Before killing their opponents, these soldiers of Christ try to save the Moors' souls. Servants of a generous and forgiving God, they offer to spare the infidels' lives if they agreed to convert to Christianity. Faithful to the end, Balán's men prefer death, except for Fierabras, the king's only son. When given the choice, the Moor's heir to the throne embraces the Cross and escapes the sword. Both children have now abandoned Islam and, apparently, their father; one for love, the other for life.

With nobody else left to defend his kingdom, Balán prepares bravely to face the Christian army by himself. Charlemagne, however, is a man of honor: he holds his men back and steps forward to fight this battle alone. As Balán advances to meet the Christian king, he beseeches his god to give him strength. In his prayers, he tells Maum about a dream he just had in which he learns that his son has abandoned him.

The fencing begins and Charlemagne gains the advantage immediately. As he raises his sword to kill the Moor, Fierabras arrives and pleads with Charlemagne to give him the chance to convince his father to accept the Cross. Charlemagne grants the young man his wish.

Fierabras succeeds in persuading Balán to convert to Christianity, convincing his father to face up to the fact that his god has betrayed both him and his men. Christians, he adds, are not only stronger, but they alone go to heaven. Sadly admitting that Christianity has triumphed, Balán agrees to go to Rome with his son and to accept the blessings of the Church.

The next scene takes place at the Moor's baptismal ceremony. Everything at first is going along well until the priest orders the Moor to renounce his infidel soldiers who died faithfully in battle, defending the honor of their king. This, Balán cannot do. Although he will gladly give up his religion—rejecting his "god" whom he even calls

"Satan"—his land and the power of his throne, the king has his limits. He will not desecrate the memory of men who have sacrificed their lives for him. He has given them his word. Outraged by the demand, he refuses to obey. If this is what he must do to convert to Christianity, he will die instead.

Balán does not resist Charlemagne's men, as they take him away and line him up for execution. Before he dies, the Moor repeats that he has lost his faith, but continues to honor the memory of those who have given their lives for Islam and their king. Addressing Charlemagne directly, he asks the great ruler to make Fierabras lord of the lands that used to belong to the Moorish kingdom. The Christians bury Balán in a majestic tomb, worthy of a man of his royal station. Like good Christian children, Fierabras and Floripes pray to God to look after their father.

The play closes with a formal speech to the audience, bidding them farewell and offering special prayers to the Virgin of Guadalupe, the Maestro de los *Moros* and the village of San Juan Amecac.

Although my friends in Hueyapan would never have agreed, Almirante Balán is clearly the hero of this version of the play. The script presented a Moorish king with real tragic dimensions. By the end of the story, the infidel Moor resembled a Christian martyr, as he sacrificed his life for his people. In Hueyapan, however, nobody sided with the Moor. Enthusiastically identifying with the victorious Christians, they enjoyed describing how Charlemagne and his vassals defeated the Moors. Those who knew the script well summarized the plot in the following way: On one side, you have the Christians— Charlemagne and his 12 vassals—and on the other side, the Moors—Almirante Balán, King of Turkey, his son, Fierabras, and his daughter, Floripes. After a great deal of fighting, the Christians finally win. The god of the Moors made grandiose claims about being all-powerful, but he was no match for the Christian God. One of the highlights of the play, several female villagers added, was the scene in which Floripes married Borgoña. Not until I returned to the United States and had the chance to study the written text carefully did I learn that the play portrayed the king of the Moors with real compassion.

In 1971, I returned to Hueyapan to observe the Virgin of Guadalupe fiesta again, fully expecting to see the play for a second time and to discuss the script with members of the cast. Unfortunately, there was no performance that year. Although I was terribly disappointed, I did have the opportunity to interview Delfino Flores, who had played the part of Charlemagne in 11 productions. His interpretation differed little from what I had already heard from other people in the village, except in the degree of detail.

Don Delfino explained that Charlemagne was the most noble character in the play. We know that this was true, because he triumphed in the end. Balán, on the other hand, was bad and therefore had to die. While the Christians prayed to the Virgin and saints, the Moors worshipped the devil or whatever, just like the Protestants or Aztecs, he added, who prayed to rocks.[26] Repeating himself, he stressed once again that the Moors took the devil to be their "*santo*."

Abandoning the script entirely, Don Delfino went on to explain the origins of the conflict between Charlemagne and Balán, offering an abbreviated account of Satan's expulsion from Heaven. In his version, the event took place in Rome. Substituting the name of Charlemagne for God and Balán for Satan, Don Delfino gave the following account: "Charlemagne and Balán were both born in Rome, but they could not get along, so Balán left for Turkey and Charlemagne stayed in Rome. While Charlemagne was a religious man, Balán worshipped evil; and so he went to Turkey and found people there to follow him."

Like everyone else who discussed the play with me, Don Delfino had little, if any, sympathy for Balán. Nobody seemed moved by the fact that the Moorish king had agreed to convert to Christianity and give up his "evil" religion, worldly riches, and land, but would not desecrate the memory of men who had died faithfully in battle to defend his name. As far as the villagers were concerned, Balán had to perish. That was the law. There was nothing to question or regret.

We often read in the anthropological literature that traditions introduced to the Indians by colonial Spaniards take on new meaning over the centuries and blend into a non-Western indigenous worldview. Perhaps, this is true in other communities, but the discussions I had in Hueyapan about the Moors and the Christians suggest something quite different. Instead of turning a medieval epic into a narrative entirely foreign to European sensibilities, the villagers I spoke to embraced the beliefs of their conquerors in terms more literal and doctrinally faithful than the version of the play that they had been performing for many years. Dismissing the text, the villagers expressed no interest at all in the complex idea, familiar to the genre of medieval epics, of a "sympathetic" Moor (Saracen). Ignoring the moral struggle in the final scene of the play, they diminish the poignancy of the story, never responding to the fact that when it came to war, the infidel Balán shared the same feudal values as the good noble Christian. He even used the logic of the rules of chivalry to challenge the priest's interpretation of Church law, refusing heroically to renounce his soldiers who had died bravely in battle.[27]

Blindly identifying with Charlemagne and his men, the villagers assumed that might made right. Thanks, no doubt, to the influence of poorly educated priests, Church doctrine prevailed in a simplified form, with no questions asked. The children in the *pueblo* in 1969–1970 reinforced this flat interpretation of the text by playing Moors and Christians the way American children once played Cowboys and Indians, before it became politically unacceptable to do so.

La Fiesta in the Mayordomo's Home

Hueyapan observed the Virgin of Guadalupe fiesta in ways similar to other communities in rural Mexico, both Indian and Mestizo. Although some of the traditions may have looked exotic to outsiders, the customs had deep Christian roots, introduced, for the most part, during the colonial period. Converted Indians began celebrating Catholic holidays under the direction of missionary priests who helped them blend Spanish practices from Europe together with "baptized" rituals from prehispanic Mexico that had been carefully refashioned to conform to Christian sensibilities.

In 1969, Zenaido Ansures had the honor of sponsoring the Virgin of Guadalupe fiesta, serving as the *mayordomo*. Two years later, Maestro Rafael would have the same privilege. This meant that the schoolteacher and Doña Juana had major responsibilities already.

Not only did they have to contribute money to help defray the cost of a fiesta that offered hospitality to hundreds of villagers for days on end, but they also had to work around the clock, assisting with the preparations. For the duration of the fiesta, Maestro Rafael and Doña Juana lived at the *mayordomo*'s home, catching what sleep they could by stretching out on *petates* placed on the floors and covering themselves with blankets they had brought from home. Doña Zeferina and Angelina stayed behind to take care of the children. Only Quico, who was not yet weaned, accompanied his parents.

Don Zenaido and his wife Doña Nasia were considered to be one of the wealthiest couples in Hueyapan. Unlike their neighbors who lived crowded together in *adobe* brick houses, the two of them lived in a spacious, brightly colored three-room establishment, whose only other occupant was their young grandson David. Made out of cement-block, the house had a large living room that doubled as the couple's bedroom, a second smaller bedroom, and a kitchen. In keeping with their status, Don Zenaido and Doña Nasia had a television set and gas stove.[28] For the fiesta, Don Zenaido set up a temporary kitchen outside, with seven fire places, to accommodate the huge cooking demands of the holiday week.

The fiesta officially began in the early evening on December 8, the day of the Immaculate Conception. Anticipating the event, children gathered in the plaza right after lunch. Whispering among themselves, they eagerly waited to join the procession that would accompany the Virgin to the *mayordomo*'s home. By 5:00, everyone was ready.

Don Zenaido led the procession, followed by Don Abogón and Maestro Rafael, the two men who would sponsor the fiesta over the next two years. The three *compadres* had carefully attached the large icons of the Virgin of Guadalupe and the Immaculate Conception to litters and women carried them out of the church. The sacred figures remained in their glass boxes, which had been gaily decorated for the occasion with white and pink paper flowers. For several days, the images would stay in the *mayordomo*'s home, until the 12th of December, the official day of the fiesta, when the villagers would form a second, more elaborate, procession and return them to the church.

When the procession reached the *mayordomo's* home, everyone entered through the living room door and turned into the adjoining bedroom, which had been transformed into a sanctuary. Doña Nasia had decorated the room with white flowers and covered the floor with *petates*, to make the surface comfortable for worshippers to kneel and pray. A small image of the Virgin stood in its glass case on a table at the back of the room. Known as the *misterio*, the little image had been in the *mayordomo's* home for nearly a year. As the men removed the large images of the Virgins from the litters and placed them on the table with the *misterio*, the villagers went down on their knees. Then, some left the room discreetly, while others remained to recite the Rosary with Francisco Hernández, the deacon of the church.

After paying their respects to the Virgin, visitors returned to the living room, where Doña Nasia greeted them warmly. Repeatedly filling the same jigger-size glass with *aguardiente*, she passed it around, encouraging everyone to have a drink. Then, she invited her guests into the kitchen in groups of seven or eight for a light supper of coffee, bread, *tortillas*, and beans. Although only 20 villagers had participated in the procession itself, by the time the evening was over Don Zenaido and Doña Nasia had welcomed 50 people. As friends and relatives waited their turn for a seat in the kitchen, they chatted amicably among themselves.

Preparations for the fiesta continued the next day, without any formal ritual. Then, on the evening of the 10th, Don Abogón and his wife, and Maestro Rafael and Doña Juana moved into the *mayordomo's* house, and they stayed there until the 14th, together with a few other *compadres* and *comadres* close to the family. In all, counting the children who had tagged along and the resident anthropologist, we were about 15. From that time onward, Doña Nasia's *comadres* would work nonstop by the open fires, cooking huge casseroles of food and getting virtually no sleep.

Before settling into the arduous routine, we were all welcomed as honored guests. First, everyone went into the sanctuary to pray to the Virgin. We then returned to the living room, found places to sit on the bed or on the chairs arranged in a semicircle, and waited patiently as Doña Nasia served us a mixture of *aguardiente* and coffee from a jigger-size glass, in a slow methodical way. Women joined the men, some of them joking informally, as they accepted the glass, about the way brandy helped people endure the cold weather. It would not make them drunk. Doña Nasia also gave her *compadres* and *comadres* a cigarette, which they put away to smoke in private, at another time.

After enjoying the *aguardiente,* we took turns going into the kitchen to have some coffee, bread, beans, *tortillas,* and a bite of roasted rabbit a special treat from Don Zenaido, whose hunting expedition earlier that day had been a great success, by 9:00 PM, the men had returned to the living room to make final plans for the coming days—and to have a little more to drink—while the women retreated to the outside kitchen to begin preparing food for the following day.

December 11th was the first day of the fiesta, officially marked as such at 11:00 AM by the celebration of Mass. The women, however, had been working since 7:00 AM. In addition to those who had spent the night in the *mayordomo's* home, other comadres had arrived, increasing the number of cooks to 20. From this moment on, Doña Nasia had enough work to keep all of them busy making plain and bean *tamales, mole colorado,* beef and turkey soups, seasoned with *pasilla* chiles, rice, boiled beans, and mounds of *tortillas.* The team of women included mothers with nursing babies, old women free of family responsibilities, and a few unreliable teenage girls who spent more time inside the house dancing with the men than tending the fires.

Although the *comadres* worked hard, they clearly enjoyed themselves a great deal. The fiesta, after all, broke the monotony of their lives, giving them the chance to spend time together, to eat lots of good food and to drink *aguardiente.* But they also complained about missing the processions and not seeing the Moros perform in the plaza. They did not, in fact, even enter the house to take part in the dancing and other social activities, for they were either too busy or felt too embarrassed about the way they looked after spending so many hours cooking. Only Doña Nasia bustled about, catching glimpses of the party inside.

By early afternoon, the troupe of actors had arrived. So had the members of two musical ensembles, one of which was a brass band that would accompany Los Moros and the religious processions and the other a *mariache* ensemble that would play in the evening in the *mayordomo*'s home. Boths groups came from neighboring villages.

Perhaps, as many as 100 people visited the house on the evening of the 11th and 50 of them stayed the night in order to take part in the procession the next day that would begin before sunrise. Despite the television blaring in one room and the dancing in the other, guests found places for themselves on the floor where they could lay down their *petates* to soften the surface and curl up in the blankets they had brought from home. By midnight, most of the men had gone to sleep and by 1:00 AM, most of the cooks had retired as well. Only a couple of women remained behind to keep an eye on the fires during the night.

Guests had a hard time finding a place to sleep in the small bedroom, where the images of the Virgin were on display. While the party was in full swing, women had filled this little sanctuary with a mound of freshly cut flowers that they would tie to the big crosses carried in the procession. Since it took a long time to decorate the crosses, several *comadres* got up at 2:00 AM and began the exacting task of reproducing floral arrangements they had learned many years ago from their mothers and grandmothers. While they worked, an old woman sang religious hymns in a beautiful haunting voice.

When the crosses were ready, Don Zenaido woke everybody up. He wanted the procession to leave the house early. Despite his good intentions, it still took over an hour before everyone was ready. Finally, by 5:30 AM, the *compadres* and *comadres* had succeeded in attaching the *misterio* and the large images of the Virgin onto litters and had lined up the women who would carry the religious icons back to the church. At the head of the procession, two men carried Mexican flags on which Don Zenaido had attached small emblems of the Virgin of Guadalupe, symbolizing the fact that the Virgin had remained a national symbol, even after the Mexican Revolution and the imposition of fiercely anticlerical laws. Following the men came a group of young girls carrying baskets of flowers. As the procession moved slowly along the streets of Hueyapan, these girls graced the path with a carpet of flower petals, preparing the way for the comadres who were carrying the *misterio* and the two large images of the Virgin. Immediately, behind the Virgins, two men held the imposing crosses that had been beautifully decorated with flowers, balancing them delicately with the full length of their

Photo 9 Rosa and a *comadre*, carrying the *misterio* in a procession during the Virgin of Guadalupe fiesta in 1971. [This year there was no brass band, only a few local guitarists.]

bodies. The remaining guests formed two lines behind the men with the crosses and everyone, male and female, carried bouquets of flowers and candles. At the very end of the procession marched the brass band, followed by two *compadres*, who had the important job of setting off firecrackers at regular intervals.

The procession took two and a half hours to go from Don Zenaido's house to the church, covering a distance an adult could have walked in five or ten minutes at a normal pace. Those participating in the procession stopped every few yards to sing hymns with Don Paco. When the deacon finished praying, they started walking again, ever so slowly, as the band filled the void with the same martial music it had been playing before and the firecrackers exploded at regular intervals, reporting to villagers, in every *barrio* of the *pueblo*, on the progress of the procession. By the time Don Zenaido's party arrived in the plaza, a big crowd had gathered, most of whom fell into line to accompany the Virgins into the church and to recite the Rosary with Don Paco.

Later that morning, a priest celebrated Mass. Then in the afternoon, as the sun was setting, a small procession formed in the church to return the *misterio* to Don Zenaido's house. The little image would remain with the family for another month, until Don Abogón, the next *mayordomo*, organized the transfer, complete with the necessary *mole*, procession, and other festivities appropriate for the occasion. Now that the big images of the Virgin were back in the church, the Moros had the villagers' undivided attention. Breaking only for meals, the players performed from dawn to dusk, until the end of the following day.

The fiesta itself continued as well for another day in Don Zenaido's home, with crowds of people stopping by to eat, drink, and enjoy the music. For the women in the kitchen, this meant that they worked almost nonstop for four days. When the party finally ended, they started in all over again at home, picking up their normal routine of demanding chores, without ever getting the chance to catch up on their sleep.

Protestants in Hueyapan

Protestant missionary groups began visiting Hueyapan and making converts in the early years of the twentieth century. According to Elvira Hernández, who belonged to an evangelical sect, Protestants first made contact with the village just before the Mexican Revolution, when her grandparents were still young. The Spiritualists (Espiritualistas) came first; then the Methodists arrived. Although these groups no longer had a following in Hueyapan by 1969–1970, several hundred Protestants divided themselves up among the Iglesia Cristiana Universal, Pentecostals, Seventh-Day Adventists, and Jehovah Witnesses, with the largest number of them belonging to the Iglesia. Predictably, Protestants never sponsored or even participated in the cycle of Catholic fiestas celebrated throughout the year. They also excluded themselves from establishing

Photo 10 Maestro Rafael and Doña Juana, the *mayordomos* of the fiesta in 1971, waiting to welcome the Virgin of Guadalupe procession, in their home.

religious ties to their Catholic neighbors. They did not, for example, exchange favors by becoming *compadres*.[29]

The Protestants built their churches in the outlying *barrios* of Hueyapan: San Andrés, San Bartolo, and San Felipe. Their decision, clearly, made good strategic sense. It would be easier to convert Catholics living up in the hills, at some distance from the church, than those residing near the center of town. How much simpler it became for villagers in the *barrios* to attend religious services closer to home.[30]

But convenience was not the only attraction. There were good political reasons as well. The Centro used the Catholic church and the San Miguel chapel as proof of their cultural superiority and of their

Photo 11 Women serving *mole* at a fiesta in Hueyapan.

ties to other Mexicans. The *barrios* did the same with their store-front Protestant temples.

Although Catholics and Protestants had little respect for each other's religion, professions of faith rarely led to political conflict. Geography, on the other hand, did play a role and since Protestants tended to live in the *barrios*, most of them identified with the so-called conservative side of disputes and were therefore associated by Catholics in the Centro with the backward "Indian" elements in town.

In fact, Hueyapan's Protestants were successful entrepreneurs and were among some of the wealthiest people in the village. Disciplined and abstemious, they did not drink or smoke or spend money on costly fiestas. Earnest and hardworking, they helped the *barrios* develop, in both material and symbolic ways. As part of their modernizing project, they welcomed the nation's growing interest in Mexico's prehispanic heritage.

Evangelical sects have traditionally worked in indigenous tongues and provided translations of significant portions of the religious service in the languages of the people they have converted. When they came to Hueyapan, they taught the villagers hymns in Nahuatl, which the residents then sang to visitors passing through as examples of the *pueblo's* indigenous traditions. Since most of the other Nahuatl songs had been introduced to the villagers by government employees, Hueyapan's Protestants saw nothing outlandish about adding liturgical music to the mix that they had learned from evangelical missionaries.

When the missionaries translated their hymns into Nahuatl, they tried hard to "purify" the language, without fully succeeding, by eliminating Spanish loan words and grammatical constructions. The Catholics cared less about mixing the two languages, as we can see in an article published in the late 1940s, in the scholarly journal *Tlalocan*, where a native schoolteacher from Hueyapan reproduced a series of prayers that were traditionally recited by the village's rainmakers, under the influence of hallucinogenic mushrooms.[31] In colonial times, Catholic missionaries encouraged villagers to borrow freely from Latin and Spanish to identify Christian symbols, even though they wanted the Indians to continue speaking Nahuatl. Protestants, on the other hand, tried to preserve, and when necessary reconstruct, the indigenous languages of the people they had come to convert. Despite the relative purity of the Nahuatl, the songs I heard were reminiscent of the ones I had learned as a child in a New England summer camp, both in melody and verse. The hymn reproduced here is just one example of how missionaries refined twentieth-century Nahuatl, banishing Spanish terms, like Dios, that had crept in over the years, in order to convert the Indians of Hueyapan from one Christian denomination to another.

The villagers sang this hymn in both Nahuatl and Spanish. To perform it in Nahuatl, however, was a bit of a challenge, because the missionaries failed to translate the lyrics to fit gracefully into the musical score. The clumsiness of the Nahuatl version introduces yet another note of irony to the evangelical project.

Song 1 Canto Bienvenido (Canto Cualle Micaqueh, or The Welcome Song).

Nahuatl Version

Sance cuicame nochintlapacme ince pancinco in Teotl,
Mauesotiga nican ticate itepancinco in Teotl.
Cualle micaqueh nognitzitzin (g)uan itocatzin tlasoh den Teotl.
Axan cecan titaquisqueh tichmahtic tecmololcuia.
Timotlasocamatisqueh cantaquisqueh antualmatzin quimachilia
    tlasotlalistleh,
Ican ce yen Teotl techmomaquilia iuitatzin paquilichle,
Anicuiga quimiquilia cuanepanolti.

Ansacuiliui monechegoxe xlapepenalme xpantzin con Teotl.
Anompa alcuiga quipiasqueh tlaxtlaualistleh tioteguitzqueh.
Cualle micaqueh nognitzitzin (g)uan itocatzin tlasoh den Teotl.
Axan cecan titaquisqueh ticmahtic tecmololcuia.
Timotlasocamatisqueh cantaquisqueh antualmatzin quimachilia
    tlasotlalistleh,
Ican ce yen Teotl techmomaquilia iuitatzin paquilichle,
Anicuiga quimiquilia cuanepanolti.

Spanish Version

Unen los santos todos los santos con dulce voz,
Con reverencia porque en presencia están de Dios.
Bienvenidos se hallan hermanos en el nombre bendito de Dios.
Hoy reunidos nos gozamos al saber que nos une su amor.
Demos gracias por ser salvos y en nuestras almas sienta gratitud,
Porque solo Jesús nos da vida y salud,
Y a la gloria alque lleve su cruz.

Muy pronto unidos los escogidos irán a Dios.
Ya en el cielo tendrán el premio de su labor.
Bienvenidos so hallan hermanos en el nombre bendito de Dios.
Hoy reunidos nos gozamos al saber que nos une su amor.
Demos gracias por ser salvos y en nuestras almas sienta gratitud,
Porque solo Jesús nos da vida y salud,
Y a la gloria al que lleve su cruz.

English Translation

All the saints (sing) together in a sweet and reverential voice,
Because they are in the presence of God.
You are all welcome, brothers, in the blessed name of God.
Today reunited, we enjoy the knowledge that His love unites us.
Let us give thanks for being saved and in our souls feel gratitude,
Because Jesus alone gives us life and health,
And glory be to Him who carries the cross.

Very soon the chosen ones will go united to God.
In heaven they will finally enjoy the fruits of their labor.
You are all welcome, brothers, in the blessed name of God.
Today reunited, we enjoy the knowledge that His love unites us.
Let us give thanks for being saved and in our souls feel gratitude,
Because Jesus alone gives us life and health,
And glory be to Him who carries the cross.

CHAPTER SIX

THE ROLE OF THE STATE IN POSTREVOLUTIONARY MEXICO: A NEW PERIOD OF "EVANGELIZATION" IN HUEYAPAN

In the early 1920s, schoolteachers came to Hueyapan to help the villagers take advantage of new opportunities opening up in the country. Representing Mexico's revolutionary government, they were part of a wider national campaign to "acculturate" the Indians, offering the inhabitants of indigenous *pueblos* the tools that they needed—both ideological and technological—to reap the benefits of social and economic reform. Twenty-five years later, social workers settled down in Hueyapan for a few months as well to help the villagers achieve the same goal. Although these ambassadors spoke about change, their words harkened back to the old colonial project. Social workers, for example, wanted to alter the same areas of daily life that colonial priests had focused on centuries before. Then, while pledging allegiance to an anticlerical state, both schoolteachers and social workers adopted the model of colonial Catholic rituals to celebrate national holidays. Finally, like the colonists before them, they continued to blame traditional cultures for the persistence of ignorance and poverty in the country—Indians remained poor, the argument went, because they stubbornly held on to their ancient customs. But unlike their predecessors, these secular emissaries of postrevolutionary Mexico spoke glowingly about the nation's indigenous past, sending mixed messages to those still identified as Indians. While schoolteachers and social workers encouraged members of indigenous communities to reject their own cultures, they also insisted that they play Indian for others and take pride in their prehispanic heritage.

Over the years, schoolteachers and social workers—known as cultural missionaries—contributed significantly to shaping Hueyapan's indigenous identity. As we examine their programs, we see how they established a pattern of swinging back and forth between promoting positive and negative images of the Indian, depending on the audience. When, for example, government officials visited the *pueblo*, they made sure the villagers welcomed their guests with ceremonies that drew on indigenous themes. In the absence of outsiders, these very same teachers and cultural missionaries criticized the villagers for being too Indian and encouraged them to adopt the practices of urban Mestizos.

Using methods first introduced during colonial times, representatives of Mexico's postrevolutionary state settled down in the community for months at a time to give the Indians the "culture" they supposedly lacked. In modern Mexico, this meant instructing the villagers to stop speaking Nahuatl to their children at home, because indigenous languages kept young people, supposedly, from learning Spanish well and Spanish was the key to their success. But this also meant training the villagers to participate in patriotic ceremonies that confirmed their place as indigenous Mexicans in a decidedly non-Indian nation.

Cultural Missions

The Department of Cultural Missions was established in 1926. By the early 1970s, it had merged with the Department of Public Education.[1] Between 1926 and 1938, the state set up regional centers to train teachers working in rural communities to participate in adult literacy campaigns and in other projects aimed at raising the standard of living in the villages. Before schoolteachers received their federal certification, they had to complete a four-week orientation program at a Cultural Missions center located in the region of Mexico where they had been assigned to work.

In 1942, the department expanded its program and began recruiting a larger number of technical specialists to send to the *pueblos*. Traveling in teams, cultural missionaries went from village to village, settling down for a few months at a time to help rural peasants help themselves. By the time I was doing my fieldwork in Hueyapan, there were 108 missionary teams working across rural Mexico in indigenous and poor Mestizo communities.

In 1970, the Department of Public Education produced a small pamphlet that explained the philosophy behind the Cultural Missions and described the various services they provided. According to the pamphlet, Cultural Missions workers were supposed to organize a series of economic, social, and cultural reform programs that would have an impact on almost every aspect of life in a rural community. The missionaries were also encouraged to coordinate their efforts with local and regional welfare agencies. Finally, they were expected to set up economic and cultural action committees in the *pueblos* that would take responsibility for managing projects introduced by the government, after the cultural missionaries had moved on to another village.[2]

The teams in later years were staffed with the following specialists: a social worker/homemaker, nurse/midwife, agricultural/livestock adviser, music instructor, mason/carpenter, and industrial adviser. In ways reminiscent of the tasks assigned to Catholic missionaries during the colonial period, every member of the team had a specific list of obligations to fulfill, both as individuals and as part of the group. First, like the mendicant orders, cultural missionaries professed a (secular) "Gospel" that they truly believed in, proclaiming that those who followed their instruction were destined to be saved. Second, continuing an old tradition, the new evangelists moved the few Indians still scattered across the countryside into new settlements so that they could manage them more easily and perform their proscribed duties. For example: dispense medicine to the ill, introduce Indians to European-style amenities that would improve their living conditions and diet, and encourage Indians to make better use of their leisure time. Through their teachings, the missionaries converted the Indians of postrevolutionary Mexico to the nation's new secular religion, creating, in the process, an entirely new set of rituals that incorporated "exotic" customs from the rural countryside. And as they assimilated traces of Mexico's prehispanic past into nationalistic ceremonies, they prepared ethnographic accounts of indigenous practices for the edification and further use of Mexico's elite.

Third, members of the Cultural Missions helped peasants in rural Mexico adjust to the economic changes taking place in the nation, teaching them how to use modern farming technology to improve the harvests. Finally, not only did the Cultural Missions rely on strategies similar to the ones used in colonial Mexico, but they ended up replacing the earlier work of their Spanish predecessors. As we have already seen, more often than not, customs identified as Indian were European to begin with or, if indigenous in origin, had already been altered to such an extent that they had little to do with prehispanic Mexico.

I was unable to interview anyone who had worked in Hueyapan as a member of the Cultural Missions. When I looked for reports on the village in the central office of the Missions, once again I was unsuccessful. I have therefore relied entirely on the impressions of local people in Hueyapan who vividly remembered their experiences with cultural missionaries. According to the villagers, members of the Cultural Missions visited the *pueblo* twice, once in 1945 and again in the early 1960s. When they first arrived, they encountered resistance. People told me that they were suspicious of them, because they thought that they were evangelical Protestants, an understandable error, given the name, and the "religious" zeal with which these cultural missionaries embraced their calling. By the late 1960s, however, the villagers had come to appreciate the help the missionaries provided.[3] The community had, in a sense, been converted. Those who had anything to say about the Cultural Missions spoke enthusiastically about the people who had come to Hueyapan. As they described the contributions that team members had made, they stressed the fact that cultural missionaries were government representatives and had no affiliation with a religious sect.[4]

Gregoria Lozada represented the opinion of many others in the *pueblo* when she summarized the impact that the cultural missionaries have had on Hueyapan: they brought "civilization" to the village. In the days before the Cultural Missions, Hueyapan had been much more "Indian." To "civilize" the villagers, the missionaries, she continued, had taught them good manners and discipline. For example, they insisted that people eat only when seated properly at a table. Doña Zeferina added that the missionaries visited individual homes, in the company of a villager, to teach people how to live better. Since everybody knew and respected her, the missionaries often asked Doña Zeferina to accompany them to help convince her neighbors to cooperate and trust the government representatives.

According to the villagers, mission workers were responsible for getting the *pueblo* to build a bridge over the Amatzinac gorge that was strong enough to support trucks and buses, thus making it possible for heavy vehicles to enter Hueyapan. In addition, these government workers encouraged *campesinos* to use chemical fertilizers and technological innovations that improved the quality and quantity of agricultural products. Influenced by members of the Cultural Missions, villagers began building homes out of *adobe*. The more ambitious also plastered and painted over the mud bricks on the outer walls of the structures that faced the street. Previously, people lived in houses made out of wood planks that were draughty and risked catching fire.

The teams' carpenters helped villagers build latrines, tables, chairs, and beds. By the late 1960s, although some villagers continued to use homemade furniture, those who had the means preferred to purchase store-bought merchandise, for they were sturdier and had more "câché." Particularly popular were the colorfully decorated straight-back chairs with straw seats, metal-frame beds with religious scenes at the head, and small storage compartments at the foot, and large armoires (*roperos*).[5]

Homemakers affiliated with the Cultural Missions encouraged women to purchase *hibachi*-like stoves to use along side the hearths that every indigenous home had.[6] They also taught women how to jar fruit and introduced them to other methods of preserving food. To encourage artistic expression, they showed women how to embroider and do other kinds of decorative sewing.

With the hope of turning the local custom of weaving into a profitable industry, team members introduced mechanical looms to the *pueblo*. In the late 1960s, you could still find a few modern looms in Hueyapan, but most women preferred to work on the backstrap loom, if they wove at all—and very few women continued to do so. People gave several explanations for this lack of interest in the new technology: First, villagers saw more opportunities for advancing themselves by making an investment in agricultural equipment than in weaving; they could make a better living for their families by improving the yield of fruit in their orchards and corn in their fields, than by producing more *rebozos* and *bufandas*. Second, they personally preferred the backstrap loom to the new technology, because the traditional *telarcito* produced a thicker, warmer piece of cloth. Third, the villagers knew that they could command a higher price for items produced the traditional way from tourists, anthropologists, and weaving aficionados.[7]

The Cultural Missions were particularly successful in introducing modern medicine to Hueyapan. In 1945, several *curanderas*, Doña Zeferina among them, attended classes in the village to learn the rudiments of modern medicine and they quickly switched to contemporary methods of healing, almost to the exclusion of their "rustic" techniques. The program also attracted about 20 other villagers, with no prior experience, to serve the village as part-time medical assistants, capable of giving intramuscular and intravenous injections and bandaging wounds.

Given the emphasis on injections, it was not surprising that the villagers referred to the newly trained healers as "the ones who inject." For most ailments, healers gave a patient a shot of penicillin and prescribed an oral antibiotic. Since anyone could purchase medication over the counter, with no prescription from a doctor, healers in Hueyapan simply went to a pharmacy in Cuautla and bought whatever the nurses associated with the Cultural Missions recommended or what the doctor in Tetela told them to do. Then, according to Doña Zeferina, after a period of trial and error, every healer developed her own list of favorite remedies. The Cultural Missions also helped the village put together a reasonably well-equipped infirmary in the home of Modesta Lavana, who lived right off the plaza.[8]

In addition to providing medical instruction, the nurses who came to Hueyapan in 1945 appointed and trained three women in the village to assume the role of public health inspectors for the school. Doña Zeferina served in this capacity. As she explained it, the inspectors attended flag-raising exercises twice a week and examined the children as they stood in line to pledge their allegiance, making sure that every pupil was wearing clean clothing and was adequately scrubbed. Many mothers complained, but they rarely rebelled. Those who did, exposed their children to the terrible humiliation of being bathed in public and themselves of being branded "lazy Indians."

According to the villagers I spoke to, members of the Cultural Missions worked with schoolteachers to organize programs that recognized the community's indigenous identity. For these special performances, they instructed young girls to dress up in *xincueites*. They also taught villagers to sing songs in Nahuatl. Then, while I never saw any of their ethnographic research, I have every reason to believe that they fulfilled their obligations, as defined in the pamphlet distributed by the Mexico City office. As for the ethnographic writings of schoolteachers, I did have the chance to read the work of two native schoolteachers, one of whom celebrated the ongoing indigenous traditions of the village in a scholarly publication intended for specialists of Nahuatl-speaking Indians; while the other bemoaned these traditions in a report prepared for the national school system.

Ethnographic Contributions

Cultural Missionaries and Schoolteachers

Nahuatl Songs
Although the villagers said that they did not have any traditional Nahuatl music, I learned seven songs that had verses in Nahuatl during my stay. Two of the pieces were introduced to the *pueblo* by Protestant missionaries. Another four were introduced either by schoolteachers or cultural missionaries and the final one was composed by Lino Balderas, who was born and raised in Hueyapan, but then spent many years of his adult life in Mexico City, singing at the Bellas Artes, the home of the Ballet Folklórico. While based in Mexico City, Don Lino attended meetings of the Nahuatl cultural renaissance movement that I describe in chapter seven. Of the four songs introduced by schoolteachers and/or members of the Cultural Missions, two are in what might be called a "pure" dialect of Nahuatl, exhibiting very little interference from Spanish. Although the themes of the songs are indisputably European, the

lyrics have been carefully stripped of any possible loan words, offering the villagers a more "authentic" rendition of their native tongue than the one they themselves spoke. In the first song, "Güilotl Istac," a man asks a white dove to sing the song he remembers hearing, when he last saw his sweetheart. In the second song, "Xipatlani Ompa," a man asks a swallow to carry a message to his beloved.

The other two songs are variations on the same melody and pattern of versification. The lyrics for "Xochipitzauac" and "In Tamalera" are in the dialect of Nahuatl traditionally spoken in Hueyapan. Considerably mixed with Spanish, the songs are playful and a bit off-color. The schoolteacher, or cultural missionary, who introduced these songs to the village probably learned them from people in the region and passed them on as he/she found them, without trying to "clean up" the Nahuatl.

"Xochipitzauac" is well known in the area, in both Nahuatl and Spanish. According to Doña Zeferina, the inhabitants of Huazulco, one of the poor Mestizo towns on the bus route from Cuautla, performed a Spanish version of the song—together with a little dance—every time they celebrated a marriage. Even though the oldest known version of the song and dance date to the eighteenth century, scholars have suggested that "Xochipitzauac" is a prehispanic survival of a rite dedicated to Xochipilli (Goddess of the Flowers) and that Catholic priests turned it into a celebration of the Virgin Mary. But when, for example, the musicologist Castellanos tries to make the case for the prehispanic origins of the ritual, he lamely bases his argument on the "simplicity" of the stanzas and the "chaste" manner with which the dance is performed.[9]

In the villagers' version of "Xochipitzauac," an old man looks back over his life, recalling moments of romance and struggles with poverty. The first stanza describes scenes from the singer's youth, when he was a young man courting his beloved. Everything, says the man, was easier then: clothing was cheap and a little money went a long way. In those days, he continues, he lived with a priest who provided him with shirts that had buttons. Now, as an old man, he has nothing; only a pair of *calzones* made out of a piece of colored cloth—he could not even afford a pair of white *calzones*, the preferred uniform of poor peasants! Finally, in the last stanza, he prepares for death and fantasizes about kissing the breast of a young maiden.

As I have already indicated, the second song written in colloquial Nahuatl is a variation on the theme of "Xochipitzauac." "In Tamalera" describes cooks at a fiesta preparing *tamales* and having a good time.[10] Once again, the influence of Spanish culture and European imports dominate: Doña Dominga (Christian name) dances with another cook and accidentally drags a silk shawl on the ground (high prestige item, identified with colonial Spain). While the women enjoy themselves, a lamb (Spanish import) scampers playfully about. The song ends clumsily with a scatological joke. The melody itself, in this and all the other songs I heard, conforms nicely to the familiar repertoire of popular music heard throughout Mexico and other parts of the Spanish-speaking Americas, easily recognized by its major-chord harmonies and regular beat.

Here I reproduce "Güilotl Istac" and "Xochipitzauac" to illustrate the contrast between the two styles of songs introduced to Hueyapan by schoolteachers and cultural missionaries.

Song 2 Güilotl Istac (Paloma Blanca, or White Dove).

Nahuatl Version

Güilotl istac itegüitz costic,
Igan ihyo nicnegui tlahtos.
Nicnegui caguis mosel igüigas
Nigan tlatenco aguatitlan.
Nega yoale cuactimonosqueh
Nan onic piaya mocualtu tlahtol.
Nicnegui caguis mosel igüigas
Nigan tolhuisque tiutzin tiutzin.

Spanish Version

Paloma blanca piquito de oro,
Con el aliento quisiera hablar.
Quisiera oír tus tiernos cantos
Por las orillas del ensinal.
Aquella noche que platicamos
Tenía presente tu linda voz.
Quisiera oír tus tiernos cantos
Para decirnos adiós adiós.

English Translation

White dove with your beak of gold,
I want to speak with your spirit.
I want to hear your gentle songs
By the edge of the stream.
That night when we (my true love and I) spoke,
Your beautiful voice was there.
I want to hear your gentle songs,
So that (she and I) might say adieu, adieu.

Song 3   Xochipitzauac (Flor Delgada, or Slender Flower).

Nahuatl Version

Xochipitzauac del alma mía,
Cualani in monana por acmo nia.
Manin mostla, manin uipla,
Tinemisque en companía.

Cuac onia nipiltontlia,
Tlen sombrero, tlen tortilla.
Axan yi niueuetzin,
Sa sombrero de a cuartía.

Cuac onia tetlan cura,
Tlen botones, tlen botones.
Axan yi niueuetzin,
Sa nogazon de colores.

Tech in copa, tech in chile,
Nictlahcali in nodespedida.
Manin mostla, manin uipla,
Ticpitzosque in cone chichile.

Doña Zeferina's Spanish Translation

Flor delgada del alma mia,
Se enoja tu mamá porque no voy más.
Sea mañana, sea pasado,
Andaremos en companía.

Cuando fuí muchacho,
¡Cuánto sombrero, cuánta tortilla.
Ahora que soy viejo,
Solo sombrero de a 25 centavos.

¡Cuando estaba con el cura,
Cuánto botones, cuánto botones!
Ahora que soy viejo,
Solo mi calzón de colores.
En la copa, en el chile,
Tiro mi despedida.
Sea mañana, sea pasado,
Besaremos la chichi de nene.

English Translation

Slender flower of my soul,
Your mother is angry because I no longer come by to see you.
(Don't worry) be it tomorrow or the next day.
We will be together.

When I was a boy,
I had so many hats and a lot to eat.
Now that I am old,
Just to buy one hat is expensive.

When I lived with the priest,
I had so many buttons, so many buttons.
Now that I am old,
I have only my pair of colored calzones.

With a drink and with a hot *chile* pepper,
I'll take my leave of the world.
(But before I do) be it tomorrow or the next day,
We will kiss the breast of some young girl.

Ethnographic Reports

Although cultural missionaries and schoolteachers did not find any Nahuatl music that was indigenous to the pueblo, they identified a number of traditions in Hueyapan that convinced them of the villagers' ongoing ties to the culture of their prehispanic ancestors. Researchers prepared reports and presented their evidence to scholars in the academy and to government agencies. I had the opportunity to read the research of two native schoolteachers, one of whom, Miguel Barrios, published his findings in a well-known journal of Nahuatl studies (*Tlalocan*).[11] His article, as noted in chapter five, described religious practices in the *pueblo* and offered several examples of prayers in Nahuatl that were invocations to Catholic saints. He also recorded stories he had heard as a child. Although Miguel Barrios did not publish versions of fairy tales about kings and princesses, like the ones Doña Zeferina enjoyed telling, his stories described the struggles of people who were forced to live in a decidedly nonindigenous world.

In one tale, "The Rich Man and the Poor Man," the wealthy landlord forces a lazy worker to separate seeds of wheat (a European import) from grains of sand, a familiar fairy-tale theme. Two other stories describe witches burning to death, a classic European punishment for people accused of possessing evil powers. In one of the stories, witches and vampires are interchangeable. Two of the stories make fun of husbands who behave in the *macho*-style widely associated with Latin American men—their wives literally castrate them for dallying with other women. Yet another story explains the influence Saint Anthony had in the choice of a name for a neighboring village.

Finally, Miguel Barrios describes a prank, called the "Deer Game," that men enjoyed playing on one another while working in the corn fields *(milpa)*. Since I cannot trace the origins of the game to either Europe or prehispanic Mexico, the jury is out on the provenance of this dirty joke. Either way, it says little about the villagers other than to suggest that they have a scatological sense of humor—something we have already noted in the song "In Tamalera." It goes without saying that pranks involving feces are hardly unique to Nahuatl-speaking Mexicans. The game consists of tricking a neighbor into grabbing a piece of cloth smeared with human feces—the cloth is supposed to be the tail of a deer.

Although Miguel Barrios did not mention it, another favorite game in Hueyapan was called "Jesus Christ." Doña Zeferina explained that you play "Jesus Christ" by persuading an innocent neighbor to be Jesus for the duration of the game. Once the poor sucker has accepted the role, the others tie him up and set fire to his hair and clothing.

The second piece of ethnographic research was never published. It was prepared by Cecilio Pérez, a native schoolteacher, who submitted the work as his thesis *(memoria)* in partial fulfillment of the requirements for certification as a rural primary schoolteacher. In his *memoria*, Maestro Cecilio was expected to describe local customs and traditions. Unlike Miguel Barrios, who was writing for a community of scholars interested in prehispanic Mexico, Maestro Cecilio had to please an administration committed to "acculturating" the Indians. Faithful to a set of assumptions that were generally accepted in the mid-1960s, he argued that Hueyapan's indigenous traditions complicated the efforts of schoolteachers to educate the village's children for the modern world. Of particular concern to Maestro Cecilio was the Nahuatl language and alcoholism. The only local customs he described positively were Catholic rituals; for example the custom during Lent of local men to dress up in "funny" costumes and run about the *pueblo*, playing harmless tricks on the villagers. He also wrote about the elaborate processions held on Good Friday, when members of the community reenacted the Crucifixion of Christ.[12] Like many others in Mexico, Maestro Cecilio did not worry about distinguishing between customs having roots that went back to prehispanic times and those that were imported to Mexico during the colonial period. What is more, he never seemed to consider the possibility that a problem like alcoholism had less to do with the survival of indigenous culture in Hueyapan, than it did with the debilitating impact over the centuries of discrimination and poverty.

These two pieces of ethnographic research offer diametrically opposed responses by "acculturated" villagers to the problem of being Indian. Although Miguel Barrios and Cecilio Pérez were both born and raised in Hueyapan, they clearly disagreed about the value of the village's indigenous heritage. No doubt the choices they made in their personal lives influenced the perspectives they had on the question. Maestro Miguel left Hueyapan for Mexico City in the early 1940s and found work there teaching Nahuatl. While he enjoyed the life of an urban Mestizo in the nation's capital, he provided members of the country's academic elite with the kind of ethnographic descriptions that they were looking for, as they constructed the image of postrevolutionary Mexico. Maestro Cecilio, on the other hand, stayed in Hueyapan and dedicated his life to improving the standard of living of his fellow villagers. Every day, he saw people struggling with extreme poverty and the "more Indian" they were, the poorer, often, they seemed to be.[13]

Despite his views on the subject, Maestro Cecilio was still a good citizen, and as such he understood the importance of promoting the villagers' Indian identity for the benefit of distinguished visitors. He, therefore, joined other teachers in Hueyapan in organizing ethnic programs for government dignitaries who came to the village on official tours of rural Morelos. As Maestro Cecilio put it, it was his "duty" to honor important guests in this way.

The School

In 1870, Maestro Cecilio's grandfather, Francisco Pérez, opened the first school in Hueyapan. A native of the community, Don Francisco learned how to read and write from a parish priest. There are no records, unfortunately, that describe what motivated him to take this important step. Perhaps, he heard about President Benito Juárez's new law that required every child in Mexico to go to school. Perhaps he simply decided to teach the village's children how to read. Whatever his reasons, he volunteered his services and shared what little he knew.

In the late nineteenth century, the village did not have a dedicated school house and classes took place in private homes. The situation changed, however, in the early 1900s, when Hueyapan welcomed teachers from neighboring towns, who insisted on building classrooms in the old municipal palace. If these teachers had any training at all, they probably studied in normal schools established by Mexico's celebrated educator Justo Sierra.[14]

Those who shared memories with me about going to school before the Mexican Revolution complained bitterly about their experiences. The teachers, they said, showed little interest in them and spent most of their time applying for jobs closer to Cuautla. As they waited to hear about a new assignment, they routinely skipped classes, ignoring their responsibilities in the village. Even when they showed up, the teachers were not very good. To add insult to injury, some of them were also terrible drunks. Still, having teachers assigned to the *pueblo* at all made a significant difference in the mindset of the villagers. By the time the Mexican Revolution broke out, the school was a permanent fixture in the *pueblo*, corrupt and inefficient though it may have been.

During the Revolution, classes met only sporadically. Impatient with the situation, in 1919, a group of villagers took the education of their children into their own hands. Since they all had farming to do, they decided to share the task and assign several villagers to take rotating shifts that would last for several months at a time. Maestro Cecilio's father, Eligio Pérez, went first. He was still a young man at the time and had not yet married. When the time came for him to step down, everyone concluded that he was doing a very good job and should remain permanently in the position. As the official teacher, he received a daily wage of 50 *centavos*.

In 1921, President Obregón established a new educational system for postrevolutionary Mexico.[15] That same year, Maestro Eligio told me, a man by the name of Rómulo F. Hernández arrived in Hueyapan, claiming to represent the president of the Republic and to have the authority to affiliate the school in Hueyapan with the new national system. But first, the *pueblo* needed qualified teachers with federal certification. If local villagers were interested, he continued—and if they could read—he invited them to go to the Ministry of Education in Mexico City on a particular day where they would get the additional training they needed. As certified teachers, they would receive a salary of two *pesos* a day.

Although several villagers were eligible, they were afraid to leave home, convinced that soldiers would stop them on the way—as they routinely did during the Mexican Revolution—and force them to join the army. Only Maestro Eligio decided to take his chances. On the designated day, he showed up at the Ministry of Education.

The reception in Mexico City exceeded all expectations. Arriving in the capital, Maestro Eligio joined other aspiring teachers and went through an abbreviated training program, at the end of which every participant received a huge bonus of 300 *pesos* in "pure silver." Nobody had a pouch large enough to hold that much money, so the *maestros* poured the coins into their hats and took off for home. Triumphantly returning to Hueyapan, Maestro Eligio's good fortune tempted others in the village to get certified as well, but it was too late.

By the early 1930s, the primary school in Hueyapan went up to the sixth and final grade. As director of the school, Maestro Eligio had a good deal of political influence in the *pueblo* and he persuaded the villagers to turn the plaza into a beautiful square (*un zócalo*), with a kiosk and flowers. A few years later, however, the villagers turned against the *maestro* for expressing freely his socialist views and they forced him to resign.

As an enthusiastic and faithful employee of the state, Maestro Eligio supported the federal government and shared the sympathies of Mexico's president, Lázaro Cárdenas, who in the late 1930s, had nationalized the oil industry and introduced other measures that placed modest restrictions on a free-market economy. To demonstrate the village's loyalty, Maestro Eligio instructed the teachers to march the children around the *pueblo*, shouting, "¡*Viva el Socialismo!*" This made people so angry that they mobilized against him. The group used this episode and an apparently unfounded rumor about teachers forcing a boy and a girl to undress in public to justify their decision to close down the school. After firing Maestro

Eligio, the antagonistic faction destroyed the *zócalo* as well. The school did not open again for another two years, and when it did, it only ran classes up to the fourth grade. As for the plaza, the villagers refused to fix it up again, preferring to use the square for bull riding—a choice more "acculturated" villagers noted as further evidence of the *pueblo's* Indianness.[16] When the school opened its doors, Maestro Eligio joined the ranks of the primary schoolteachers. His days as director were over.

This period of intense conflict between schoolteachers and villagers reflected the general mood of the country, when Cárdenas was president, throughout the state of Morelos and other parts of the nation. As we saw in earlier chapters (two, three, and four), the villagers themselves took part in a regional struggle during those years and the nature of their involvement defined the terms of local conflicts as well. Most of the antischoolteacher faction in Hueyapan supported the Morelos rebel leader Tallarín, who was rampaging the countryside in the late 1930s and early 1940s, killing teachers and other government employees.

Although Tallarín's movement eventually disappeared, bitter disputes continued to erupt between schoolteachers—many of whom had been born and raised in Hueyapan—and other members of the community. These conflicts, what is more, had a negative impact on the education of the community's children. After losing confidence in a specific group of teachers, the villagers did little to restore the school system they had lost, leaving Hueyapan without a full course of study at the primary school level until 1960. When I arrived in Hueyapan in 1969, there was still no secondary school in the village. If a family wanted their children to continue going to school, they had to send them to Tetela, Tlacotepec, or even farther away.[17]

During the year I lived in Hueyapan, control of the village's schools remained essentially in the hands of Maestro Eligio's family. Although Maestro Eligio himself had retired many years before, his sons were carrying on the tradition. Maestro Demetrio was director of the school in the Centro, Maestro Cecilio was director of the school in San Felipe, which went up to second grade, and a third son, Maestro Octavio, was director of the San Bartolo school, which went up to the third grade. The only other school in the village was in the

San Andrés Barrio and it was not, in the year I lived in Hueyapan, in the hands of a member of the family, or, for that matter, in the hands of any other resident of the *pueblo*. Like San Bartolo, the San Andrés school went up to the third grade.

Primary School Textbooks

Primary schoolteachers in Hueyapan gave lessons in geography, national language (grammar), history, civics, arithmetic, and natural sciences. To guide their instruction, teachers relied on a series of textbooks and accompanying workbooks that the National Commission of Free Textbooks distributed to every community affiliated with the national school system. The material reviewed here came from the books that were used in the 1960s and early 1970s to teach history, civics, and language—books that boldly espoused the dominant ideology of a Mestizo nation and had a clear bias toward urban, not rural Mexico. When Indians appeared on the pages of these books, they were depicted as historic relics of prehispanic times or poor humble Indians of modern Mexico who needed the help of Mestizo children to assimilate.[18]

In Hueyapan, children found the descriptions of prehispanic Indians as alien to their own experiences as did children living in Mestizo towns, but they recognized themselves in the portraits of contemporary Indians. What is more, since the reading selections idealized the experiences of Mestizo children, any pupil in the village—who could dream just a little—wanted to live the way other Mexican children did and to stop being Indian. The message was clear: if they did not assimilate, they would remain marginalized and poor, just like the Indians who appeared on the pages of these books—smiling, gentle observers, who rarely took part in any of the fun.

In the first grade, the textbook introduces the children to the cheerful homes of Mestizo families. The illustrations depict colorfully painted two-story houses, constructed out of cement or red brick. Inside, we see familiar wood-frame chairs with straw seats, beds, chests of drawers, armoires, tables, curtains, and rugs. Kitchens have gas ranges, refrigerators, and electric blenders.[19]

First, graders also meet the members of an idealized Mestizo family: the affectionate mother, the hardworking father, and the dutiful children who love going to school. Even the dullest pupil in Hueyapan could not help but see the contrast between his or her morning routine and that of the lucky little boy in the reader who starts his day with a wake-up kiss from his smiling attractive mother, followed by a warm bath and a well-balanced breakfast, served to him at the kitchen table. As we have already seen, Doña Juana's children get up by themselves, straighten out the wrinkles in the clothing they slept in and perform a series of household chores before having breakfast, served from the hearth by their silent, overworked mother, who remains kneeling over the fire making *tortillas*.

The first explicit reference to Indians in the first-grade reader appears in a poem entitled "Indian Boy" (by Gastón Figueira). A young Mestizo invites an Indian boy to play with him, explaining to those who may not take it for granted that all children in the Americas should love one another. Acknowledging his privilege, the Mestizo offers to teach the Indian how to read, because all children in the Americas want to learn. Two sketches accompany the poem. In the first, we see a young boy dressed like a Mestizo, wearing modern-day pants, a shirt, and shoes. He is leading a second boy by the hand who is dressed in white *calzones*, a hat, and sandals. The skin color of the Mestizo child is perceptibly lighter than that of the Indian, but definitely not white. In the second picture, the boys are seated. The Mestizo has placed his arm around the Indian's shoulder and is showing him how to read.

On the last pages of the textbook, first graders receive a short lesson in history about Hidalgo, the priest who led Mexicans into battle against Spain in 1810 in the War of Independence. Called the "Father of the country," the children learn that Hidalgo loved the Indians and taught them how to read, repeating the message of the earlier lesson: Good Mexicans treat Indians with kindness and give them the education they need to participate in the wider society. Although first graders do not read about Mexico's prehispanic heritage, the textbook suggests the important place this legacy has in the history of Mexico by including a picture of Cuauhtémoc (the last Aztec emperor) in a lesson that encourages children to participate in school clubs.

The second-grade textbook expands on the theme of how dutiful Mestizos help Indians assimilate and how worthy Indians take advantage of the opportunities made available to them. In the early chapters of the reader, we meet Pedro, his sister Carmela, and their parents. The family lives in Mexico City, in a comfortable middle-class home with a maid and a pet dog. Pedro's father is a doctor who works in a public health clinic. One day, Pedro's father reads in the newspaper that a cyclone has severely battered the states of Oaxaca and Veracruz, causing damage to the very region where Pedro's grandparents live. Alarmed by the news, Pedro's father drops everything and takes off for Oaxaca to make sure that everyone is all right.

When he returns, he reports that the grandparents are fine, but that he has met a young boy, by the name of Martín, who "did not have a father" and whose mother was killed by the storm. Given the situation, Pedro's father decided to take the child back to Mexico City and invite him to live with the family. Pedro and Carmela welcome the young boy warmly. In the picture illustrating the moment when Pedro's father arrives with Martín, we see that the young boy has a darker complexion than everybody else and does not dress like the other children—he is wearing colored *calzones*, sandals, and a hat.

At first, the story says nothing specific about Martín's ethnic origins, but the pictures provide all the necessary clues. So does the text, describing Martín's mother as having had her son out of wedlock. The next chapter makes everything explicit.

When Martín goes to school with Pedro, the teacher asks the new boy to tell the class where he comes from. Embarrassed by the question, Martín shyly replies that he is from Oaxaca. Reassuring the child that he has nothing to be ashamed of, the *maestra* replies that they are delighted to welcome to their class somebody who was born in this historic state, because they have just finished reading about another *Oaxaqueño*—"an intelligent and brave little Indian boy who went on to become president of the Republic."

The following lesson describes the life of Benito Juárez, a man who, against all odds, overcame his Indianness and became a great national hero—Benito Juárez was adopted by a priest. The message could not have been clearer: Martín and other Indian children are different from Mestizo children, but if they try hard, or, even better, if they have the good fortune of being adopted by non-Indians, they too can rise above their indigenous station and make important contributions to Mexico.

The second-grade reader also introduces children to the broad outlines of Mexican history. Without making an explicit connection between earlier periods and the nation today, the children read about the Aztec Empire, and the discovery of the New World; the Spanish Conquest of Mexico, the War of Independence and the period of reforms under Benito Juárez. In the workbook, they read as well about the great nineteenth-century educator Justo Sierra, who is quoted as saying that the Indians must progress in order to assure the social development of the country.

The emphasis shifts slightly in the third grade. Instead of describing the role Mestizos should play in helping the humble Indians, the textbook describes the nation's indigenous past, making explicit reference to the fact that the peoples of prehispanic Mexico are the noble ancestors of the Mestizos. Beginning with the big game hunters of Paleolithic times, who crossed the Bering Strait and settled in Mexico thousands of years ago, the reading selections go through all the major pre-Columbian cultures, period by period, ethnic group by ethnic group: the Olmecs, Mayas, Teotihuacanos, Toltecs, Chichimecs, postclassic Mayas, the Nahua tribes, Tarascans, Mixtecs, Zapotecs, and Aztecs. It also presents the history of Spain around the time of the Spanish conquest, introducing the subject with the following words:

> In the first pages of this book, we learned that we are Mexicans and that we must love and serve our country. We have also learned the interesting history of the first inhabitants of our country whom we call indigenous, because their ancestors came here many years ago. In the following pages, we will study the part another people played in creating Mexico as we know it today.

Given the government's interest in promoting an image of the Mexican people as the descendants of two great races and cultures, it is not surprising that the schoolbook version of the Spanish conquest minimizes the atrocities committed by Cortés and his men and focuses instead on moments of mutual aid and compassion. For example, the Tlaxcalans and Cholulans had brutal encounters with the Spaniards, but appear on these pages only as willing accomplices, eager to help the conquerors defeat their common enemy, the Aztecs. The same comforting gloss is given to the story of Cortés' Indian mistress, baptized Doña Marina, who spoke Nahuatl, and several other indigenous languages well, and who served as the official interpreter.[20] In an equally conciliatory spirit, the textbook devotes more space to the missionary priests and the work they did in "teaching the Indians customs" than to the cruel *encomenderos*. After describing the support the Indians received from Catholic priests, the third-grade reader ends with a brief review of the Mexican Revolution.

In sum, as the third graders read about the Indians and the Spaniards, they learn almost nothing about the long history of abuse that indigenous groups experienced, dating back to the sixteenth century. Skipping over the painful process involved in creating the Mestizo people of Mexico today, the matter is presented as a *fait accompli*. The children must wait until the fourth grade to learn anything about the complexities of the colonial period or the first 100 years of the nation's independence. And what they learn is not very much.

In the fourth grade, children read about the origins of the Mestizo people in the colonial period, but once again the process receives only a couple of introductory sentences:

> Over three centuries [1521–1810], two races and two cultures blended together: the indigenous and the Spanish. And from this blending came the people of present-day Mexico, the people to whom you belong.

In Hueyapan, however, the children have learned just how little they belonged. They did not bathe or brush their teeth every day, or live in pretty well-furnished homes with gas ranges and refrigerators. They were much more like the Indian boy they met in the first-grade reader and Martín whom they met the following year. As for their parents, they resembled the gentle, smiling figures dressed in Indian clothes who appear on the margins of the book, doing nothing more than watching Mestizo children having fun as they played games at school. A nagging question, therefore, remains: since children in Hueyapan were clearly different from the Mestizo children portrayed in the texts, did they not have a different history as well? For, if everyone shared the same experiences in Mexico, why were there still so many Indians in the country today, nearly 500 years after the Spanish conquest?

According to the fourth-grade reader, the story goes like this: after the heroic death of Cuauhtémoc, kindly priests converted the Indians to Catholicism and cruel *encomenderos* exploited their labor. But from that moment on, the text does not distinguish between the experiences of Indians and those of poor Mestizos. Both groups suffered abuses by enemies of the Mexican people (usually landowners) and enjoyed the protection of the nation's heroes (often priests, before the Mexican Revolution). As for the criteria used to distinguish between Indians and Mestizos, the readings say virtually nothing. All we know is that by the time we get to modern-day Mexico, the country still has a sizable indigenous population, and those so identified need the help of Mestizos to change and assimilate.

In the fifth and sixth grades, the textbooks teach Mexican history in the context of North and South America. National themes appear in the language arts workbooks, intended for teaching grammar. Although Indians are not mentioned at all in any of the sixth-grade reading materials, they are the subject of several lessons in the fifth grade. Here we see indigenous people as tourist attractions. Students read about the adventures of children from Mexico City who take a class trip to the south of the country to visit archeological ruins in the Yucatán and Chiapas. Their guide tells them that there are 81 distinct archeological zones in Mexico and 12,000 registered sites. The students also travel north to meet the Tarahumara Indians and learn about their indigenous customs, the difficult lives the Indians have led, and the positive steps the Tarahumara are taking to improve their situation, like sending their children to school.

National Holidays and School-Run Assemblies

To enrich the curriculum provided in the textbooks, teachers organized elaborate programs for their students and other members of the community on national and state holidays. In Hueyapan, these programs reinforced the lesson the children learned in class: in

Mestizo-oriented Mexico the villagers were still Indians. With these ceremonies, teachers continued the process of incorporating the villagers into the postrevolutionary cultural system, while preserving their distinct indigenous identity. After convincing the villagers that they should learn to live and act like Mestizos, schoolteachers organized assemblies that emphasized the fact that the villagers were still Indians.

As I have already suggested, government representatives of postrevolutionary Mexico adopted many of the same strategies used by Catholic missionaries during colonial times. Their reliance on religious forms of instruction was particularly obvious in the way schoolteachers organized the community on patriotic holidays. Not only did they borrow the idea of "baptizing" indigenous customs by "nationalizing" them, but they also adopted the general model of the Catholic fiesta system, using it to structure their own secular ceremonies. Patriotic holidays, like Catholic fiestas, included processions, with decorated portraits of national "saints" (Hidalgo, Morelos, and Zapata), "religious" services led by members of the government's "clergy" (schoolteachers, etc.), and a *mole* feast for the community, in the home of the sponsor (*presidente de fiestas patrias*). For the graduation ceremony marking the completion of primary school, which was not a national or state holiday, but still followed the same pattern, parents even selected godparents for their children and dressed their sons and daughters up as if they were celebrating their First Communion.

Finally, just as every *barrio* in Hueyapan sponsored a fiesta on the day of the saint for which it had been named, it also assumed responsibility for the appropriate national or regional holiday, hosting the event for which the *barrio* had named a school, plaza, or main street. San Felipe, for example, sponsored the fiesta celebrating the Mexican Revolution, because it had a school called November 20, named after that day in 1910 when Francisco Madero and a small band of followers declared war on President Porfirio Díaz and successfully persuaded the landless peasants of Mexico to join his struggle for social and economic change. San Bartolo sponsored the fiesta commemorating the death of Zapata because it had named its main plaza April 10, after that day in 1919 when Emiliano Zapata was killed in an ambush, and so forth. Whenever possible, processions marched along streets in Hueyapan that bore the appropriate historical names, just as the procession on Good Friday went up Calvary Street.

Over the 1969–1970 academic year, teachers organized about 25 patriotic assemblies in Hueyapan, of which eight were major *pueblo* celebrations. For purposes of this discussion, I have limited my comments to two: the fiesta commemorating the death of Emiliano Zapata, and an official ceremony organized to welcome Felipe Rivera Crespo, the PRI's candidate for governor of the state of Morelos. The two events offer a clear contrast between the way schoolteachers treated the question of being Indian in Hueyapan for the villagers themselves and for distinguished outsiders. The two ceremonies illustrate as well how schoolteachers relied on more than just the structure of the Catholic fiesta system. They also embraced the Church's negative attitudes about indigenous cultures, sharing the conviction of Catholic priests that the only way to save the Indians was to convert them.

The Zapata Fiesta

The anniversary of Zapata's death was not an important holiday in Mexico in 1970 except in Morelos where the revolutionary hero was born and killed.[21] For people in Morelos, the 10th of April was almost as important as the 20th of November, the official day throughout the country for celebrating the Mexican Revolution. In Hueyapan, the ceremony began on the evening of April 9 in San Bartolo, with a short program sponsored by the school in an open air theater constructed specially for the fiesta in the main plaza of the *barrio*. The program included a number of patriotic speeches and recitations (formulaic orations and poems), delivered by teachers and their pupils. Children also performed a comedy skit and folk dances, representing various regions of the country. Not until the following morning did the formal presentations focus in a systematic way on the Mexican Revolution and the death of Zapata.

At 5:00 AM, Maestro Demetrio turned on the record player and amplifying system in the Centro, waking up the entire village to the blaring sounds of *ranchero* music. Between songs, he announced that students were expected to be in the plaza by 6:00 AM to take part in the flag-raising exercises. One by one, sleepy children, wrapped up in wool *rebozos* and *gabanes*, wandered into the square. By 7:00, enough people had gathered for the patriotic ceremony to begin: a teacher hoisted the flag up the pole while the children sang the national anthem. Dismissing their pupils, the teachers sent them home to have breakfast, dress, and make their way up to the San Bartolo Barrio to join others in the community who would soon be assembling for the procession.

By 10:00 AM, there must have been about 1,000 people in the San Bartolo plaza and the teachers started lining the villagers up. First came the major officers of the community, including the *presidentes de fiestas patrias*, who had the honor of carrying the portraits of Zapata, Hidalgo, and Morelos. The national "*saints*" were decorated with green, white, and red streamers, the colors of the Mexican flag. Next came the brass band hired from a neighboring *pueblo* for the occasion by the *presidente*, then the schoolchildren, and finally, the public at large. Beginning on Calle Emiliano Zapata, the procession turned onto Calle Popo (named after the majestic volcano Popocatepetl that stood above the *pueblo*) and then onto Calle 10 de Abril.

As the procession made its way back to the plaza, a few men broke away to set up the benches, so that the "religious service" might begin. After everyone found a seat, Maestro Octavio asked his fellow villagers to rise and observe a minute of silence in memory of Zapata. Before sitting down again, they sang the national anthem. As director of the San Bartolo school, Maestro Octavio had the privilege of delivering the main oration of the morning. In his speech, he described with eloquence how Emiliano Zapata sacrificed his life for "Land and Liberty." The *maestro* reviewed the history of Zapata and the Mexican Revolution, praising the rebel leader's selfless heroism and recalling the act of betrayal that led to his death. As he spoke, the schoolteacher sounded like a village priest describing the death of Jesus Christ. Drawing on Mexico's "deep myth of culture,"[22] Maestro

Octavio created the "Passion of Zapata." The speech ended with the following words:

> Don Emiliano Zapata never wanted power; he used his sword to fight ambition and treason. Calling out to the fields, he identified the land as the reason for this struggle. He sought freedom with great dignity . . . and that is why, Mexican peasants, you should never forget Emiliano Zapata who gave us land to use, for our sustenance and for our future. In gathering together here today, we have come to praise Zapata publicly and express our gratitude, our affection, our respect for this man who died for the land. His battle cry, "Land and Liberty," was heard throughout the nation.
>
> Citizen General Don Emiliano Zapata, we swear to you that we will always remain ready to face every kind of danger so that the land we farm will always be free. We will repeat as often as necessary your saying that "the land must belong to those who cultivate it with their own hands."
>
> The present agrarian reform has advantages. It assures social justice and better crops; it teaches the peasants how to end their suffering; it teaches them how to use agricultural machinery; it introduces new ways of farming; it opens up unused fertile land; it builds roads and schools. Article 27 of our Magna Carta pays tribute to the Plan de Ayala, which was written for the benefit of the Mexican people and for a better future for Mexico.
>
> Ladies and Gentlemen, Zapata died for the land.
>
> Thank you.

The program continued with several more speeches and recitations by students, mostly about Zapata but also about other national heroes and related patriotic themes. Several children sang a ballad about Zapata, while still others offered the assembled a few folk dances, like the ones we had seen the night before, and another comedy routine. Finally, the program ended with the national anthem.

Absent from all the speeches and artistic performances was any attempt to integrate the local history of Hueyapan into the ceremony celebrating the life of Zapata. Everyone knew the names of the villagers who had fought in the Revolution, some of whom were still alive. Everyone knew people in the older generation who had stories to tell about what life was like in Hueyapan during those years. Nobody even thought to mention that two members of the community had actually signed the Plan de Ayala.[23] Instead, teachers and students described the sacrifices others had made for the people of Hueyapan so that they might be free. From Christ to

Photo 12 Children in the San Bartolo Barrio dancing during the fiesta commemorating the death of Emiliano Zapata. They are dressed in colonial Spanish costumes. Zapata's photograph, decorated with streamers in Mexico's national colors, holds the place of honor, much like the image of a Catholic saint.

Zapata, the villagers learned to thank outsiders for virtually everything they had, be it their religion, their land, or what people loosely called "culture."

The village's history and traditions were apparently so unimportant that schoolteachers did not even dress children up in the traditional clothing of the village. When they performed, they wore costumes associated with other regions of Mexico, everywhere but Morelos. As they waited for the music to begin, teachers introduced the dancers to the audience with announcements like the following: "And here come some *charros* (dudes) from Jalisco and some women from Puebla to perform a beautiful typical dance called 'Jarabe Tapatío.' "

During the program, people mentioned Indians explicitly only twice; the first time to pay tribute to Mexico's indigenous past—a little girl recited a poem that described the heroic death of Cauhtémoc, the last emperor of the Aztecs, who died without ever revealing to the Spaniards where his people had buried their treasures. The second time the subject was mentioned, it was in a denigrating skit—a modern-day indigenous woman confesses her sins to a Catholic priest. Performed by two teenagers, the one playing the Indian spoke in a stylized Spanish riddled with grammatical mistakes and errors in pronunciation. Called "Confessions of a Little Indian Woman (*indita*)," the one-act play takes place in a church. Seated by the confessional booth, the Indian woman asks the priest for forgiveness as she describes all the things she has done that have angered her husband: she flirted with another man, stole money out of her husband's trousers, and so forth. After she confesses, the young woman tries to defend her behavior by saying that she did not really mean to do any harm. Like a good father, the priest forgives the "naughty" woman and absolves her of her sins, but not before giving her a piece of his mind.

When the school program ended, Padre Diego celebrated Mass on a hill overlooking San Bartolo. Imitating the *mayordomo* system introduced by colonial priests, the *presidente de fiestas patrias* paid for the Mass and hosted the festivities that followed the religious service. Whereas *mayordomos* relied on their *compadres* and *comadres* to assist them with the cost and preparation of the *mole* feast, the *presidente* depended on villagers with *ejido* lands—*campesinos* who had benefited from Mexico's land reform—to help out with the meal and pay for the dance that followed later that evening.

The Welcoming Ceremony for Lic. Felipe Rivera Crespo (PRI Candidate for Governor of the State of Morelos)

In February 1970, the PRI's candidate for governor of Morelos came to Hueyapan on a campaign tour. In a country that had, effectively, a one-party system, everyone knew that this candidate would win.

Still, tradition prevailed and Felipe Rivera Crespo had to go through the motions. This meant traveling to villages across the state of Morelos. In addition to giving him a little publicity, these visits supposedly offered *campesinos* the opportunity to inform the next governor about the special needs of their communities. Anticipating this important event, schoolteachers met with the elected officials of Hueyapan to plan the welcoming ceremony.

Although teachers rarely encouraged villagers to celebrate their Indian identity, for this occasion, they used all the influence they had—overriding the opposition of others—to convince the villagers to put on an indigenous show for the candidate. In this context, they argued, their ethnicity was an asset. Yet, given the purpose of the candidate's visit, a folkloric performance was particularly out of place. The villagers, after all, were planning to ask the new governor to help Hueyapan lose its Indian identity. They wanted him to provide the community with more economic, political, and social opportunities than it presently had.

Even though they had very little indigenous material to work with, the teachers managed to cobble bits and pieces together. In the end, they succeeded in producing an ethnic show that drew on a few local customs, but in a way that was as foreign to the villagers as were the many other innovations introduced to the *pueblo* over the years by schoolteachers and representatives of other government agencies. Despite the incongruities, the program achieved what it set out to do: Rivera Crespo left the village believing that Hueyapan was a place where people had preserved their prehispanic traditions. When he became governor of the State Morelos, he would be able to count on the village to help him fulfill his patriotic duty of paying tribute to the nation's indigenous heritage.[24]

The performance itself was simple. Four teenage girls waited for the candidate's party at the entrance to the village. They were dressed in the traditional costume of Hueyapan, which only a few old people still wore (black *xincueites*, embroidered cotton blouses, black wool *rebozos* and *ixcactles*) and they carried a large wreath of flowers. When Rivera Crespo arrived at the bridge, the girls gave him the wreath, welcomed him in Nahuatl and Spanish, then accompanied the candidate and his entire entourage to the San Miguel plaza. Before the school house in

Photo 13 Young girls dressed in *xincueites* at a ceremony in the San Miguel plaza, honoring government dignitaries. The headdresses worn by the girls in the last row are not traditional in Hueyapan, but are imitations of a costume found in parts of Oaxaca.

the plaza, Maestro Demetrio and Rivera Crespo exchanged formal greetings. Then, a sixth-grade boy recited a poem in Nahuatl and Spanish that is frequently attributed to the prehispanic poet king of Texcoco, Netzahualcoyotl. Known as "Nonantzin" (My Mother) the poem was published in Spanish translation in the second-grade language arts workbook. With the help of a few other villagers, native schoolteachers translated "Nonantzin" from Spanish into Hueyapan's dialect of Nahuatl.[25]

The program finally turned to more serious matters and several villagers presented petitions to the candidate, requesting support for individual projects. Speaking for Hueyapan's self-proclaimed progressive faction, Maestro Rafael asked Rivera Crespo to endorse the *pueblo*'s longstanding desire to secede from the municipality of Tetela. Maestro Rafael explained that the present arrangement interfered with the community's desire to progress more rapidly. Hueyapan, he added, was bigger than Tetela and the villagers were tired of being governed by people who represented a minority and favored the interests of the smaller settlement. The candidate listened politely, embraced Maestro Rafael three different times, and promised to do what he could. Others asked Rivera Crespo to help improve the roads between Hueyapan and Tlacotepec and between Hueyapan and Tetela, build a permanent marketplace off the plaza, provide running water for the entire village, provide funds to renovate a house that the *pueblo* had made available to schoolteachers, and establish a more adequate health clinic. In addition, almost every *barrio* asked the candidate for funds to build special facilities, like a basket ball court. Even Hueyapan's musical ensemble (*Los Norteños*) presented the candidate with a petition, asking him to provide members of their group with *charro* costumes—they wanted to look like musicians from Jalisco, whose style of music they performed.

Making no distinctions, the candidate embraced every petitioner warmly and promised to do what he could to meet the needs of the people of Hueyapan. He then excused himself and left for Tetela. Eager to see what he would say at the municipal seat, some of the schoolteachers joined Rivera Crespo's party. As they departed, the *maestros* instructed the villagers who remained behind to plaster the walls of Hueyapan with campaign posters.

For several days, people were enthusiastic and optimistic about Rivera Crespo's visit, but soon cynicism set in. As one schoolteacher put it, he did not expect Rivera Crespo to honor any of their requests. The entire tour was nothing more than a publicity stunt. Given his pessimism, I asked the teacher whether he planned to vote for Rivera Crespo in April and for Echeverría in the presidential elections the following July. My question surprised the *maestro*: of course, he would vote for them; he was Mexican after all.

Photo 14 A poster found all over Hueyapan after the campaign visit of the PRI's candidate for governor of the state of Morelos. In addition to photographs of the national party's candidates, the poster reproduces a drawing of the Mexican Constitution and three heroes of the Revolution—Carranza, Madero, and Zapata. Although the drawing suggests a strong and unified political legacy the actual story is not so idyllic: Zapata turned against Madero and Carranza in the early days of the Revolution and, in 1919, Carranza arranged to have the Morelos leader killed. Madero was killed as well in 1913, in a plot organized by Victoriano Huerta.

I visited Hueyapan several times while Rivera Crespo was governor of Morelos and saw for myself that the skeptical *maestro* had predicted the future accurately. The few changes that did take place while he was in office could not easily be attributed to the promises he made in the winter of 1970 (see chapter three). What the visit did achieve was precisely the opposite of what the villagers had wanted: it reinforced the community's identity as an Indian *pueblo*.

Chapter Seven
Cultural Extremists

In the 1950s, members of a Nahuatl renaissance movement came to Hueyapan to encourage the villagers to preserve their indigenous heritage. Based in Mexico City, they visited the *pueblo* as part of their effort to build a following in Indian communities where people still spoke the language of the Aztecs. Supporters of the movement firmly believed that their attempt to revive prehispanic traditions would help the nation become powerful once again, the way it was in the early sixteenth century, in the days before the Spanish conquest. For reasons I hope will become self-evident, I refer to members of this renaissance movement, and of groups similar to it, as "cultural extremists."

National politicians and federally funded anthropologists vigorously opposed the cultural extremists on scholarly and ideological grounds, dismissing their project as utterly absurd. Responding in kind, cultural extremists accused members of government and the academic establishment of being anti-Indian and, by extension, anti-Mexican. Perhaps, the most infamous confrontation occurred in the late 1940s, when a self-proclaimed historian by the name of Eulalia Guzmán announced to the press that she had discovered the grave of Cuauhtémoc in Ixcateopan, Guerrero.[1]

Upon hearing the news, archeologists sponsored by the Mexican government went down to Guerrero to examine the remains. Instead of finding the bones of a single individual who might arguably have been the last Aztec emperor, they identified the skeletal parts of at least five different people, including women and children. But it was too late. The discovery had aroused a great deal of enthusiasm. Partisans simply refused to listen to what the specialists had to say.

Fueling the debate, regional newspapers published inflammatory editorials that accused the archeologists of being traitors to Mexico. One paper recommended that they be shot.[2]

Cultural extremists were still causing trouble in 1969, forcing political leaders to take public stands against them. In the early days of his presidential campaign, Luis Echeverría felt obliged to set the record straight, explaining to reporters why the PRI disagreed with those who proclaimed that Mexicans should reject their ties to Spain and identify only with their indigenous ancestors. Repeating his party's widely accepted line, Echeverría argued that Mexicans were blessed with a double heritage, both Indian and Spanish. They should embrace their mixed origins and celebrate the traditions of their Mestizo nation.

A few days later, a reporter interviewed Alfonso Caso, director of the National Indigenist Institute (INI), and asked the distinguished anthropologist to comment on Echeverría's statement. The interview appeared in *El Día*, one of Mexico's government-sponsored papers. Receiving a two-column spread, the headline read, "Showcase *Indigenismo*—'To Reject the Spanish, One of the Two Sources of Our National Identity, Would be a Painful Mutilation': Caso." Agreeing with Echeverría and calling the extremists "raving indigenists," Alfonso Caso presented the case against them in the following way:

> These *indigenistas*, whom I would call "raving indigenists," claim that we should abandon Spanish and speak Nahuatl. And why Nahuatl? Why not Maya, or one of the other 60 or so languages still spoken in the country? These raving indigenists do not understand that Spanish is our national language, a means of communication for all Mexicans.
>
> Look, as you know, I have dedicated my life to the study of ancient Mexican cultures. Thanks to the work of modern-day anthropologists, we have succeeded in gaining world-wide recognition for the achievements of these ancient Mexican cultures. That said, we must never forget that Spain brought to Mexico European culture, which is itself descended from Mediterranean culture. And this earlier culture flourished from Egypt to Chaldea, passing through Palestine, Greece, and Rome, and culminating in the works of great thinkers and artists in the Renaissance. Having inherited traditions from two great cultures, we must affirm our personality by continuing to drink from both their fountains. In this way, we will preserve our own style and be more and more ourselves.[3]

In the same article, Caso defended Mexico's indigenist policy and described the ways the state fulfilled two obligations: paying tribute to the nation's prehispanic past and helping to raise the standard of living of Indians today. The government, he explained, created "two distinct but intimately connected institutions: the Institute of Anthropology and History (INAH). . . which studies Indians in the past and present, and the National Indigenist Institute (INI) which . . . takes the improvements of modern civilization to the Indians."[4]

The cultural extremists vehemently opposed INI's acculturation policy, arguing that indigenous customs were far superior to those identified with so-called modern Mexicans. They also rejected the ideological campaign of celebrating the nation's Mestizo identity. As far as they were concerned, the people of Mexico had not blended their cultures and races—or at least not willingly—and they never would. According to the extremists, the Spanish and other European invaders simply imposed their traditions on the Indians, interfering with the "natural evolution" of true Mexicans. Conceding the obvious, that there were many Mestizos in the country today, they referred to these racially mixed people as the unfortunate descendants of raped Indian women. Violated and robbed of their indigenous heritage, they had no choice but to imitate the ways of their White European colonial rulers. The nation had suffered for centuries under the domination of outsiders, but the time has finally come to rise up and take radical action: expel the foreigners and educate the Mexicans in their own traditions. This was the only way to return the nation to its former racial and cultural grandeur.

Although they firmly believed that they held different positions, cultural extremists and representatives of the government had a lot in common. At times, it was difficult to tell them apart. This was particularly true when representatives of the state paid tribute to Mexico's indigenous past.[5]

To begin with, members of both groups shared similar backgrounds—for the most part, they belonged to the urban middle classes. They also shared similar ideas about who the Indians were, describing them as people whose traditions had roots going back to prehispanic times. Although state representatives and cultural extremists proposed different solutions for helping the Indians, they all gave the same explanation for why indigenous communities still existed today: geographic isolation. Indians, they claimed, lived in remote parts of the nation and had little access to the conveniences of an industrialized society. Protected, therefore, from the full impact of modernity, Indians maintained ties to the ancient ways of their prehispanic ancestors. Both groups took pride in Mexico's indigenous heritage as well and paid tribute to the nation's prehispanic past by assigning to present-day Indians the task of serving as living links to a time before the Spanish conquest. Finally, both sides developed elaborate strategies for saving the Indians—the government by turning Indians into Mestizos and the extremists by turning Mestizos into Indians.

I was interested in the ideas and programs of the cultural extremists because they represented the latest attempt by a group of non-Indians to address the nation's so-called Indian problem. As we have already seen, factions among the ruling elite have debated the issue since early colonial times, and introduced a number of different solutions. Over the years, the methods have varied, from the kindly approach of missionary priests to the biting whip of the cruel *hacendados*, but everyone shared essentially the same goal: to destroy indigenous traditions and to "civilize" the Indians. Traumatized and beaten, Indians became part of New Spain in the sixteenth century, a society dominated by the values of Europe, and were forced to work for the economic well-being of a decidedly non-Indian state.

Throughout the colonial period and the first 100 years of independence from Spain, non-Indians occasionally rose up to defend the Indians. But more often than not, they did so as part of a wider political agenda, caring little about reviving indigenous traditions. They wanted instead to give Indians a chance to succeed in a world that had left prehispanic Mexico behind. When, in rare cases, these champions fought to restore an indigenous way of life, what they had in mind were traditions identified with an earlier period of colonial rule, when Indians were protected by Catholic priests.[6] In the days following the Mexican Revolution, members of the government sympathetic to Indians paid tribute to the nation's prehispanic past, but they firmly continued the old colonial campaign of "acculturating" the Indians. This double agenda pulled in opposite directions, eventually inspiring a new group of advocates to challenge the ideals of the Mexican Revolution and to urge fellow citizens to rise up once again—to revive the traditions of prehispanic Mexico. No longer satisfied with acts of veneration to the nation's indigenous past, they wanted to take the next radical step and reconstruct the cultures of prehispanic Mexico. Their image, however, of this indigenous past, relied more on European fantasies than on anything resembling historical fact.[7]

Since Hueyapan was a Nahuatl-speaking *pueblo*, the villagers met cultural extremists interested in reviving Aztec traditions. Elsewhere in Mexico, Indians encountered extremists dedicated to other prehispanic peoples. In the 1940s, for example, Yucatecan communities encountered enthusiasts of Maya culture.[8] In the late 1960s, as the interview with Caso in *El Día* suggests, activists calling for an Aztec revival were making the most noise and giving the government a big headache.[9]

When I came to Mexico in July 1969, I made contact with the Movement for the Restoration of Anauak (El Movimiento), one of the most important organizations in cultural extremist circles at the time. Over a period of several months, I participated regularly in the Movimiento's weekend meetings in Mexico City and in their very occasional midweek activities. Although I grew disillusioned with the group early on and moved to Hueyapan, I maintained close ties to the Movimiento until Christmas, returning on weekends to attend their events.

In Hueyapan, I quickly learned that the villagers knew all about the Movimiento. They assumed, in fact, that I was part of the group, or at least interested in indigenous cultures for the same reasons. In the eyes of the villagers, there was little difference between an anthropologist like me, who wanted to learn Nahuatl, and a cultural extremist. Before I had the chance to ask about the group, the villagers introduced the subject and told me about their experiences with the Movimiento in Mexico City and Hueyapan.

The Movimiento in Mexico City

A lawyer by the name of Rodolfo F. Nieva founded the Movimiento in the late 1950s. Before creating his own circle of

cultural extremists, Nieva belonged to the Indigenous Confederation of Mexico, whose leader was a linguist by the name of Juan
Luna Cárdenas. According to Eliseo Cortés, who knew Juan Luna
well, the Indigenous Confederation had been in existence since, at
least, the late 1930s.

Nobody I met in Mexico City could tell me why the Movimiento
broke away from the Indigenous Confederation. In Hueyapan, however, Juan Maya suggested that Juan Luna and Rodolfo Nieva had
different agendas—the former devoted his time and influence to
recreating the Aztec religion and the latter to promoting political
change. Juan Luna's group disbanded before I got to Mexico, so I
never saw any of their ceremonies. According to Don Eliseo and Don
Juan, the Indigenous Confederation worshipped the gods of the
Aztec pantheon, in particular Huitzilopochtli and Texcatlipocatl.[10]
Although members of the Movimiento told me that they too had
adopted the Aztec religion, I never saw them pray to a prehispanic
deity. They commemorated the triumphs of Aztec military heroes
instead and paid tribute to vague "cosmological" concepts.

As head of the Movimiento, Rodolfo Nieva organized a political
party (El Partido de la Mexicanidad), a newspaper (*Izkalotl*), the
name of which means, "reappearance," a school for teaching Nahuatl
(Mexikatlahtolkall) and innumerable political, cultural, and com-
memorative gatherings. Before long, his efforts attracted the attention of illustrious people, including the controversial Eulalia
Guzmán and the former president of Mexico, Miguel Alemán.[11] By
1964, the group's campaign to revive the Nahuatl language had
gained international notice as well, prompting *The New York Times*
to publish an article about their activities. Taking its information
from a Reuters Press Agency release, *The New York Times* did not
mention the Movimiento by name, but it described the First
Congress of the Nahuatl Language that the group had just sponsored
and mentioned the Nahuatl grammar, *Izkalotl*, that members of the
Movimiento had recently published. According to the article, the
grammar was being used in the schools of an "Indian community,"
located on the outskirts of Mexico City.[12]

In September 1968, Rodolfo Nieva died and the Movimiento
went quickly into decline. Although the founder's brother Jorge and

sister María del Carmen were now in charge, they did not have Rodolfo's charisma, or, in the case of Jorge, much enthusiasm for the cause. Jorge, in fact, had so little interest in the Movimiento that he turned almost everything over to María del Carmen, who, while deeply devoted, had little aptitude, she confessed, for political matters. Playing to her strengths, she organized cultural gatherings instead. A retired teacher, who had served many years as an inspector for the federal school system, María del Carmen Nieva spent most of her time introducing young people to Nahuatl.

By the time I met the group in July 1969, the Movimiento had reduced its activities to occasional outings, a few cultural ceremonies, and regular classes in Nahuatl on Saturday afternoons in Maestra María's del Carmen's home. In memory of their founder, members paid lip service on important occasions to Rodolfo Nieva's more ambitious political agenda, giving speeches that tried to imitate his fiery rhetorical style. The Movimiento also continued to publish the group's newspaper, but at irregular intervals, perhaps two or three times a year. Finally, Maestra María del Carmen tried to preserve her brother's philosophy and militant voice by writing the book that she assumed he would have wanted to write. Calling it *Mexikayotl*, she published it one years after his death.

Members of the Movimiento reported that the group had somewhere between 400 and 800 members in Mexico City alone and many thousands in the countryside. Perhaps, that was true when Rodolfo Nieva was alive, but it was no longer the case in 1969. During my time with the Movimiento, I never attended a gathering that attracted more than 25 people, nearly half of whom were young children. With the exception of one little girl, who was the daughter of the *maestra*'s maid, the children came from middle-class homes.

Of the 13 or 14 older members of the Movimiento, over half of them were teenagers finishing up their final years in preparatory school. The most impressive individual in this group was called Cuauhtémoc and he served as president of the Movimiento's effort to recruit new members from preparatory schools across Mexico City. The son of an agrarian engineer, Cuauhtémoc planned to pursue the same career as his father and had just been accepted at the prestigious National School of Agriculture in Chapingo (state of Mexico).[13]

Most of the other students in the group were girls and three of them belonged to the Movimiento's corps de ballet.

As for the adults, they included three schoolteachers, Maestra María del Carmen's maid, two small-scale entrepreneurs, an engineer, and a landowner who rented out fields to peasants. Known as Señor Castillo, the landowner was the most picturesque member of the group and he played the role of the Movimiento's "pet Indian." When I asked him to tell me about where he came from, Señor Castillo explained that he had grown up in a Nahuatl-speaking village in the state of Mexico and could still remember a little of the language. With the approval of everyone, he always attended meetings dressed up in a *charro* costume. To add a final note of irony, Movimiento members had comparatively light skin and Maestra María del Carmen drew attention to this fact by dying her hair a flaming red.

According to members of the Movimiento, the history of Mexico justified their desire to restore "Nahuatl culture." As Maestra María del Carmen explains in *Mexikayotl*, the ancient inhabitants of the Americas originated here on these continents. They were not—as Europeans would have us believe—the descendants of paleolithic peoples who wandered across the Bering Strait at the end of the Pleistocene period. The Western Hemisphere was called Ixachilan (Inmensidad or Vastness) and those who lived here belonged to a single race, which the Movimiento called Ixachilankatl.[14] Across the Americas the Ixachilan race divided itself into a number of distinct ethnic enclaves that occupied wide territories. One of these groups called themselves the Nahuah (or Nahuatl people) and they lived in an area called Anauak, which extended south as far as Nicaragua and included all of North America.[15]

The Movimiento divides the history of Anauak into five epochs: Olmekatl, Maya, Teotiuakatl, Toltekatl, and Mexikatl. During the Maya period, the Nahuatl people expanded well beyond their own borders and had a major impact on the cultural evolution of Western Civilization. According to Maestra María del Carmen, the Mayas already knew that the earth was round 2,500 years ago and had boats sturdy enough to circle the globe. Setting sail from the Atlantic coast of Anauak, the explorers passed through the Straits of Gibraltar and arrived in Egypt, where they showed the Egyptians how to build pyramids and introduced them to the central concept of the Nahuatl religion: Teotl or creation.[16]

When the Egyptians asked the Nahuatl people where they had come from, they responded, "*atlantike*" or "by the sea." And so the Egyptians called them the people of "Atlantis." The Nahuatl explorers moved on to Greece where they influenced Solon and later Plato. More than anyone else, Plato captured the spirit of Nahuatl culture in his writings, in particular in *The Republic* where he incorporated the idea of the "Nahuatl family" (Kalpull)—the kinship and land tenure system of Anauak—into the culture of the Mediterranean.[17] Thanks to the influence of Nahuatl culture in Greece, elements of the tradition reappeared in Rome, and eventually served as the foundation of Christian theology, albeit in a sadly corrupted form. The Christians, we learn, took the Nahuatl god (Teotl) from Roman culture and then "dressed it up with all the religiosity and mysticism of the Jewish people." We know that the Christians borrowed their concept of God from Teotl, because the disciples of Jesus called Him Deus, the Latinized version of Teotl, instead of Yaweh (Jehovah), the name in Hebrew for the God of Israel.[18]

With the fall of the Roman Empire and the rise of individual European kingdoms, dialects of Latin assumed the status of bona fide languages and Deus became Dieu in French, Dìo in Italian, and Dios in Spanish,

> which is the way it [Teotl] returned to us, suffering the fate of all the raw materials we produced and continue to produce. We export these materials, foreigners transform them and then send them back to us at a higher price. And what a price we Mexicans have paid for Teotl, who returned as the Dios of the Christians! A price that has made us the victims of great crimes, committed by those who conquered our nation and forced our ancestors to accept the Catholic religion. A price that almost caused us to lose the instinctive nature of the Mexican people![19]

As María del Carmen Nieva tells the story, on August 12, 1521, the day before Cortés conquered Tenochtitlán, the Ueyi Tlahtohkan, ruler of the Great Confederation of Anauak, ordered the Nahuatl people to preserve their culture in secret and to pass it down by word of mouth from one generation to the next, until the Mexican people were ready to throw off the yoke of foreign domination.[20] The autochthonous inhabitants of Mexico obeyed the decree and now the moment had finally come to rise up and expel the foreigners so that Mexicans might practice once again their nation's legitimate culture.

As to how and when the Revolution would take place, the book said absolutely nothing, nor did any other publication produced by the Movimiento that I had the opportunity to read. Nobody bothered to describe the political, social, or economic program for the new state either, except in the very vaguest of terms. We learn, for example, that Movimiento members planned to use the generative and creative forces of Teotl. Describing themselves as "cosmological socialists," they identified, to a certain extent, with the ideas of Karl Marx, but they criticized the nineteenth-century revolutionary philosopher for limiting himself to material socialism. In *Mexikayotl*, María del Carmen Nieva added that Marx relied on a poor imitation of the Nahuatl doctrine of the Kalpull, having taken his understanding of the concept from Plato.[21] In Mexico, however, members of the Movimiento would not make the same mistake, for they would build their new political system according to the teachings of the original doctrine on the "Nahuatl family." They would also make Nahuatl the official language of the country.

In preparation for the moment when Mexicans would rise up and expel the foreigners, members of the Movimiento would educate the Mexican people culturally, politically, and psychologically. In their newspaper *Izkalotl*, they tried to mobilize citizens with revolutionary slogans, printing them in bold letters: "The superior Anauak world of our ancestors"; "Spanish colonization, Mother of all our troubles and miseries"; "The Nahuatl language will unite the Mexicans"; "It is the duty of every Mexican to learn his Mexican language"; and "We must insist that they teach us our true history."[22] The articles themselves offered historical analyses, reported on cultural activities sponsored by the Movimiento, and on archeological finds made across the country—Aztec calendar stones were particularly popular. Every issue of the newspaper also included a language lesson and crossword puzzle in Nahuatl.

The historical essays provided critical readings of the past that challenged conventional interpretations. Focusing on Spanish atrocities during colonial and postcolonial times, the authors frequently mused about the terrible consequences of Columbus' error: for centuries, the people of Mexico have had to bear the burden of being called Indians, just because Columbus thought he had arrived in India! Rejecting the name entirely, *Izkalotl* called the indigenous people of Mexico Mexicanos, Nahuah, or Autóctonos. The newspaper referred to the Spaniards by the derogatory term Gachupines[23] and called Mexicans who "collaborated" with foreigners Malinchistas, associating them with Cortés' Indian mistress Malinche—a designation derived from the Nahuatl version of the woman's baptized name, Marina.[24]

In an effort to encourage the Mexican people to pay tribute to their "autochthonous" history, the Movimiento created a calendar of important dates and held ceremonies on the appropriate days. On July 6, for example, members gathered to celebrate a major Aztec victory against Cortés and his men that took place on that day in the year 1519. Known in the Spanish Chronicles as "*la noche triste*," (the sad night), the Movimiento renamed it "*la noche victoriosa.*" In 1969, members held a ceremony on Avenida de la Reforma, right in the center of Mexico City, at the foot of the statue of Moctezuma's brother Cuitláhuac, who was the hero of that historic day. At the time of the battle, Moctezuma was already in prison, the victim of his own good nature, having trusted the Spaniards and welcomed them into the imperial city as honored guests. Cuitláhuac was a military man and considerably less naive. After his brother was arrested, he took matters into his own hands and attacked the Spaniards and their Indian allies, killing them mercilessly and chasing the survivors out of Tenochtitlán. It would take the conquistadors another two years to defeat the Aztecs, by which time Moctezuma had been killed and Cuitláhuac had died in a small pox epidemic—an Old World disease imported to Mexico by the Spanish that eventually killed millions of Indians.[25]

Izkalotl reported that the ceremony attracted a large crowd.[26] In fact, the turnout was poor; maybe 20 people in all. The mood, however, was good, and the ritual went off as planned. An agile young man scaled the steep pyramidal platform that supported the imposing statue. At the foot of Cuitláhuac, high above the assembled, he placed an arrangement of flowers shaped in the form of the

Figure 3 Naui Olli, the Insignia of the Movimiento.

Movimiento's symbol (see figure 3). He then blew on a conch shell, officially opening the ceremony with a haunting sound that evoked ancient times. Down below, a boy beat on a Plains Indian-style tomtom, while a young girl walked back and forth, solemnly waving a smoking receptacle of *copal* incense. After the religious ritual, members of the group gave fiery speeches, calling on Mexicans to recognize their true heritage. And with that, the ceremony came to an end. The entire event took about 30 minutes.[27]

Since the Movimiento looked ahead to an autochthonous future, it participated in programs that offered indigenous alternatives for modern Mexico. On October 21, for example, it cosponsored an event with a group of hair stylists called El Grupo Mexicano de Belleza (Mexican Beauty Group). Held in the fashionable Teatro del Bosque, located in Mexico City's Chapultepec Park, the theme of the evening was: How to be "chic" and "autochthonous too." As announced in the program, the show began with a "Nahuatl ceremony," performesd by the Anauakxochitl (Flower of Anauak) Dance Group and introduced by María del Carmen Nieva, who was identified for the occasion as Maestra Izchalotzin. Dressed in a floor-length Spanish-lace gown, the *maestra* made some remarks about the meaning of the dance, explaining that we were about to see "an act of veneration to our race," a "philosophy without words," a visual representation of the creative forces of the "natural" Mexican.

When she finished speaking, Maestra Izchalotzin stepped to one side and a young maiden appeared on stage, blew a conch shell, and lit some copal incense. A group of 11 women and girls then joined the conch player and performed the "Autochthonous Dance of Happiness." They were dressed in white linen—*huipil*-style blouses, the tops of which were decorated with representations of the Movimiento's symbol, and full skirts, with colorful stripes. In their hair, the dancers wore wreaths of red flowers, and around their ankles, a string of dried fruit of the *coyoli* plant that made a rhythmic rattling noise every time the women lifted their feet.

While the dancers performed a simple hopping step, moving slowly around in a circle, the *maestra* played an "indigenous" drum, maintaining an even beat. Several days later, I asked a dancer about the choreography. She told me that Maestra María del Carmen had composed the piece herself. As they rehearsed the dance, she continued, the *maestra* explained that every step had meaning.

The entire ceremony lasted about 20 minutes. After receiving a polite round of applause, the dancers took their leave, making room for the second act. Ten women appeared on stage, one of whom was dressed in the traditional costume of the Yalalteca Indians, with her hair tied up in the distinctive style of this indigenous group from Oaxaca. The other nine models were dressed in modern clothes and each one wore her hair in a contemporary variation on the Yalalteca theme. For those of us in the audience who might want to reproduce a modern-day version of the Yalalteca look, the Mexican Beauty Group provided diagrams and instructions in the program (figure 4). They also included photographs of several of the models whose hairdos suggested easy alternatives to the basic set.[28]

The private get-togethers in Maestra María del Carmen's home tended to be much more informal. On these occasions, members of the Movimiento did not bother with the ritual blowing of the conch shell or the waving of incense. Nor did anyone rehearse for the assembled the basic ideas of the Movimiento's philosophy. For the most part, the meetings were social gatherings that touched lightly on "cosmological" and political themes. On December 22, however, the Nahuatl New Year, people made more of an effort to turn the evening into a ceremonial event. Members of the Anauakxochitl Dance Group

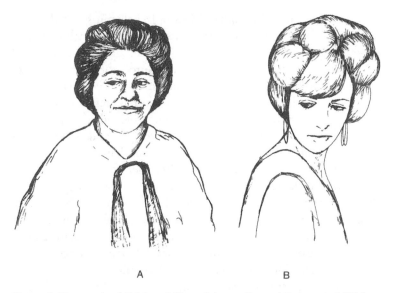

A   B

Figure 4 How to be "Chic" and "Autochthonous" too (A) A typical Yalalteca hairdo. (B) A variation of the Yalalteca hairdo as presented by the Grupo Mexicano de Belleza (Mexican Beauty Group) in Mexico City on October 21, 1969.

performed and guests played a game similar to Bingo (Lotería), using symbols of the Aztec calendar. Near the end of the evening, Maestra María del Carmen called everyone together to see a slide show of some archeological treasures, mostly calendar stones, photographed by guests who had recently returned from tourist trips around the country.

On Saturday afternoons, children of Movimiento members attended Nahuatl classes in Maestra María del Carmen's home. Based on lessons taken from a primer that she had published with other members of the group, every week the *maestra* gave her students lists of vocabulary to memorize, providing them with derivations of place names, like Mexica and Tenochtitlán. She also taught her pupils how to invent terms for such modern-day conveniences as the automobile and train, by combining root words from the prehispanic language. Airplane, for example, became *tepoztototl*, or iron bird (*tepoztli* + *tototl*). Her students, however, never learned any grammar or the rudiments of making simple sentences.

Cultural Extremists in Hueyapan

Villagers identified cultural extremists as one more group of urban Mexicans who had come to Hueyapan to teach the Indians about their Indian identity. Once again, outsiders arrived in the *pueblo* with the aim of saving the villagers' indigenous souls and helping them acquire the "culture" they "lacked." This time, however, the villagers learned that the culture they lacked was their own "autochthonous" heritage. Clearly, the Indians could never win. They never seemed to meet the ever-changing expectations that different groups of non-Indians had for them. For centuries, people blamed them for being too Indian, now they complained that they were not Indian enough.

In the end, cultural extremists persuaded only a handful of villagers to join their movement. More people were interested in losing their indigenous identity than in reinventing it. I could not, however, dismiss the extremists entirely—if for no other reason than that the villagers themselves took the group seriously. What is more, they saw little difference between these extremists and other outsiders—tourists, anthropologists, government workers—who came to Hueyapan in search of Mexico's indigenous heritage. In the eyes of the villagers, we all shared the same goals: to help the *pueblo* conform to our image of the Indian. Every time strangers, who appeared relatively wealthy, drove into town, villagers assumed that they had come to Hueyapan in search of Indian culture. And usually they were right.

Of all the people I knew in Hueyapan, Eliseo Cortés had the greatest sympathy for the cultural extremists. He became interested in their activities in 1939, after attending a Nahuatl congress in Milpa Alta.[29] In 1945, he met Juan Luna Cárdenas, who, he was told, was serving as head of the linguistics division of a governmental agency.[30]

A schoolteacher in Hueyapan encouraged Don Eliseo to go to Mexico City to ask the linguist for a scholarship for one of his sons who wanted to continue his studies beyond the village's primary school. Juan Luna Cárdenas welcomed Don Eliseo warmly and the two men became good friends. Although the villager received nothing for his son, he returned to Hueyapan with several copies of a Nahuatl grammar, compliments of the linguist.

Several years later, in the early 1950s, Don Eliseo, Juan Maya, and two other villagers went to Mexico City to study Classical Nahuatl at Juan Luna Cárdenas's school, a private establishment that the linguist had opened. Known as In Uey Tlatekpanaliztli (The Great Society of Aztec Fellows), Juan Luna's brother taught most of the language classes there and another colleague, by the name of Juan Chávez Orozco, offered courses in how to read calendar stones. Chávez Orozco was a painter, Juan Maya told me, who had studied with Diego Rivera and had ties to Bellas Artes in Mexico City. The painter took his students to see some calendar stones that were on exhibit on the Calle Moneda in Mexico City and lectured them at length, offering elaborate interpretations. Recalling what he had learned, Juan Maya explained that the calendar stones described the history of the world in such detail that they even told the story of the founding of Hueyapan. Although primary schoolteachers back home had taught the villagers that the first settlers of the *pueblo* came from Xochimilco, Juan Chávez Orozco told his students that the original inhabitants were the Metzintin. Not until the Age of Petl,[31] after the First Flood, did the Xochimilcas finally arrive.

Juan Luna Cárdenas paid Don Eliseo to give a few classes in the Nahuatl language at the school, but not enough to cover his expenses. The others received no assistance at all. As a result, the four villagers abandoned their studies and returned home. Looking back on the experience, Juan Maya observed that aside from the Hueyapan contingent, the other students lived in Mexico City and had high-paying jobs as teachers, lawyers, or engineers. The villagers, on the other hand, were poor. The only means they had for making a living was the land. Although they left after only a few weeks, the experience inspired Don Eliseo to preserve the Nahuatl language in Hueyapan and revive the culture of the Aztecs.

With the help of Juan Luna Cárdenas, Don Eliseo opened a school in the *pueblo* in 1956 to teach "pure" Nahuatl, uncorrupted by Spanish. For several years, the linguist visited the village regularly and gave classes in the school, attracting about 50 students. He also held rituals in Don Eliseo's home to celebrate the Aztec religion. Finally, like the Catholic priests in colonial times, Juan Luna served as a mediator in local land disputes.[32]

In the late 1950s, Juan Luna Cárdenas stopped coming to the *pueblo* and the students lost interest, which in turn led Don Eliseo to close down the school. By the time I arrived, only a handful of villagers still cared about "pure" Nahuatl. Among the faithful was Lino Balderas, the villager who had spent many years of his life in Mexico City, singing in the chorus of the Ballet Folklórico.[33]

Over the years, Don Lino got to know Juan Luna and Rodolfo Nieva well. With their encouragement, he tried to make a name for himself by recording songs in his native tongue. Although he did not have a great deal of success, he did produce a Nahuatl version of the traditional Mexican Birthday song, "Las Mañanitas." As noted in chapter six, Lino Balderas composed songs in Nahuatl as well. In one of his compositions, a man woos a beautiful young maiden with lovely blond hair. He also translated into Spanish a Nahuatl poem that Juan Chávez Orozco had transcribed from the *ozomatl* (tiger) glyph of an Aztec calendar stone. But perhaps most important of all, at least from the perspective of scholars of Nahuatl, was the fact that Lino Balderas served as a native informant for the distinguished linguist and philosopher of ancient Mexico, Miguel León-Portilla.

Accepting the fanciful account of a cultural extremist from Hueyapan, León-Portilla published a prayer that Lino Balderas claimed his "old mother" recited to the prehispanic rain god Tlaloc.[34] In contrast to the Nahuatl prayers published by Miguel Barrios,[35] this one was recorded in "pure Nahuatl," so "pure," in fact, that when Elvira Hernández went over the text with me, she pointed out several expressions that the villagers did not use and probably never did.[36] What is more, as I have already noted, nobody in Hueyapan had prayed to prehispanic deities for centuries, with the possible exception of a handful of followers of Juan Luna Cárdenas, such as Eliseo Cortés and Lino Balderas. Even the *pueblo's* rainmakers, who relied on the effects of hallucinogenic mushrooms, called on Dios and Catholic saints to protect the villagers from drought.

By the time I met Lino Balderas, he was a broken man. A few years before I arrived in Hueyapan, he had been in a terrible car crash that left him crippled and severely brain damaged. Under the circumstances, I did not interview him, but relied instead on others to describe his experiences. Villagers reported that Don Lino never succeeded in making a viable living in Mexico City from any of his artistic endeavors. After years of trying, he came back to Hueyapan, disappointed and bitter, complaining that people had taken advantage of him.

Still, Lino Balderas established a name for himself in Mexico City as an Indian, and the recognition he gained made a vivid impression on people back home. So did the fact that he returned to Hueyapan dejected and poor. His story served as a cautionary tale for villagers dreaming about getting ahead by exploiting their Indian identity.

Adelaido Amarro also had dealings with cultural extremists. One day, in 1965, when he was selling fruit in Mexico City at the Manzanares Market, Don Adelaido met an acquaintance of his who came from the lowland Mestizo community of Jumiltepec. His friend told him about the Movimiento and took Don Adelaido to Rodolfo Nieva's office to meet the founder of this urban-based group. Recalling the incident, Don Adelaido said that Lic. Rodolfo greeted him warmly, delighted to have the opportunity to exchange a few words in Nahuatl. Although the Mexico City lawyer did not speak the language well, the two men conversed for a while in Don Adelaido's native tongue. Lic. Rodolfo then extended an invitation to the villager to join the Movimiento and asked him to help make the case in Hueyapan for offering classes in Nahuatl at the local school. After accepting to serve as the Movimiento's representative, Don Adelaido asked the lawyer to send him a formal letter, authorizing him to act on behalf of the group. Otherwise, he explained, his neighbors would think he had made the whole thing up, while wandering around the streets of Mexico City drunk.

Rodolfo Nieva agreed to the request and sent a letter to Hueyapan. Don Adelaido showed the communication to Maestro Rafael, who was serving as director of the school at the time. Although his good friend and neighbor endorsed the idea, Maestro Rafael never assigned a teacher to the task of giving classes in Nahuatl.

A year later, Rodolfo Nieva sent Don Adelaido an invitation to a Nahuatl congress in the state of Morelos. By the time the notice reached Hueyapan, however, the event had already taken place. Deeply disappointed, Don Adelaido, with the help of Maestro Rafael, sent a letter back to Lic. Rodolfo, asking the lawyer to send more information about how people in Hueyapan might participate in future meetings. The letter informed the lawyer as well that Maestro Rafael would organize classes in Nahuatl. Lic. Rodolfo never replied to the letter and with that the villagers lost touch with the Movimiento. A year and a half later, Rodolfo Nieva died.

Don Adelaido was intrigued by the idea of the Movimiento, but not by the people he met in Mexico City. As he put it, they were all rich professionals who had the time to educate themselves about ancient Mexico. He, on the other hand, had a large family to feed and could not afford to remain in the Distrito Federal and associate with people who did not even offer him something to eat, let alone a job or a place to sleep. Nevertheless, the Movimiento convinced him that he should capitalize on his family's indigenous traditions.

Recognizing the exceptional talent of his wife as a weaver, Don Adelaido contacted the head of the Cuernavaca branch of the Burlington Textile Mills who had a passionate interest in indigenous textiles. Known to the villagers as the Engineer (*el ingeniero*), Juan Dubernard had been recruiting men from Hueyapan since 1953 to take menial jobs in his factory. Then, in 1960, he began collecting textiles from the village that were woven on the backstrap loom.[37]

Before long, Don Adelaido had convinced Juan Dubernard that Doña Epifania was the best weaver in town and the engineer began doing business almost exclusively with her.[38] Whenever his wife had a new piece to sell, Don Adelaido took Doña Epifania to Cuernavaca to see the engineer at the factory. On these special occasions, he asked her to wear a *xincueite*, something she almost never did at home, for Don Adelaido knew that Juan Dubernard would receive them more warmly if Doña Epifania arrived dressed like an Indian.

A bit of a cultural extremist himself, the engineer complained that the Cultural Missions were "ruining things" by introducing the villagers to modern weaving technologies. In his opinion, they should do exactly the opposite and, following his example, make the weaving in Hueyapan more authentic than it already was, by teaching the villagers how to use prehispanic dyes. According to Doña Epifania, nobody in Hueyapan knew anything about these ancient methods of coloring before the *ingeniero* showed them how to do it. When I asked Doña

Zeferina, whose memory stretched back maybe 20 years farther than Doña Epifania's, she said the same thing: she had no memory of a time when weavers in the village used prehispanic dyes.[39] That said, if people like us (the textile fancier and anthropologist) really wanted Doña Epifania to try, she was happy to do so, but first, we would have to show her how.

CHAPTER EIGHT

THE ANTHROPOLOGIST AND
THE INDIANS

I may have been the first anthropologist ever to live in Hueyapan for an extended period of time, but I was not the first in my discipline to do research in the village. Nor was I the first American. A few years before I arrived in the *pueblo*, anthropology students from the Escuela Nacional de Antropología did some preliminary fieldwork there, commuting back and forth from Mexico City. An anthropological linguist affiliated with Harvard had already visited Hueyapan as well, in the hope of finding a native speaker of Nahuatl who might be willing to spend a semester in Cambridge working with her and her students.[1] By the time I showed up, therefore, the villagers knew all about people like me. And anthropologists, they concluded, were basically the same as cultural extremists.

When villagers asked why I had come to Hueyapan, I explained that I wanted to learn Nahuatl. That was all they needed to hear. Eager to please, they pulled out their repertoire of well-rehearsed routines. Some offered to sing little songs in Nahuatl, others to recite the schoolbook poem "Nonantzin," and still others to teach me the words for "train" and "airplane" in the language of the Aztecs. Weavers set up their backstrap looms and demonstrated how to make garments out of wool with their prehispanic technology. Those who had nothing special to show simply greeted me in Nahuatl and laughed as I tried to reply.

At first, I could not believe that anyone would take an anthropologist like me for a cultural extremist. I had just left Mexico City, after all, because the Movimiento had offended me. In the end, however, I appreciated the villagers' insight. By making the connection, they forced me to see the similarities that existed between "them" and "me."

When I began doing research in 1969 on the Movimiento, I expected to find a grassroots organization with a large indigenous constituency. To my disappointment, I encountered a group of light-skinned middle-class urban professionals who considered themselves spokesmen for the Indians. Yet, even after I rejected this political movement and changed the focus of my research, I continued to share the Movimiento's understanding of who the Indians were. In choosing Hueyapan, I identified, I believed, an indigenous community whose culture had preserved the legacy of prehispanic Mexico.

Having embraced their nation's revolutionary project, Mexican anthropologists in the early 1970s cared less about proving that present-day Indians were living links to the past than they did about turning indigenous people into modern Mestizos[2]—and they were vigorously criticized by North American colleagues for maintaining these views and for playing an active role in their country's acculturation program. But even Mexican anthropologists, who identified with the nation's *mestizaje* project, promoted the idea that Indians belonged to different cultures. Government workers, they argued, needed to study indigenous customs, before they could help the Indians make a transition from tradition to modernity.

There exists today a rich body of ethnographic literature about Indians in Mexico, some of which reaches back to colonial times. Excellent syntheses are also available, relieving me here of the formidable task of making one myself. [3] Suffice it to say that over the years, as scholars have refined their analytical skills and asked more sophisticated theoretical questions, their basic premise has remained the same—be they North Americans, Mexicans, or Europeans. Eric Wolf and Rodolfo Stavenhagen, for example, have described in detail the ways indigenous communities are tied to each other and to the wider society, both economically and socially.[4] But they continue to talk about present-day Indians as geographically isolated and culturally distinct. Charles Gibson and George Foster have written extensively on the "heritage of conquest" and the brutal imposition during colonial times of Iberian traditions.[5] Yet, many scholars play down the impact of this terrible trauma on indigenous cultures, preferring to focus on heroic moments instead, on the part of the Indians—as if one side of the story negated the other! Pedro Carrasco has even taken the argument a step farther by proclaiming that "Tarascans will pass their Christianity test with honors if we compare their religion with the folk religion of southern Europe,"[6] but respected anthropologists continue to describe rural Catholic traditions as resilient survivals from prehispanic times—conclusive evidence of cultural resistance rather than the work of colonial priests who had creatively "baptized" indigenous rituals when they converted the Indians to Christianity.

I do not deny the obvious fact that life in a so-called indigenous *pueblo* is different from life in a Mestizo town. But I object to the way anthropologists talk about these differences. By using the term Indian, in all its euphemistic guises, we have helped to preserve a cultural category constructed in the sixteenth century. Based on the logic of a colonial caste system, the term provides an ethnographic excuse for why certain people in Mexico remain marginalized and poor.

My strong sense of indignation reflects the concerns of anthropologists like myself who came of age in the late 1960s, during a period of political unrest on university campuses in the United States and abroad. As students, we looked critically at the legacy of colonialism in a postcolonial world, while we marched for civil rights and against the Vietnam War. These political concerns raised questions in our minds about why anthropologists worked almost exclusively among "exotic" peoples in far off lands or impoverished citizens back home. Who benefited from our research? Who got hurt? Even though we became anthropologists with the best of intentions, the time had come, we now argued, to open our eyes and take a good look at what we were doing. Contributing to this sense of urgency was the fact that we had recently learned about members in good standing of the American Anthropological Association who had voluntarily participated in counterinsurgency operations sponsored by the U.S. government.[7] Shocked by these revelations, a group of us formed an organization called Anthropologists for Radical Political Action to discuss our concerns about the future of the discipline. Minority groups within the American Anthropological Association began caucusing as well.

By the early 1970s, many of us had reached the conclusion that our scholarly interests should clearly reflect our political commitments.

Embracing the position of the American women's movement, we solemnly proclaimed that the "personal was political." Our research, by extension, should focus on questions closer to home. It soon became fashionable for middle-class social scientists to study members of the middle class, for women to study women, Blacks to study Blacks, Native Americans to study Native Americans, Jews to study Jews, and so on. Influenced by my peers, I decided to leave Mexico. The experiences in Hueyapan may have changed my life and taught me a great deal about oppression and poverty, but now I was going to work with my own people and encourage the Indians to do the same.[8]

The situation in Mexico was particularly compromised, I believed, because anthropologists enjoyed a privileged position in government circles, as policymakers for indigenous affairs and as special consultants on the nation's prehispanic heritage. Since the Mexican Revolution, federal agencies had been generously sponsoring anthropological research about indigenous cultures. Much of the work was technical and programmatic. But some of it was written for the general public as well. Reinforcing old stereotypes, these popularized texts offered idealized images of indigenous Mexico that were easily reproduced in schoolbooks and museums and on monuments in the street.

As I have tried to show on the pages of this book, this national celebration of the country's prehispanic heritage has been a mixed blessing for the Indians themselves, at times even insulting. To illustrate the point, Doña Zeferina used to tell the following story: She once met a man in Mexico City who owned an *itzcuintli* (Mexican Hairless), a very rare and expensive breed of dog that the Aztecs raised and fattened up for food. The animal is squat and completely hairless, except for a few coarse bristles on its belly and back and tufts of soft fur on its head and tail. Having never seen an *itzcuintli* before, Doña Zeferina remarked that the dog was quite ugly. Surprised by her reaction, the man explained that she was looking at an Aztec dog, domesticated by her ancestors. She should be proud of it. To which she replied that she was no Aztec. And, what is more, that his dog was still ugly!

CHAPTER NINE
BEING INDIAN REVISITED

Everyone knows what cultural anthropology is about: it's about culture. The trouble is that no one is quite sure what culture is

—Clifford Geertz

Simply put, the cause of cultural nationalism in Africa has been to make real the imaginary identities to which Europe has subjected us

—Kwame Anthony Appiah

Introduction

The first edition of *Being Indian in Hueyapan* closes with one of my favorite anecdotes from Doña Zeferina's repertoire of personal stories. I recorded the incident in ethnographic time, outside of history, even though I had rejected this anthropological convention throughout most of the book. In doing so, I turned the timelessness of traditional ethnography away from its usual subjects—from people living on the edges of modern society—and directed it toward the urban elite. The incident itself occurred in the 1930s, when Doña Zeferina was working as a maid in Mexico City. For my purposes, however, the date was irrelevant. The encounter she had on a particular day, with a particular man and his prized "Aztec" dog, stood in for every encounter between the urban rich and the rural poor. The script never changed. You could always count on members of the Mexican upper classes to identify people from the impoverished countryside as living links to the nation's prehispanic past.

Clever, perhaps, but not very persuasive. It was too late to invoke the timeless convention of ethnographic writing at this stage of the game, on the final page of the book–even as a rhetorical flourish.

Either history mattered or it did not and I had based my argument everywhere else on the strength of the historical evidence.

Doña Zeferina's story also overstated my case by rejecting the idea that she had any ties to the Aztecs. When I spoke in my own voice, I was less categorical. I never denied that she came from a community where traces of the prehispanic past lingered on. But while acknowledging the obvious, I suggested as well that during the year I lived in Hueyapan, I learned more about ties to medieval Europe than I did about prehispanic Mexico.

So why did I use this misleading anecdote? Because I wanted Doña Zeferina to have the last word on the Indian question, a subject hopelessly confused in the literature, but one that rarely represented the confused perspective of her own point of view. The anecdote also summarized my primary objective for writing the book: to challenge the terms of an interminable debate about indigenous culture and the meaning of identity in contemporary Mexico.

What worried me in particular was the category itself and the criteria used for identifying someone as Indian—criteria, I argued, that were constantly shifting, depending on the year and the cultural hand-me-downs *du jour*. Over the centuries, as people belonging to the ruling classes in Mexico adopted new customs and rejected the old, they exported their castoffs to remote parts of the country, frequently demoting these recycled practices to the lowly status of Indian. As a result, while the cultural markers were frequently changing, the social position of Indians in Mexico stayed essentially the same. Indians remained Indian by virtue of the fact that they continued to lack what the Mexican elite continued to acquire.

Now in the first decade of the twenty-first century, the same tension persists between change and no change, but with interesting variations on this very old theme. Looking for ways to describe the current situation, I came across a "corollary" to the famous proposition "*plus ça change, plus c'est la même chose*—"*moins ça change*," states the corollary, "*moins c'est la même chose*" (the less things change," the less they remain the same).[1] And as I look back over the last 35 years, "*moins ça change continue*" with a vengeance. Indigenous communities are still steeped in poverty, the way they were in the late 1960s and for centuries before that. But the less things change, the less the discourse on Indians remains the same.

As Mexico makes its "transition to democracy," the government embraces the language of diversity. People speak more today about granting Indians their indigenous rights than they do about helping them participate in a culturally unified Mexico. Ethnic pluralism has replaced the revolutionary image of a single people with a double heritage—the Mestizo nation has given way to a multicultural state.

In 2001, the national legislature in Mexico passed a new law to protect the country's indigenous cultures and to help them flourish. This *ley indígena* strengthened an earlier constitutional amendment, passed in 1992, that had already affirmed Mexico's commitment to multiculturalism.[2] From this point onward, the nation officially accepted the responsibility for honoring not only the memory of its prehispanic past, but for preserving the cultures of indigenous people in the present as well.

The *ley indígena* has aroused a great deal of controversy. Many say it rings hollow, for it acknowledges only part of the cultural agenda of the indigenous rights movement, while it rejects the political entirely. The law itself, however, represents a significant change in the way the state speaks about Indians. Recent mobilizations have clearly forced the issue and influenced the language of the new legislation, even though their leaders dismiss the law as nothing more than window dressing.

In the early 1990s, indigenous communities throughout Latin America began organizing across ethnic lines, creating a pan-Indian movement that demanded political autonomy for Indians and the rights of indigenous citizens to practice their own customs. The quincentennial celebration of Columbus in 1992 offered the perfect opportunity to stage massive demonstrations against the ethnocidal practices of the Spanish Crown, the Catholic Church, and the present-day governments of countries with sizable populations of people still identified as Indians. Responding to global economic and political forces, the new movement represented a coalition of many different groups, whose leaders ranged from indigenous intellectuals to self-styled revolutionaries, to members of the Catholic clergy and Protestant evangelists, to anthropologists identified with the generation of 1968.[3]

The coalition called for establishing the autonomy of indigenous communities and for recognizing their right to govern themselves according to "traditional forms of authority." I focus this discussion on the part anthropologists have played in the process, expanding on the subject of the concluding chapter of the first edition of this book ("The Anthropologist and the Indian"). Anthropologists, I suggest, have encouraged indigenous people in recent years to become their own "cultural specialists" and have urged them to demand their right to be different.

Opinions may vary about what gave rise to the indigenous rights movement in Mexico—and to the role anthropologists have played within it as ideological guides. Scholars, however, generally agree that the movement grew stronger as the nation abandoned its isolationist policies and began participating actively in the global economy. And as Mexico's leaders prepared the country to open its doors wider to international markets, they relied more heavily on the advice of economists than they did on the advice of their friends in Anthropology, with whom they had had a very special relationship since the days of the Mexican Revolution. These changes, in turn, led the governing party to question the idea of a unified culture, inspired in large part by anthropological notions about the Mestizo. As a result, after years of exercising a great deal of influence on public policy, Anthropology lost its centrality to the national project. And as the discipline's star faded in government circles, anthropologists found a new source of light in the political opposition.

Coincidentally or perhaps not so coincidentally, after years of working with the leadership of the country to help Indians move from tradition to modernity, anthropologists switched gears. Today, we see them training members of indigenous communities to become specialists of their *usos y costumbres*. Speaking as advocates of traditional cultures, they encourage Indians to claim their indigenous citizenship and demand protection from the Mexican Constitution for the right to practice their ancient customs.

To trace these changes, I will briefly review the history of Mexican Anthropology, focusing in particular on the discipline's decline over the last 30 years as an influential arm of the government and on the simultaneous rise of interest in indigenous rights on the part of anthropologists. But first, I will say a few words about the way I edited the new edition of this book and comment on the reasons I wrote *Being Indian in Hueyapan* the way I did. This digression gives me the opportunity to address methodological and ethical issues of mutual concern to anthropologists of my generation in Mexico and the United States.

Writing Ethnography

Ethnographic Research in the early 1970s

As I mentioned in the preface of the new edition of the book, I never lost touch with Hueyapan or the family with whom I lived. Given the notes I kept over the years, I could have written a new monograph, describing the village as it had changed/or not changed over the last 35 years. But I rejected that option, preferring instead to look at the period of my initial research as a particular moment in history and to focus on the meaning of the moment. With that goal in mind, I edited the book heavily with the hope of strengthening the argument I had made in 1975. I also added new notes to each chapter to update and/or comment on points I had made in the original manuscript. In these notes, I only addressed issues that related to the text itself and saved for this chapter experiences I had at the University of Chicago that influenced the way I wrote the book.

When I entered graduate school in the mid-1960s, Anthropology had not yet entirely abandoned Malinowski's ideal of a good ethnography. As I understood it, if you chose to work in either a rural community or a "tribal" society, you produced a traditional monograph—a choice many of us, myself included, decided not to make. I had avoided the problem when I entered the field by choosing to study the Movimiento, but in the end I had to face it. Once I left this urban-based group and settled down in Hueyapan, I accepted my fate. I simply assumed that now I would have to write about everything: from the village's economic, religious, and kinship systems to child-rearing practices and healing, to forms of land tenure and house building. At the University of Chicago, younger members of the faculty had rejected the exercise in their own research, having come to the conclusion, as Clifford Geertz would put it many years later, that "walking barefoot through the Whole of Culture was really no longer an option."[4] Some of these same professors, however, encouraged their students to try their hand at producing an old-fashioned ethnography in their PhD theses, the way abstract painters, I imagined, first taught their students the techniques of figurative drawing.

When I came back to Chicago to write my doctoral dissertation, the department was paying particular attention to the ethnographic method as it was originally conceived by Malinowski in Great Britain. Bernard Cohn, who was chairman at the time, had invited Raymond Firth to spend a semester in residence and to give a special seminar for graduate students like myself, who had just returned from the field. Firth had recently retired from the London School of Economics and was making a tour of American universities in the early 1970s. Not only was he one of Malinowski's best students, but his work on Tikopia was considered a great classic. I loved reading *We, The Tikopia* and listening to the master make sense out of the problems each of us faced as we tried to organize countless pages of field notes into systematic analyses. He was truly an inspirational teacher.

But the person who influenced me the most was the anthropological linguist Paul Friedrich. A loner in many ways, Friedrich belonged to no faction in the department or to any one school of thought within Anthropology. He was, however, very much a member of the post–World War II generation. Like his contemporaries on the faculty, Friedrich conducted his fieldwork in the 1950s, while colonial empires were crumbling and dragging paradigms of British Anthropology down with them. As I was studying with him in Chicago, he was putting the finishing touches on *Agrarian Revolt in a Mexican Village*. Based on his doctoral dissertation, the book became an immediate success and remains to this day one of the best pieces of political anthropology ever written. Deeply involved in his research on Tarascan-speaking Indians, Friedrich trained me to think historically and politically, to define a specific problem and to focus primarily on that. But he also strongly believed in the importance of doing fieldwork in the traditional sense of the term and in presenting the people with whom I had lived in as full an ethnographic context as possible. Under his careful, discerning eye, I tried to do it all, experimenting with the model, but respecting it all the same. In the process, I hoped to address some of the criticisms members of my generation had of classic ethnographies by rejecting the timelessness of the ethnographic present and doing historical research. I also limited the description of everyday life to the home of one family (à la Oscar Lewis, some might say, but with different goals in mind),[5] before widening the perspective to include the entire community and focusing specifically on the question of Indian identity.[6]

Although I gave a great deal of thought to the problem of writing ethnography, I did not see my efforts, as I might have today, as an exploration into the possibilities and constraints of this "literary genre." The challenge for me was one of strategy, not style. I was looking for a way to make my argument in as convincing a manner as I could. As I conceived of it, the case relied on gathering the kinds of data often found in traditional ethnographies, but not in the works of contemporary anthropologists. Few people seemed interested in material culture anymore—with the exception of archeologists, but even they tended to reject the work of colleagues whom they dismissed as "dirt archeologists" for devoting more time to looking for artifacts than to generating grand theories.[7] Fashionable or not, I firmly believed then—as I still do today—that in order to address the theoretical questions that interested me, I had to keep my eyes on the ground and look at the "stuff" outsiders referred to when they talked about Hueyapan's Indian culture: the textiles the villagers wove; the ingredients they used in making *mole* and medicine; the prayers they recited and the mushrooms they ate, as they beseeched the heavens for rain; the syntax and lexicon of the language they spoke.

In Chicago, everyone learned to think about "culture" as a system of symbols. I accepted the formulation and tried faithfully to apply it, but the culture I was studying was constantly changing and being reinvented. I needed another analytical approach. And another methodology. With the help of Paul Friedrich, I started digging—in the archives and in the field.[8]

The Politics of Ethnographic Fieldwork

Equally important to me were the ethical implications of doing anthropological research, a burning issue in the 1970s and an ongoing subject of controversy at the present time. Today, however, we debate the issues as we watch the subjects of anthropological inquiry leave their homes in the former colonies of Europe and the United States and settle down in poor neighborhoods in our cities and towns, moving from the "margins of the modern world to its center." And as the children and grandchildren of the people we studied abandon their communities and emigrate to the West, American Anthropology—in contrast to Mexican Anthropology—has become increasingly influential in the wider academic and policy communities. Commenting on the discipline's rise in popularity, Clifford Geertz observes that anthropologists have responded by fighting among themselves—even more than they used to do—for the honor, I would add, of representing the discipline to the outside world. Turning up the volume on time-worn controversies, they are arguing in particular about the use of methodologies and the nature of legitimate research: "a new form of an old, all-too-familiar debate, *Geisteswissenschaften* vs *Naturwissenschaften*, has broken out afresh, and in an especially virulent and degraded form—déjà vu all over again." If forced to take sides, Geertz favors "those more inclined to a free-style view of things" over those whom he calls the "paradigm hunters." But he has lost patience with virtually everyone: "Those more inclined to a free-style view of things are afflicted with their own variety of failure of nerve, save that it is less methodological than moral. They are not much concerned about whether 'me anthropologist, you native' research is rigorous than whether it is decent. About that, however, they are *very* concerned."⁹ He then criticizes the kind of breastbeating I indulged in with abandon in 1975, in the final chapter of the book (and I quote him at length):

> The trouble begins with uneasy reflections on the involvement of anthropological research with colonial regimes during the heyday of Western imperialism and with its aftershadows now; reflections themselves brought on by accusations, from Third World intellectuals, about the field's complicity in the division of humanity into those who know and decide and

those who are known and are decided for, that are especially disturbing to scholars who have so long regarded themselves as the native's friend, and still think they understand him better than anyone else, including perhaps himself. But it hardly ends there. Driven on by the enormous engines of postmodern self-doubt—Heidegger, Wittgenstein, Gramsci, Sartre, Foucault, Derrida, most recently Bakhtin—the anxiety spreads into a more general worry about the representation of "The Other" (inevitably capitalized, inevitably singular) in ethnographic discourse as such. Is not the whole enterprise but domination carried on by other means?: "Hegemony," "monologue," "*vouloir-savoir*" "*mauvaise fois,*" "orientalism"? "Who are we to speak for them?"

This is hardly a question that can simply be dismissed, as it so often has been by hardened fieldworkers [by which Geertz means "paradigm hunters"], as the grumbling of café or gas-station anthropologists; but one could wish it were being met with less breastbeating and lashing out at supposed failures of mind and character on the part of bourgeois social scientists, and more attempts actually to answer it . . . . The changing situation of the ethnographer, intellectual and moral, brought on by the movement of anthropology from the margins of the modern world toward its center, is as poorly addressed by crying havoc as it is by crying science. Mere malaise is as evasive as mere rigor, and rather more self-serving.[10]

"Mere malaise" led me to turn away from Mexico and start a new project in France, but not before seeing the book published in Spanish. By 1977, the year *Ser Indio en Hueyapan* came out, things had already begun to shift, in a direction that persuaded me to move even farther away. A younger generation of anthropologists had replaced the old school of *indigenistas* in Mexico. I knew who they were and had met several of them before while I was doing fieldwork in Hueyapan (e.g., Lourdes Arizpe, Guillermo Bonfil, Andrés Medina, Guillermo de la Peña, Arturo Warman). The more militant among them were predictably hostile to Americans of all political stripes—even to people like me who shared their critique of U.S. foreign policy—and I sympathized with the position they took. What I did not understand until 1977 was that we actually disagreed, if not about imperialism, about indigenous peoples in Mexico.[11]

Although we shared a predilection for Marxist modes of analysis, my critics in Mexico disagreed with the way I used class to address the Indian question. And over the years, the divisions between us grew as more anthropologists of the generation of 1968 took an interest in Indians. In the late 1960s, a number of key players were still working in Mestizo villages and/or urban slums. But others had already changed their area of research and were taking positions in the mid-1970s that were very different from my own. Where I saw oppression, they saw resistance. Where I saw "culture" being used to justify the fact that Indians lived in desperate poverty, they saw the glimmerings of ethnic pride.[12]

Debates about indigenous cultures were hardly a local mater. The idea of diversity had captured the imagination of a new generation of leftist intellectuals around the globe. As students demonstrated in 1968, in Tokyo, Warsaw, Prague, Paris, New York, and Mexico City, they questioned the Soviet Union's interpretations of Marxist doctrines and went back to the texts.[13] For me, this meant looking critically at the "national question" and at the ways the Soviet Union had turned indigenous cultures into folklore—a version of which I saw in postrevolutionary Mexico. For a growing number of my contemporaries in Mexico, this meant celebrating difference—an ironic turn of events given how many of them had previously challenged American anthropologists for making Indians look exotic.

Although I was taken by surprise, I should have seen it coming. I went to Mexico, after all, to look for groups that might parallel the Black Power and Red Power movements in the United States. What interested me in particular was the cultural ideology of these political mobilizations. When at first I saw members of the Movimiento draw parallels between themselves and the Black Power movement, I thought I had found the Mexican equivalent of what I was observing in the United States. But of course, I had not. What is more, the Movimiento was not the only group in Mexico identifying with radicals in the Civil Rights movement, or with others struggling for the rights of minorities in different parts of the world. Members of the student left were doing the same, and they were destined to have a far greater impact on Mexican politics than the Movimiento.

Despite the obvious differences between the student left and the Movimiento, the two groups had important things in common. Like the Movimiento, student activists—in particular those who were studying Anthropology—identified the struggles of separatist movements in other parts of the world with the injustices Indians faced in Mexico. And like the Movimiento before them, veterans of the student left began training Indians to fight for their rights as indigenous citizens of the state.

Anthropologists of the generation of 1968 were also influenced by Liberation Theology. A number of them had even joined the clergy—at least for a few years, before renouncing their vows. Having radically interpreted the intentions of Vatican II, progressive priests were heroes in Latin America and had successfully won the support of leftist intellectuals, who were defiantly resisting the anti-clerical PRI. For this new generation of anthropologists, some of whom had lost their jobs after 1968 at the National School of Anthropology, it was the Jesuit-run Universidad Iberro-Americana that gave them a home. Welcoming them warmly, La Iberro-Americana opened its doors widely to an excellent group of young scholars—both secular and religious—who went on to build a first rate department of Anthropology there.

Some may say that I am painting the picture with very broad strokes, generalizing in places where distinctions need to be made. The story, of course, is more complicated. For example, while reviewing the history of Mexican Anthropology, Emiko Saldívar has ably shown that the agency used to implement indigenist policy (INI) continued to promote assimilationist programs in indigenous communities long after the old guard had retired.[14] These programs, however, still had to compete with an attractive alternative that was also supported by members of INI, and had captured the imagination of people around the world. Then, although people like Guillermo de la Peña may fit the description I made of Mexican anthropologists who used to write about Mestizos and now write about Indians, his analysis of the rise of indigenous rights avoids taking sides in aimless debates about cultural survivals.[15] Based in Guadalajara, De la Peña participates actively in international conversations with thinkers in Europe, Canada, and the United States about the politics of recognition and distribution. Historically grounded and philosophically sophisticated, scholars like him make it possible to have the kinds of exchanges I had wanted to have over 30 years ago. So do U.S.-based anthropologists like Claudio Lomnitz and Deborah Poole. They too keep their distance from romanticized images of an indigenizing Mexico, while offering historically nuanced analyses about the history of race and class in Mexico and the rise of indigenous intellectuals today.[16] The impressive research of colleagues like these has enhanced our understanding of how Indians became a social class in Mexico, without losing the stigma, both racial and cultural, of an anachronistic indigenous identity. Their contributions, I believe, have also strengthened the argument I was trying to make. Let me offer one example from the work of Claudio Lomnitz, which is representative, I think, of some of the best analyses being done today on the history of Mexico's Indians.

Recent Historical Research on
Race and Class in Mexico

In *Exits from the Labyrinth*, Claudio Lomnitz describes Mexico's evolution from a caste society to a class society. After gaining independence in the nineteenth century, the country did away with Indianness as a legal category. Abolishing the caste system, it merged the country's two republics—one Spanish, one Indian—into one. With these legal and administrative changes, the term "indian became synonymous with a combination of material poverty and cultural 'backwardness.' " Indianness, in other words, designated an individual's class position, but it had ethnic/racial overtones as well. In the eyes of the upper classes, poor Mestizos became Indians, particularly poor peasants who were living in impoverished regions of the country, while the relatively richer ones became White.[17]

Lomnitz describes how "the passage from a caste to a class society" does not eliminate ethnic distinctions. Cultural markers remain in place: "The nineteenth century kept the European and the Indian in opposite poles of an ideological system, and it also created (this was its novelty) an image of a dual society: one was a national society of citizens and social classes, the other was an Indian society of autarchic communities that, despite the national society's best efforts, survived."[18]

After the Mexican Revolution, policymakers took a fresh look at Mestizos and Indians. In the new narrative, Mestizos became the heroes of Mexican history, while the Indians became a major social and economic development project for the country. Called Indigenismo,

Mexico assumed the task of modernizing the Indians while it simultaneously expressed pride in the country's prehispanic past:

> The phenomenon of indigenismo is interesting in several respects, for it served to reformulate the relationship between race and nation. Instead of seeing Indians as a nation encompassed by a Europe-oriented nation, indigenistas chose to see Mexico as the product of a clash between two independent and opposed nations, that of the Spaniards and that of the Indians. The new hero of the epic of Mexican nationality became the mestizo, who was physically both Indian and Spanish, and whose spiritual qualities avoided both the atavisms of Indian culture and the exploitative nature of the European . . . The choice of the mestizo as the new protagonist of nationality allowed both for the construction of a strong national state which buffered the influence of foreign power and for a retention of the Eurocentric goals of progress. Moreover, indigenistas used the image of the Indian community— which . . . retained its hierarchical organization in a way that mestizos never did—as a model of nationality. This was the purpose of Chávez Orozco's (1943) study of Indian "democratic institutions," it was behind Alfonso Caso's lists of "positive" and "negative" Indian traits, and . . . is also Bonfil's (1987) strategy. In the recreation of a national community, the Indian comunidades served as a model of hierarchy, and thus as the antiliberal element that was necessary for the strong state and the "mixed economy" that was being proposed.[19]

In other words, by maintaining the idea of the Indian *comunidad, indigenistas*, and their critics (from the generation of 1968) agreed with one another in so far as they both recognized a set of hierarchical arrangements as a positive feature of indigenous cultures and endorsed the incorporation of these antiquated arrangements into the organization of the PRI. Apparently, it did not bother them very much that these hierarchical arrangements had been previously used to establish a governing structure in colonial New Spain for controlling the Indians and managing interactions between la Républica de indios and la Républica de españoles—for the benefit, of course, of the latter. Today, we call these ancient arrangements *usos y costumbres*.

A Brief History of Anthropology in Mexico and the Rise of Indigenous Rights

Excellent work has recently appeared on the history of Mexican Anthropology and on the emergence of indigenous rights in the country. I rely heavily on some of it, in particular on the contributions of Courtney Jung, Claudio Lomnitz, Carmen Martínez, Guillermo de la Peña, Emiko Saldívar, and Saúl Velasco, in addition to my own more limited research, conducted since 1969–1970, despite declarations to the contrary that I would abandon indigenous Mexico as a subject of further study.[20]

The Early Period

As Claudio Lomnitz sees it, "Mexican anthropology has had multiple births," beginning with the writings of sixteenth-century friars, like Fray Diego Durán, who described the early history of Hueyapan and the conquest of the village by the Spanish.[21] Lomnitz traces these multiple births through the writings of Creole patriots and antiquarians in the seventeenth and eighteenth centuries and through a number of publications in the nineteenth century, including *Anauak*, an exceedingly unflattering book by the British anthropologist E.B. Tylor that looked forward to the day when the United States took possession of Mexico. Lomnitz also mentions *El Libro Rojo*, published in 1870, the first in a series of magisterial volumes by Vicente Riva Palacio and Manuel Payno. Their work became the model for constructing the image of a unified Mexico, one that acknowledged past suffering while it defined opportunities for positive change. This homogenizing theme would be further elaborated upon during the dictatorship of Porfirio Díaz in the writings of the great educator Justo Sierra, who espoused a "vision of national evolution," that gave coherence and unity to the diversity of Mexico.[22]

One of the most influential anthropologists in the Porfirio period—during the years leading up to the Mexican Revolution—was the archeologist Alfredo Chavero. Summarizing his contributions and those of other early anthropologists, Claudio Lomnitz makes the following observation:

> The special role of Chavero and other early anthropologists was to suggest a certain isomorphism between the past and the present. By creating a single racial narrative for the whole country, these anthropologists could shape the internal frontiers of modernization while upholding a teleology that made progress and evolution an integral aspect of Mexican civilization. Moreover,

this strategy involved using history to moralize about the present, which was an immensely popular activity in Mexico that had significant grassroots appeal.[23]

In *México a través los siglos* (1888), Chavero supported his argument with "an evolutionary scheme for pre-Columbian history that implicitly organizes hierarchical relations between the races in the present."[24]

The Years Following the Mexican Revolution

After the Mexican Revolution, anthropologists used the logic of evolutionary theory to justify introducing programs to indigenous communities that would prepare the Indians for the challenges of modern Mexico. In the name of progress, they endorsed the government's goal of creating a unified nation that encompassed everyone. To achieve their revolutionary objectives, anthropologists recommended assimilation. Indians had to stop being Indians and become members of Mexico's national culture.[25] As early as 1917, President Carranza appointed Manuel Gamio as director of the Department of Anthropology, a newly constituted branch of the Ministry of Agriculture. Revolutionary factions were still fighting with one another at the time, but Carranza anticipated winning the war and was thinking about the future. He therefore urged Gamio to develop an ambitious indigenist project that would incorporate Indians into the wider society.

A student of Franz Boas, Gamio embraced the intellectual biases of the Porfirio period as well. He endorsed, for example, the vision of Justo Sierra that was modeled on the ideals of the French Revolution and that espoused the universalistic values of the Enlightenment. Everybody in the country would share a common language and identify with the same history and traditions. Education, Gamio believed, would prepare the backward peoples of Mexico for their revolutionary future.

In order to ease the transition, Gamio trained anthropologists to study the traditions of Mexico's indigenous peoples. Before initiating change, the nation's leaders needed to understand the local cultures of the country and be sensitive to the special needs of the Indians.

Following Boas, he trained his staff to embrace diversity, before sending them off to study the Indians on the Valley of Teotihuacan Project:

> We . . . suggested to our personnel that they shed the prejudices that can arise in the minds of civilized and modern men when they come into contact with the spirit, the habits and customs of the Teotihuacanos, whose civilization has a lag of four hundred years. We advised that they should follow strict scientific discipline in the course of their actions, but that they should make every effort to temporarily abandon their modes of thought, expression, and sentiments in order to descend in mind and body until they molded to the backward life of the inhabitants.[26]

As this passage suggests, Gamio's tolerance for others had limits. He reserved the right to make value judgments. Some cultures, clearly, were better than others and the weaker ones had to go. His *indigenista* project was supposed to help make that happen.

From Cárdenas (1934–1940) to
Díaz Ordaz (1964–1970)

When Lázaro Cárdenas became president 17 years later, very little had changed. The Indians of Mexico were still desperately poor, visibly more so as a group than those identified as Mestizos. A native of the state of Michoacán, which had a large indigenous population, Cárdenas was familiar with the problem and took the matter of indigenous affairs very seriously. One of the difficulties, the president suggested, was that policy makers still did not know who the Indians were. The nation would not be able to address matters effectively until it had a better understanding of these people. Speaking before specialists of indigenous affairs, Cárdenas proclaimed, "Our problem is not to preserve the Indian, or make Mexico Indian, but to make the Indian Mexican."[27] To help the nation determine who the Indians were, Cárdenas called upon anthropologists to come up with a clear definition. Responding to their president's request, members of the discipline studied the question carefully and eventually settled on a formulation proposed by Alfonso Caso and elaborated upon by Gonzalo Aguirre Beltrán: Indians were people who lived in peasant communities located in marginalized areas of the country. These *regiones de refugio* should become the targets of intensive campaigns of cultural integration. In 1940, the year Cárdenas stepped down as president, the newly formed Interamerican Indigenous Congress held its first meeting in the city of Pátzcuaro, in Cárdenas's home state, establishing formal links across the Americas between Indian groups and government-sponsored agencies.

Less interested in the "Indian problem" than his predecessor, Miguel Avila Camacho paid little attention to the special needs of Indians. But Miguel Alemán, the next president after him, shared the concerns of Cárdenas. In 1948, two years into his term, President Alemán established INI (the National Indigenous Institute) and appointed Alfonso Caso as the director of the institute, a position the distinguished anthropologist held until 1970.[28]

Official Indigenismo

Recent scholarship on the subject has divided the history of INI into four distinct periods (Official Indigenismo, Participatory Indigenismo, Ethno-Development and Legal Indigenismo). The first one lasted until 1976. During the early years of Official Indigenismo, one of INI's primary objectives was to create on-site centers in the *regiones de refugio*, in parts of the country identified as having high concentrations of indigenous people. Anthropologists assigned to these outlying regions had two major responsibilities: (1) to give rural Indians the skills that they needed to become part of a modernizing Mexico and (2) to study and record the indigenous traditions they had come to eradicate. INI opened its first center in the highlands of Chiapas, in the same part of the country where American anthropologists from Harvard University and the University of Chicago established a center in the 1950s to train graduate students.

In the 1960s, while Díaz Ordaz was president, Mexican anthropologists were still focused on doing work with indigenous peoples living in *regiones de refugio*, but a new generation of students was coming of age and expanding the field to include research on non-Indians as well. Rural Mexicans were on the move during those years, abandoning the countryside by the millions in search of work in the cities. As people observed these demographic changes, anthropologists began studying the phenomenon among non-Indian *campesinos*, whose communities were emptying out faster than were the more isolated indigenous *pueblos*. Others turned their attention to the migrants themselves who were crowding into the urban slums,[29] while still others took a new look at indigenous Mexico and challenged the wisdom of INI's indigenist policies.[30]

Shifting populations and high levels of unemployment led to new forms of political unrest, first among railroad workers, then among workers more generally, and finally among students, many of whom came from working-class backgrounds themselves. As they participated in demonstrations, student activists learned what it meant to oppose a political system that had little tolerance for public displays of criticism. Their confrontations with police became increasingly violent and finally exploded at Tlatelolco on October 3, 1968, where hundreds of demonstrators, reliable sources tell us, were mowed down by machine guns.[31] This terrible event shocked the international community, tarnishing Mexico's reputation in the eyes of the world only days before the nation hosted the Olympic Games. In the following year, as the country got ready for the next round of presidential elections, *campesinos* coordinated their ongoing political struggle with the urban movement, embarrassing the government even further by staging raids and kidnappings in rural areas with alarming regularity, threatening the lives of politicians and millionaires.[32]

The Presidency of Luis Echeverría (1970–1976)

When Luis Echverría became president in 1970, he promised to address the grievances of all marginalized groups, including the Indians, while he continued to crack down on dissidents. To respond to the problems of indigenous Mexico, he appointed Gonzalo Aguirre Beltrán to replace the venerable Alfonso Caso as Director of INI, giving the Institute leadership and prestige with someone long associated with Official Indigenismo. As anticipated, Aguirre Beltrán continued to support INI's assimilationist policies that were first introduced by Alfonso Caso. But Echeverría had personal ambitions that extended beyond Mexico and its ideal of a culturally uniform state. When it served his purposes, he also celebrated folkloric images of the country, catering to the tastes of foreigners who liked seeing Indians in Mexico.

It was common knowledge at the time that Echeverría was hoping to become director general of the United Nations after he stepped down as president of Mexico in 1976. Perhaps, that was why he volunteered to host the UN's first international conference on the status of women. The meeting took place in Mexico City in June 1975.

The UN Conference on the Status of Women: An Ethnographic Digression[33]
In the mid-1970s, I was actively involved in the American and French women's movements. Working closely with an international group of feminists, I volunteered to go to Mexico City, with a few other colleagues, for the 1975 UN conference to try to organize simultaneous tribunals on crimes against women in different parts of the world. Before the opening session, Echeverría staged a big welcoming ceremony at Tlatelolco, for official delegates only. Individuals like myself, who represented formal and informal nongovernmental organizations (NGOs), were not invited. We gathered instead at the Centro Médico, a large conference center located in downtown Mexico City, in the Colonia Doctores. I did not, therefore, witness the performance, but I heard a great deal about it. Echeverría, I learned, had decorated the occasion with Indian women, dressed in full indigenous regalia. These women, people told me, had come from all over the country. After the ceremony, the Indians showed up at the Centro Médico, still dressed in their ethnic garb, to take part, if they wished, in the various sessions organized by NGOs to address women's economic and social problems.

As the Indians arrived and began wandering about, I noticed two women, at the far end of a large hall, dressed in black wool *xincueites*, the costume typically identified with Hueyapan. Needless to say, I was curious. Excusing myself from the people I was with, I ran over to see who the Indians were, and found myself facing Zeferina Barreto and here next door neighbor Hermenegilda Pérez. My two friends greeted me warmly, delighted to see me, but not at all surprised, even though I had not told them I was coming to Mexico. Everyone back home, they noted triumphantly, expected me to show up at an international meeting concerned with the problems of women.[34] I, on the other hand, was flabbergasted. Never in my wildest dreams did I imagine seeing Doña Zeferina participating in a spectacle like this, or anyone else from Hueyapan for that matter.

The two women explained how it happened: A few weeks earlier, the governor of Morelos sent a *maestra* to the *pueblo* with a special invitation from the first lady of Mexico. The *maestra* explained that Mrs. Echeverría had asked the governor to send two indigenous women from Morelos to Mexico City to help her welcome a distinguished delegation of foreigners. The governor decided to give Hueyapan the honor of representing their state and instructed the village to select two women who could sing in Nahuatl and dress in the *pueblo*'s traditional costume. As they filled me in on the details, I realized that the governor my friends were talking about was Rivera Crespo, who, while running for office in 1970, had come to Hueyapan on a campaign tour and had received an "indigenous" welcome.[35]

After the governor's representative departed, the *ayudante* called a town meeting and the villagers voted to send Hermenegilda Pérez and Elvira Hernández. Both of them sang beautifully in Nahuatl and Spanish. Elvira, however, was a young mother in 1975 and could not take off for a few days, so Doña Zeferina stepped forward to take her place. Even though the old woman did not sing very well, she knew many songs and had plenty of stage presence. Neither she nor Doña Hermenegilda wore *xincueites* at home, but they each owned a skirt and agreed happily to put it on for this special occasion.

After settling the matter of who would represent Hueyapan, the villagers drew up a petition to give to the first lady. The petition asked Mrs. Echeverría to help the *pueblo* participate more effectively in modern-day Mexico than it did at the time by responding to their urgent needs. They then repeated the same list of requests they routinely made to visiting politicians, like Rivera Crespo: better roads, more educational facilities, and a new health center. On the appointed day, the two women left for Mexico City with a basket of fruit and the petition.

Following instructions, Doña Zeferina and Doña Hermenegilda went straight to Tlatelolco. When they arrived and saw the huge crowds, they knew that they would never be able to meet Mrs. Echeverría there. But that did not deter them. Once the ceremony ended, they hailed a taxi and told the driver to take them to Los Pinos, the official residence of presidents in Mexico. As the car pulled up to the entrance, a guard opened the gate, accepted the petition, and the basket of fruit and that was the end of that.

By the time we bumped into each other at the Centro Médico, Doña Zeferina and Doña Hermenegilda had reconciled themselves to the fact that they would never hear from the first lady, and they were terribly disappointed. With their consent, I tried to publish a story about their experiences in *Xilonen*, a newspaper named after the Aztec corn goddess that was circulating daily for the benefit of those who were attending the conference. The article was never published.

When we met again the next morning, Doña Zeferina announced that she had had enough. Before heading back home, she took advantage of being in Mexico City to visit the Manzanares Market and replenish her stock of toys. Doña Hermenegilda was also fed up, but she stuck it out till the bitter end, hoping to meet a government official who might help her get scholarships for her daughters. She never did.

Perhaps, the most painful moment of all came at the end of a session dedicated to discussing the problems of rural women in the Third World. After the invited speakers gave their formal presentations, members of the audience were invited to participate as well and Doña Hermenegilda decided to make an intervention, still hoping to persuade a government official to give scholarships to her daughters. Speaking into a microphone, she introduced her remarks by thanking the organizers of the UN conference for making it possible for her to attend, expressing her gratitude with the kinds of obsequious phrases traditionally used by Indians when addressing people of higher status than them. Misinterpreting the meaning of Doña Hermenegilda's words, young radicals in the back booed and shouted obscenities, accusing the woman of being a party hack who was planted there by the PRI.

Opposition to Official Indigenismo
That, I repeat, was 1975. Five years earlier, members of the new generation of anthropologists had begun challenging Echeverría's

indigenist policies and openly criticizing the work of Aguirre Beltrán. Veterans of the student movement, they had vigorously opposed Echeverría on other grounds as well, in particular on his willingness to use police violence to intimidate his opponents. As Díaz Ordaz's Minister of the Interior in 1968, they held him partially responsibile for the murder at Tlatelolco of hundreds of students and workers and would hold him fully responsible in 1971 for the death of 36 students during a second demonstration that occurred while he himself was president.[36]

Taking issue with the nation's indigenist policies, five anthropologists published a collection of articles that took the government to task for the way it addressed the Indian problem in Mexico. Giving their book the ironic title *De eso que llaman antropología mexicana* (What people call Mexican Anthropology), the volume included pieces by Guillermo Bonfil and Arturo Warman, both of whom would later play central roles in redefining the role of anthropologists in Mexico.[37] Although many colleagues respected these five anthropologists for the courage they had shown, others criticized them for being opportunistic, anointing them sarcastically, along with two other social scientists, as *los siete magníficos* a nickname that has stuck to the present day.[38]

As Claudio Lomnitz tells it, "the year 1968 marked a watershed for Mexican national anthropology because the student movement reflected a shift in the relative importance of Mexico's urban population. Correspondingly, the *magníficos* and others no longer called for absorbing Indians into the nation, but argued for a more theoretically inclined anthropology" that engaged issues of concern to the international academic community.[39] But Mexican anthropology had always used a "theoretically inclined" approach, from the days of Porfirio Díaz to the present. The problem was that the relationship between "a national anthropology and its metropolitan counterparts . . . had more often been one of mutual convenience than of true dialogue, because anthropologies . . . devoted to national development must consistently choose modernization over cultural variation, and . . . balance studies of local culture with a national narrative that shapes the institutional framework of the field."[40]

After 1968, the new generation of anthropologists stopped playing this balancing act. Taking their distance from the national project, they joined forces with a wider political community that opposed the model of a strong nation-state and a single unified culture. As Courtney Jung notes, "During the 1970s indigenous rights activists, many of them anthropologists, began to organize across state lines, through conferences, a growing body of scholarly literature, and direct appeals to international bodies."[41]

In 1971, for example, Guillermo Bonfil attended a meeting in Barbados, sponsored by the World Council of Churches. This was the first of two gatherings aimed at drawing anthropologists, church activists, and indigenous leaders together to develop a collaborative network and a set of joint strategies. Among other initiatives, the participants drafted declarations that called for the creation of multicultural states in the Americas. It was here in Barbados that the idea of "Indianismo" was born. In opposition to Indigenismo, Indianismo identified "the liberation of the Indians" as its primary goal—to free indigenous people from the so-called civilizing project of the West.

The first meeting in Barbados resulted in a plan of action that would turn decision-making power over to indigenous communities. Intellectuals would step back and let the Indians step forward. The final document, however, made clear that intellectuals did not plan to fade into the woodwork, but would provide the movement with "anthropological knowledge" about the ruling society, collaborating in this way in the liberation of indigenous peoples.[42] As Saúl Velasco put it, "indigenous people would gradually assume the obligation and freedom of creating their own programs and demands, but always under the attentive guidance of intellectuals who would accompany them and attempt to orient them when they needed to make a decision."[43]

The work of anthropologists at meetings like these influenced the thinking of international human rights organizations, including the UN, that had been relying on members of the discipline since 1948, when it first formulated its Universal Declaration of the Rights of Man.[44] In 1966, the UN supported the rights of peoples around the world to cultural self-determination. It then strengthened its position on the subject in 1976 (International Agreement for Economic, Social, and Cultural Rights), and again in 1989, with the frequently cited Convention 169 of the International Labor Organization (ILO). Although the ILO Convention explicitly denied indigenous and tribal peoples political autonomy within recognized states, it supported their rights to economic, social, and cultural development.

As we take a closer look at the 1970s, we see that the new generation of Mexican anthropologists began changing direction at about the same time as the leadership of the PRI. After years of holding on to the great revolutionary project, the ruling party had started the arduous process of dismantling it—a process that included abandoning the unifying theme of a national anthropology and replacing it instead with a new image of Mexico as a multicultural state. The transformation, of course, did not happen over night, but with the benefit of hindsight, we can easily trace the changes back at least as far as the final years of the presidency of Luis Echeverría. Then, when López Portillo took office in 1976, things began changing more rapidly. After that, it was only a matter of time before the Mexican government endorsed the ILO's Convention 169 (1989) and the legislature recognized the rights of Mexico's indigenous peoples in Article 4 of the nation's Constitution (1992).

Having written my book during the Echeverría years, I did not see what was coming. Instead of anticipating the changes as they were unfolding, I continued to criticize the dying national project that gave indigenous communities a double message: Be Mexicans at home and Indians in the street. In particular, I focused my attack on the ways the government used Indians to play Indian for others. My contemporaries in Mexico were similarly locked in to a set of assumptions based on the past. Like me, they continued to challenge the dying revolutionary project, attacking moribund programs that were on the way out, or undergoing major changes. They, however, directed their criticism at the other end of the problem, namely at Mexico's policy of assimilating the Indians. In sum, as I accused the state of keeping the Indians Indian, my counterparts accused it of ethnocide.[45]

Identifying Mexico's indigenous peoples with marginalized groups in other parts of the world, the authors of *De eso que llaman antropología mexicana* praised Mexican Indians for courageously resisting the forces of change, applauding them for successfully defending their cultures against interventionist policies to assimilate them. Indigenous cultures, of course, had changed over time, but their customs and worldviews—the argument went—were significantly different from those of non-Indians. And as the *magníficos* criticized the government's traditional indigenist policy—which was, I repeat, in the process of disappearing—they encouraged anthropologists to show indigenous people how to govern themselves according to their own traditions. Indians, they proclaimed, should elect tribal councils and become guardians of their own cultures.[46]

From López Portillo (1976–1982) to Vicente Fox (2000–2006): Legitimating the New Anthropology

Participatory Indigenismo

Relations between the new generation of anthropologists and the *indigenista* establishment improved somewhat after López Portillo became president. The author of a book on the prehispanic god Quetzalcoatl, López Portillo considered himself a champion of cultural pluralism.[47] Under his leadership, he wanted to see INI preserve the ethnic diversity of the nation, while it also strengthened the economic foundations of rural Mexico. With that goal in mind, López Portillo created a new position to direct both INI and COPLAMAR (La Coordinación General del Plan Nacional Para Zonas Deprimidas y Grupos Marginados) and to coordinate the projects sponsored by the two agencies. The person selected for the job was Fernando Ovalle. A political insider who was not an anthropologist, Ovalle put an end to nearly 30 years of Indigenimso Oficial and introduced his new program of Indigenismo de Participación inviting the Indians to work closely with INI in identifying the projects that the institute would sponsor in their regions and communities.[48] Redefining the ways they brought about change, INI announced that they had abandoned their top-down approach and would now look for more collaborative projects to help indigenous people help themselves, both economically and culturally.[49]

In 1976, INI had 60 regional indigenous centers. Four years later, the institute had 130.[50] Very small groups, who were virtually unknown, now had centers of their own that were encouraging them to take pride in their indigenous identity. As I noted in an article in the *American Ethnologist*, by the mid-1980s, INI had already produced 28 ethnographic films about indigenous people in Mexico, some of which showed Indians demanding their indigenous rights.[51]

López Portillo's administration also made changes in the way the census counted speakers of indigenous languages. In 1970, when Echeverría was president, the census reported that Mexico had a population of just over 60 million people, of whom a little over 3 million spoke indigenous tongues. That same year, the census divided the languages into five basic linguistic families: Nahuatl, Maya, Zapotec, Otomi, and Mixtec and, within these families, identified 59 dialects, 31 of which were considered important enough to be listed by name. In 1980, when López Portillo's administration was doing the counting, the census reported that the population of Mexico had increased by nearly 7 million people, and the number of speakers of indigenous languages had risen to a little over 5 million (5,181,038), a disproportionately high number, given the increase of the total population. This time, what is more, instead of identifying five language groups with multiple dialects, the 1980 census recorded speakers of 40 distinct languages, including Pame, a little known language spoken by Indians who lived in Central Mexico, north of Mexico City.

According to the 1980 census, Pame speakers existed in numbers worthy of being reported in three different states (Hidalgo, Querétero, and San Luis Potosí). Yet, in San Luis Potosí, for example, we find that ten years earlier, Pame was not represented at all as a separate language or dialect. Presumably the Indians identified with this group had been lumped together in 1970 with the speakers of other unidentified indigenous tongues, the number of whom came to 1,500. In 1980, however, the San Luis Potosí census reported 4,670 speakers of Pame alone, a surprisingly high number if measured against the information provided in the previous censu. Predictably enough, in the intervening years, INI had established a center for Pame Indians in the area and an employee of INI had used the new facility as the base for making a documentary film about the group's culture. The last scene of the movie features a schoolteacher from the area campaigning for indigenous rights.

Counting the Indians: A Demographic Interlude
Since the presidency of López Portillo, the census has become an interesting measure of the different ways administrations have been repositioning themselves on the question of ethnic diversity in Mexico. As already noted, the 1970 census listed five indigenous language groups and mentioned 31 dialects by name. In 1980, the census recognized 40 distinct languages. By 1990, the number had jumped to 92 languages and dialects and in 2000, the number slipped back slightly to 85.[52] Out of a total population in 1990 of a little over 70 million people, 7.5 percent, or 5,282,347, spoke an indigenous tongue. Ten years later, in the 2000 census, out of a population of nearly 84 million, the number of speakers of indigenous languages had risen to 6,273,016, but their percentage in the total population had dropped slightly, to 7.3 percent.[53]

Although anthropologists have debated the issue for decades, language has almost always been recognized as the clearest marker of one's indigenous identity. But it has rarely been recognized as the only one. In the 1940s and 1950s, the census identified a number of different so-called indigenous traits, including specified types of communities, housing, clothing, and food—if you walked barefoot and ate *tortillas* you were an Indian. During the long period of Official Indigenismo, when Alfonso Caso and Gonzalo Aguirre Beltrán were directors of INI (1948–1976), the community an individual lived in was considered more important than the language he or she spoke. But as time went on, economic forces depleted the population of isolated Indian villages. After 1968, as members of the new generation of anthropologists rebelled against the assimilationist policies of *indigenismo*, they did everything they could to make sure that Mexico counted every Indian, no matter where the person lived or what language he or she spoke. To achieve this goal, Rodolfo Stavenhagen, for example, changed the terms of the debate entirely. Writing from Paris, where he was working for UNESCO, he dismissed the importance of individual traits. The question at hand was ethnocide and the Mexican state was systematically underestimating the size of its indigenous population.[54]

Sharing a similar point of view, Guillermo Bonfil asserted that it was a waste of time to argue over individual traits, because the very idea of the Indian was a colonial construct:

> a supraethnic category containing no cultural content from any specific group ... The Indian came into being when Columbus took possession of Hispaniola in the name of a Catholic King and Queen. Before Europe discovered America, the inhabitants of the continent lived in many different societies. Their descendents today represent a wide range of ethnic groups that are difficult to categorize. One thing, however, is clear: indigenous people cannot be identified by their language.[55]

Luis González provided historical evidence to support Bonfil's position: even as far back as the mid-1800s, a single linguistic group might include more than one ethnicity, while individuals speaking entirely different languages might belong to the same group.[56] Barbas and Bartolomé went further still, presenting evidence of indigenous communities in Oaxaca that were ethnically mixed, comprised of people who spoke more than one language. These communities, they suggested, defined "residential identities," not indigenous enclaves.[57]

To resolve a debate that had produced little more than utter confusion, the 2000 census tried to simplify the matter by turning the question over to the Indians themselves. This new initiative supported the position of those seeking an all-inclusive definition: Indians are Indians if they say they are Indians. But when given the option, fewer people stepped forward to assume their identity as Indians than to acknowledge the fact that they spoke an indigenous tongue. When we look at question #20 on the 2000 census (*cuestionario ampliado*), which invites people to identify themselves as Indian, if they wish to, the number of Indians drops to 5,259,022, or 6.1 percent of the nation's total population—approximately a million people fewer than the number of those identifying themselves as speakers of indigenous tongues, and a percentage point lower.[58]

The numbers, however, may increase in the next census, if the government continues to subsidize special economic incentives for indigenous communities. In Morelos, for example, a state agency is making grants only to women in indigenous *pueblos* to encourage them to develop small industries. Given this new source of funding, exclusively available to indigenous communities, the residents of Mestizo *pueblos* in the area surrounding Hueyapan have been reclassifying themselves as indigenous.[59]

Meanwhile, "*moins ça change* . . ." In 1990, over 80 percent of the indigenous population of Mexico was living below the poverty line, as compared to 17.9 percent of the non-Indians. What is more, the higher the density of indigenous people living in a particular *municipio*, the higher the level of poverty.

Ten percent of the population in Mexico was illiterate in 1990, but over 40 percent of those who spoke an indigenous language—64 percent of the women and 36 percent of the men. In localities where 70 percent or more of the inhabitants were Indian, the level of illiteracy was 46 percent. If we look at yet another measure of poverty, Indians were more likely to live in homes that lacked plumbing than were non-Indians.[60] The statistical data gathered from the 2000 census are not very different.

Ethno-Development

López Portillo's Indigenismo de Participación eventually failed, in part, Emiko Saldívar suggests, because it did not let the Indians participate. INI maintained control over poorly conceived projects, managing them badly with a top-heavy bureaucracy.[61] When de la Madrid became president, he recognized the need for change. He had, what is more, an eager team of anthropologists ready to help him. Members of the generation of 1968 presented the new president with a plan that addressed the supposed weaknesses of the previous administration. Ignoring the fact that López Portillo was already supporting multiculturalism, they urged de la Madrid (1982– 1988) to adopt a program that did little more than carry forward in a more focused way what the previous president had begun to do—to sponsor projects that would promote cultural self-determination.[62] The main architect of this new phase of Indigenismo was Guillermo Bonfil. Calling his program Ethno-Development, he described it as a policy that used "the social capacity of a people to construct their own future, a project defined according to their values and aspirations, taking advantage of what the people have learned through their own historical experiences and the real and potential resources of their culture."[63]

President de la Madrid appointed the anthropologist Salomón Nahmad to become the next director of INI, but Nahmad moved too quickly and did not last very long. After 18 months on the job, Nahmad was ready to turn INI's regional centers over to local indigenous organizations. De la Madrid accused his director of fraud and threw him into jail, provoking an international protest. Five months later, the anthropologist was free, but de la Madrid did not reappoint him. He named the lawyer Miguel Limón to the post instead, a man he knew well and could trust. With the change in leadership, Ethno-Development survived, but in a modified way that provoked criticism from people like Bonfil.[64] Although the new anthropologists bitterly rejected Limón's watered-down version of Ethno-Development, Mexico was now clearly on the way to becoming a multicultural state.

Legal Indigenismo

When Carlos Salinas began his term as president in 1988, he introduced yet another set of changes known as Legal Indigenismo. During this fourth period, we see INI abandoning entirely its programs of welfare-distribution and encouraging the active participation of indigenous peoples in implementing new initiatives for Indians. These are also the years when the language of indigenous rights takes hold as the dominant discourse on Indians.[65]

President Salinas made Arturo Warman, a celebrated anthropologist of the new generation, the director of INI. When Warman took over in 1988, he found himself managing an underfunded and overly bureaucratic organization that had suffered the strains of Mexico's economic decline during the previous administration. President Salinas encouraged Warman to strengthen INI again and help it become the dynamic institution it had been before, during the López Portillo period. In a document outlining the new goals of INI, Arturo Warman called for greater integration of the institute with other agencies of the government and for greater participation of indigenous communities in the projects INI sponsored. The three-page document endorsed as well the radical proposal of Nahmad and Bonfil to turn regional centers over to indigenous communities, but not until the state deemed the Indians ready to manage them adequately.[66]

In 1992, Arturo Warman left INI, but his successor continued the same policy. Before taking over as director, Guillermo Espinosa headed an NGO agency that financed development projects in Huichol communities in the state of Jalisco. During his tenure, Espinosa encouraged the formation of indigenous associations in the private sector, arguing that Indians needed the support of legal organizations that were independent of the state. During the same period, INI actively discouraged indigenous communities from depending on government agencies for economic support. The idea of Mexico as a welfare state was coming to an end.[67]

Arturo Warman, in the meantime, was promoted to the post of secretary of the Agrarian Reform. In that position, he played a critical role in dismantling the *ejido* system, the heart of Mexico's agrarian reform and a powerful symbol of the Mexican Revolution— the importance of which Warman had eloquently described in *We Come to Object: The Peasants of Morelos and the National State*.[68]

Warman held influential political posts rather late in the game, well after the state had abandoned its project to create a culturally homogeneous Mestizo nation and had stopped using anthropologists to justify its assimilationist policies—or its ethno-development policies for that matter. Despite Warman's personal prominence, the landscape had clearly changed. As Claudio Lomnitz observes,

> The pattern of absorption of Mexican anthropology by the state is in some respects quite different . . . from the times when anthropology had a central role to play in national consolidation. The multiplication of state-funded anthropological institutions in the 1970s and 1980s seemed to respond more to the growth of the educational apparatus and to state relations with certain middle-class sectors than to the need for anthropologists as technocrats. The existence of certain highly visible anthropologists in government masks the relative decline of the political significance of a national anthropology for the Mexican state.[69]

Out of the limelight, anthropologists took positions as researchers and professors in the myriad of institutions that had grown up over the years in different parts of the country. No longer needed to shape national policy, many of them embraced the cause of the indigenous rights movement, some as theorists, others as activists, some as both. In the early years of the twenty-first century, the more philosophically inclined are participating in international discussions about the politics of recognition and distribution, inspired by the works of Charles Taylor,

William Kymlicka, among others.[70] In the process, anthropologists have abandoned Anthropology as a source of intellectual insight and with it any interest in old-fashioned notions about culture, even though the movements that have captured their imaginations are carving their ethnic identities out of the "stuff" anthropologists used to study.[71]

Since Carlos Salinas signed the NAFTA agreement, an event marked spectacularly by the Zapatista uprising on January 1, 1994, the influence of anthropologists has continued to decline. When Ernesto Zedillo became president the following December, he needed lawyers more than he needed cultural specialists to guide him through a series of difficult negotiations over the indigenous rights treaty, known as the San Andrés Accords. In 1996, Zedillo finally signed a decidedly watered-down version of the original document, and then he sat on it for the remaining four years of his term.[72] As for the various factions within the indigenous rights movements, they too needed lawyers more than they needed anthropologists, as well as writers and intellectuals—the discipline did not matter—with the star power necessary to gain media attention for their cause.[73]

In the summer of 2000, the PRI finally lost a presidential election, ceding power to Vicente Fox, the candidate of the conservative party PAN. One of Fox's earliest initiatives was to pass *la ley indígena*, a piece of legislation that successfully extracted whatever teeth remained in the San Andrés Accords, while it carefully preserved the language of multiculturalism. This law was further weakened in April 2001, in response to the EZLN's month-long march through indigenous Mexico, ending in Mexico City, that demanded legal and economic rights for indigenous citizens. Then, in December 2002, Congress voted to transform INI into La Comisión Nacional para el Desarrollo de los Pueblos Indígenas. The new commission focuses more on economic development than on indigenous rights, which are now, theoretically, protected by the Constitution.

Hueyapan

Back in Hueyapan, the villagers have spent the last 35 years facing challenges similar to those faced by other rural Mexicans. When Congress amended the Mexican Constitution (Article 27) in 1992 and dismantled the land reform system, this radical economic change had a negative impact on many people in the *pueblo*. Then, when Salinas signed the NAFTA agreement in 1994, things deteriorated even further. Today, it costs more to cultivate corn and make *tortillas* by hand than to buy them ready made, produced with flour processed in the United States.

Over the last 20 years, uncounted numbers of young men from Hueyapan have left the village to look for work in the United States. Virtually every household has someone—or recently had someone—who risked the dangers of crossing the border illegally in search of better opportunities than they had at home. In 2005, people born and raised in the *pueblo* are picking fruit and vegetables on American farms, caring for gardens in exclusive suburbs, or doing menial jobs in big cities—washing dishes in restaurants, selling flowers on the street, and lifting boxes in Korean groceries. Not everyone made it to the other side of the Rio Grande. Some ended up in northern Mexico instead and are working in factories on the border. Those who found jobs in these *maquiladoras* may have become more Indian there than they ever were at home, like the Mixtecos from Oaxaca about whom Carmen Martínez has written so effectively.[74]

According to the 2000 census, there are more women living in Hueyapan than men (3,048 females and 2,833 men), a fact borne out in reality even more dramatically than in the numbers recorded by the state. Many men, apparently, claim residency in the village, but do not live at home. Leaving their wives and children behind in the care of their own mothers, they spend most of their time far away from Hueyapan, looking for work to support their families.[75]

In the early years of the new millennium, Hueyapan looks more like an urban slum than a "sleepy Indian village." Visitors still see *adobe* brick houses like the ones I described over 30 years ago, but many people today live in red-brick and cement structures, similar to the ones found in Mestizo towns. These newly constructed houses lack rustic charm, but they provide their proud occupants with indoor plumbing and other amenities identified exclusively in 1970 with the conveniences of city life.

Today, travelers approach the center of town on asphalt roads scarred with potholes, revealing below the cobblestone streets that

Photo 15 Sign above store on the corner of Calle Morelos and the San Miguel plaza advertising an express mail service to the United States (2001). Calle Morelos is the bus route to Santa Cruz, Puebla.

had been there for centuries, perhaps since colonial times. Arriving in the San Miguel plaza, visitors see that the Centro remains the hub of business activity, but it looks very different from the way it did before. Crowded with trucks, buses, private cars, and collective taxis, it is hard to picture the square as it used to be in the late 1960s. Walking back toward the hills and away from the plaza, those who knew the *pueblo* 30 years ago finally see a familiar sight—of Popocatepetl looking down on Hueyapan as if nothing had changed. These days, however, the majestic volcano is a source of anxiety—a point driven home all over town on brightly painted signs that warn villagers to pay close attention to the "Smoking Mountain," for, it might suddenly erupt the way it threatened to do in 2000. But the biggest shock of all is the garbage. Defying occasional efforts on the part of the government to haul it away,[76] huge mounds of refuse spill over the sides of the once-beautiful gorges that separate the five *barrios* from each other—plastic bottles and tin cans that will never decompose and blend into the soil, like the biodegradable waste of earlier times.

Despite all the changes and signs of modernity, Hueyapan remains an Indian *pueblo*,[77] a status that qualifies the women in town to apply to the Fondo Estatal de Mujeres Indígenas de Morelos for loans to support local businesses.[78] In 2001, groups of women borrowed money at a favorable rate (3 percent) to cover some of the expenses of the following projects: medicine for a cooperative pharmacy; fertilizer for fruit orchards; grain to fatten up chickens; merchandise for a small store that sells clothing and shoes; equipment for a small furniture factory (here women took out the loan for their husbands and brothers); materials to stock small sewing and weaving workshops that produce modern and indigenous clothing; and materials for the production of "indigenous" herbal creams, made with a base of Vaseline.

Over the years, since I first lived in Hueyapan, initiatives to promote indigenous culture have come and gone. In the mid-1970s, for example, the village had a resident priest who decorated the church's altar with *gabanes* and a Huichol Indian cross. Although he was from the state of Michoacan and learned Nahuatl only as an adult, he arranged to translate the prayers recited during Mass into the language of the Aztecs—in an effort, no doubt, to compete with the growing popularity of evangelical sects that routinely preached in indigenous tongues. There were vague efforts as well, during the years of Participatory Indigenismo, to create small factories in Hueyapan that made *gabanes* and *rebozos* on mechanical looms with store-bought thread, in addition to those that manufactured modern-style sweaters—neither effort survived. Things really took off, however, in the 1990s, after the uprising in Chiapas, when representatives of INI, CONACULTA (Consejo Nacional para la Cultura y Artes), and the CEDH (Comision Estatal de Derechos Humanos), among others, invited villagers to participate in programs in Cuernavaca and, more locally, in Mestizo *pueblos* that were in the process of reinventing themselves as Indian.

Modesta Lavana was perhaps the first person in the village since 1969–1970 to become a "professional" Indian. Once Hueyapan had its own doctor in residence, her medical clinic lost importance and she moved to Cuernavaca to live with her daughters. There she received a warm welcome from people interested in promoting indigenous cultures and eventually found work at INI and CONACULTA. Maestro Rafael's son Arturo, who also lives in Cuernavaca and teaches primary school there, has established a considerable reputation for himself in the state of Morelos as a song writer, essayist, and poet. In 1999, he won a national competition sponsored by CONACULTA for an ethnographic essay he wrote about Hueyapan, which records a version of Doña Zeferina's story about the magical cave (El Encanto) that I describe in chapter two. He has also served as secretary of the Consejo Autónomo Estatal de Pueblos Indígenas, an NGO concerned with promoting the autonomy of indigenous communities in Morelos. Finally, he was elected vice president of Muosieual Sentlalistle Temoanchani, A.C., a society dedicated to promoting the Nahuatl language. And there are others, including Aurora Sánchez, a sister of Padre Diego Sánchez who works at the Instituto de Educación Básica del Estado de Morelos (IEBM) where she is in charge of matters concerning the education of the state's indigenous people.

Government agencies have come to Hueyapan as well to promote indigenous cultures. For example, the Consejo Nacional de Fomento Educativo (CONAFE) has established a bilingual nursery school staffed by federally employed teachers. The village doctor, Marcelino Montero Baeza, has also played a major role in promoting the Nahuatl language by creating The Nahuatl Cultural Group of Hueyapan. A native of the village, in the late 1990s, he and his group sponsored several levels of language instruction and the classes ran successfully for several years. Other members of the group include the doctor's wife Delia Ramirez Castellanos, who is a schoolteacher, and my old friend and Nahuatl instructor Elvira Hernández, who had served as a linguistic informant in the 1960s and 1970s at Harvard University and Indiana University, giving students the opportunity to learn Nahuatl from a native speaker.

The group's school has very few students in 2005, but interest in learning the language persists. Elvira Hernández, for example, is taking courses in Nahuatl herself in Mitla (Oaxaca)—when she can get away—at the Summer Institute for Linguistics. This evangelical organization has a major international reputation for training linguists around the world to translate the Bible into indigenous tongues.

Over the years, Dr. Marcelino's efforts to promote Nahuatl in Hueyapan have received the generous support of the state. In the early years of the new millennium, CONACULTA and the XLVIII Legislature of the H. Congress of the state of Morelos have helped the doctor and his colleagues publish five books in Nahuatl, the first two in 2000, and the last three in 2004. As this revised edition of *Being Indian in Hueyapan* goes to press, his group is preparing a dictionary of the Hueyapan dialect of Nahuatl.[79]

In 1998, the Nahuatl Cultural Group of Hueyapan began organizing annual festivals to celebrate indigenous languages and cultures. The group held these celebrations on the 4th of August, Hueyapan's saint's day, which has traditionally drawn large crowds from neighboring *pueblos*. For these public celebrations, the group got outside assistance as well.

In 2001, for example, the festival received support from CONACULTA and the Casa de los Escritores en Lenguas Indígenas, as well as from the local *mayordomo* and the governments of Hueyapan and Tetela. The program that year included three formal lectures on the linguistic and cultural diversity of Mexico and performances of eight different songs and poems in Nahuatl, several of them by children from Hueyapan who were studying the language with members of the village's cultural group. In 2004 and 2005 (the year this book went to press), the festival did not take place.[80] Finally, INI and the Human Rights Commission of Morelos have been distributing copies of documents that outline the human rights of indigenous peoples in the state of Morelos and in Mexico more generally. These pamphlets quote directly from the relevant passages of the Mexican Constitution and legislation passed in Morelos, all of which confirm the multicultural composition of the nation, and assert Mexico's commitment to protect indigenous "languages, cultures, *usos, costumbres*, resources and specific forms of social organization" (Article 4).

The villagers, in other words, are now fully informed about their cultural and legal status as Indians and about the role the state expects them to play, this time around. The more progressive and educated members of the community have embraced the new program with enthusiasm, just as the last generation of progressives embraced the nation's assimilationist project. In the old days, villagers learned to take the Indian out of their everyday lives. Now they are learning to put it back in, with the help of human rights organizations and government agencies that actively encourage them to practice their *usos y costumbres*.

Some might conclude from what I say here that I oppose the idea of teaching Nahuatl to children or of encouraging women to preserve the ancient tradition of weaving on the backstrap loom. On the contrary. I am all in favor of practicing these customs, especially when the desire to do so comes from the villagers themselves. But something else is going on here that demands serious attention. As Charles Hale pointed out a few years ago, multiculturalism does not imply necessarily the triumph of an indigenous conquest. There is no contradiction between the growing interest today in Indian cultures and the expanding influence of global capitalism.[81]

Let me end on a more optimistic, if anecdotal, note by returning to Doña Zeferina and her family, focusing in particular on her granddaughter Maribel Vargas. As I report in chapter one, everyone, including the resident anthropologist, commented on the fact that Maribel resembled her grandmother. Having the same strength of character and driving intelligence, we all expected the little girl to realize the dreams that Doña Zeferina had for the family. Living up to expectations, Maribel today belongs to a new generation of politically engaged intellectuals, many of whom grew up in poverty, or near poverty, in indigenous villages like hers. Although raised in a period of intense assimilation, she rejects the old PRI's agenda of denigrating the ways of modern-day Indians and of celebrating the Mestizo. But she still relies heavily on the language and culture of the ruling classes, convinced that she needs a broad and inclusive education to be able to contribute in a meaningful way to solving the problems of the nation's poor.

When I met Maribel in 1969, she was turning six and was eager to begin school. Six years later, she finished primary school with distinction and won a scholarship to attend a boarding school in Cuernavaca (Palmiras). Graduating in 1979, she continued her studies in a normal school in Cuautla, to prepare herself to become a primary schoolteacher. From Cuautla, she went on to

Querétero, to the Escuela Normal Superior, where she received her *licenciatura* in Spanish. In 1983, Maribel began teaching primary school in the village of Jilotepec, in the state of Mexico.

Over the years, between my short visits to Hueyapan, Maribel wrote letters to me, to give news about herself and the family. Then, in the spring of 1990, I invited her and her sister Rosa to accompany their 85-year old grandmother to New York. They were all guests of SUNY, Purchase, where I was teaching at the time. Doña Zeferina was the main attraction. All dressed up in a *xincueite* (see photo in preface)—her idea, not mine—she gave a talk to over 100 students on what it was like to live for a year with an anthropologist. Her descriptions were hilarious, mostly at my expense, and the students loved them. Maribel and Rosa spoke as well to smaller groups of undergraduates about the challenges school teachers faced in rural Mexico. While in New York, they also visited two primary schools, both public and private, in a poor neighborhood in the South Bronx and on the exclusive Upper East Side of Manhattan.

Eager to learn more about life in the United States, Maribel decided to come back to New York the following year to study English intensively for six months. When she returned to Mexico in 1992, she resumed her teaching in the village of Tezoyuca, near the city of Texcoco. In 1994, she settled down with Apolinar Osorio Ruíz, a colleague of hers who came originally from Oaxaca. And in 1995, she gave birth to their daughter Abril.

Maribel and Apolinar moved to Tezoyuca proper in 1998, to live in the same town where they were teaching, in part to give Apolinar a base for his political ambitions. Two years later, they built their own house, which they designed themselves and decorated with furniture made in Hueyapan. In the same year, the left-leaning PRD won the local elections and Apolinar became secretary of the government (*ayuntamiento*) of Tezoyuca, a position he held until 2003, when the PRD was voted out.

While teaching primary school in Tezoyuca, Maribel has also been training primary schoolteachers at an annex of the National Pedagogical University, and studying part-time herself for a Master's degree at the main branch of the university. Apolinar has followed a similar trajectory. In their free time, both of them read widely and take part in the same political and academic debates that concern progressive intellectuals throughout the country.

One day, in the fall of 1999, I gave Maribel a call to see how she was doing. At the time, I was serving as Dean of the Graduate Faculty at the New School for Social Research. After giving me the latest news about everyone in the family, she told me that she was taking a course in philosophy and ethics. Whom was she reading, I asked. "You might know one of them," she replied. "She lives in New York. Her name is Agnes Heller." "Of course, I know her," I said. "I'm her Dean." At which point, Maribel countered, without losing a beat, "Why do academics like you only talk to each other? Why not reach out to people like us? We need to hear from you!"

Accepting the challenge, I asked Agnes Heller if she would come to Mexico with me to meet Maribel and give a talk at the Pedagogical University. Agnes accepted immediately. Although she had been to Mexico many times before, she had only spoken to students in privileged university circles, confirming Maribel's point. Friends at the New School had already told me that our Hungarian colleague was revered in Latin America and throughout much of the Third World, as she was in Central Europe, for her writings on politics and ethics as well as for her personal courage and integrity. But I still had not grasped the extent of her influence.[82]

By 1999, 18 of Agnes Heller's books had been translated into Spanish, among them *Everyday Life* that every normal school student reads as part of the required curriculum. The more Maribel learned about Agnes Heller's work, the more she wanted to dedicate herself to studying it seriously. When the time came to select a subject for her MA thesis, she decided to use Agnes Heller's concept of "everyday life" as the theoretical basis for analyzing the training of primary schoolteachers at the annex of the National Pedagogical University where she teaches. (Maribel graduated with honors in the fall of 2004 and her thesis was published the following year in a book series edited by her professor.)[83]

After I told Maribel that Agnes would come to Mexico and speak at the Pedagogical University, Maribel shared the good news with her professor Luis Eduardo Primero Rivas, who immediately took charge and organized a conference for the end of May (2000), entitled, "Education, Humanism and Postmodernity." When the time came, the Hungarian philosopher gave a provocative keynote address on "Why Democracies Need a Cultural Elite," offering her listeners a welcomed critique of the ways modern capitalism had distorted the ideals of democracy in the United States, but in terms that made cultural relativists uncomfortable.

The conference was a huge media success and attracted close to a hundred students, all of whom were deeply engaged in Agnes Heller's work.[84] The following day, Agnes spoke again to 500 students, at a second event organized by Maribel. When she extended the invitation, Maribel made it clear that she expected us to address her students as well at the annex of the Pedagogical University in Ecatepec, a working-class city outside Mexico City, located about an hour away from the DF (Distrito Federal). It was not enough to participate, she insisted, in a conference for comparatively privileged students in Mexico City. We needed to meet her students too. And so we did the next morning in Ecatepec, where hundreds of aspiring teachers crowded under a huge tent to hear Agnes Heller give the same talk she had delivered the day before.

Almost everyone attending the lecture in Ecatepec was raised in a rural village like Hueyapan, in a community that had little in common—one would think—with Budapest or New York, where Agnes Heller divided her time. Yet the questions students asked suggested that the writings of this Hungarian philosopher had made a deep impact on them. Drawing on her work, they pressed her to help them think about matters of critical concern to them as school teachers in Mexico.

The next day, Maribel and Apolinar took us up to Hueyapan, where Doña Zeferina, Doña Juana, and other members of the family were waiting to receive us. Deeply attached to the village of her birth, Maribel spoke at length about her desire to preserve her indigenous language and the traditions she grew up with. She hoped, she said, that others who came from similar backgrounds would do the same. Apolinar agreed that this was very important, even though he himself spoke only Spanish. For both of them,

Photo 16 Maribel Vargas standing in front of her home in Tezoyuca, State of Mexico (2001).

Photo 17 Doña Juana making *tortillas* in the kitchen on Calle Morelos, as if nothing had changed (2001).

however, their political work was elsewhere. They were dedicating their lives to reading widely and critically, preparing themselves to give rural Mexicans the education they needed to take their place in a world that extends far beyond the impoverished communities where they were born. It was their job, they believed, to introduce young teachers to the life of the mind and to help them become informed citizens of Mexico—with the skills necessary to strengthen the nation's democratic institutions and the courage to challenge global economic forces that threaten to undermine them.

GLOSSARY OF SELECTED TERMS

Adobe	Bricks made out of mud.
Aguacate	Avocado. The word comes from the *Nahuatl* ahuagatl.
Agave	A large cactus-like plant with long fleshy protrusions. Also known as the century plant, the *agave* produces strong fibers that can be woven into cloth and a liquid that can be fermented into a beer-like beverage called *pulque*, or further distilled into mescal and tequila.
Aguardiente	The term refers to a local brandy made out of sugarcane.
Alcalde	Mayor
Atole	A very thick beverage made with corn-gruel, served for breakfast on fiesta days.
Atrio	Courtyard. The term often refers to the courtyard of a church.
Ayudante	Technically the term means assistant. In Mexico it identifies the chief political officer of a satellite village of a municipality. The *ayudante* reports to the *alcalde* who is based in the municipal seat. Hueyapan's *ayudante* reports to the *alcalde* in Tetela del Volcán.
Barrio	An officially demarcated part of town. Hueyapan has five *barrios* (San Miguel, San Jacinto, San Andrés, San Bartolo, and San Felipe).
Barranca	Gorge.
Bufanda	Scarf. The term used in Hueyapan for the wool scarf men wear in the chilly seasons of the year.
Cal	A chalk-like substance (lime), added to the water used to stew corn kernels in the preparation of the *nixtamal*.
Calle	Street.
Calzones	Often translated as pajamas. The traditional white linen pants and shirt worn by *campesinos* in Mexico.
Campesino	Often translated loosely as peasant—someone of modest means who lives in rural Mexico and makes a living by farming.
CEDEH	Comisión Estatal de Derechos Humanos.
Centavo	A fraction of a *peso*. There are 100 *centavos* to 1 *peso*.
Centro	In Hueyapan, the *Centro* refers to the *barrios* of San Miguel and San Jacinto, which together constitute the center of town.
Charro	The term used in Mexico to identify the costume worn by musicians performing ranchero music in mariache bands (voice, string, and brass ensembles). The costume imitates the style of dress historically associated with owners of *haciendas* before the Mexican

	Revolution—tightly fitted black jackets and pants with silver studs up the side, black boots, and broad rimmed *sombreros*.
Chicharrón	Deep fried pork rind.
Chiles	Hot peppers.
Chirimía	Spanish term for shawm, a European Renaissance instrument of the oboe family. The inhabitants of Hueyapan and of neighboring towns consider the *chirimía* to be an indigenous instrument. See p. 247, n. 37.
Chocolate	Prehispanic Mexican spice, which, when sweetened, became a world-famous delicacy. The term comes from the *Nahuatl*.
Comal	Round disk, traditionally made out of clay, used to cook *tortillas* and *tamales*. The *comal* dates to prehispanic times and the word comes from the *Nahuatl*.
Comadre	Name given reciprocally to women who have entered into a spiritual relationship blessed by the Catholic Church, for example, the godmother and mother of a child.
Compadre	Name given reciprocally to men who have entered into a spiritual relationship blessed by the Catholic Church, for example, the godfather and the father of a child.
CONACULTA	Consejo Nacional para la Cultura y Artes
CONAFE	Consejo Nacional de Fomento Educativo
COPLAMAR	Coordinación General del Plan Nacional Para Zonas Deprimidas y Grupos Marginados.
Corregidor	The manager of a *corregimiento*. He was always of Spanish or Creole origin.
Corregimiento	An administrative unit in colonial Mexico, where there were no Spanish cities, that identified lands and districts owned by the king of Spain.
Curandera	Female form of curandero, meaning healer.
Dame de comer	Give me something to eat.
Distrito Federal	The Federal District (DF)—Mexico City.
Ejidos	After the Mexican Revolution of 1910–1920, the Mexican government initiated a major land reform program. Land grants, known as *ejidos*, were expropriated from large land-holdings and given to landless peasants and to villages. Individuals and villagers could not sell *ejido* land until 1992, when President Carlos Salinas changed the law.
Encomienda	The term used in colonial Mexico for land grants made by the king to the conquistadors. These grants included not only a parcel of land but rights to the labor of the people living there as well. After a generation or two, *encomiendas* reverted to the Crown.
Encomendero	The individual in charge of an *encomienda*. In collaboration with Catholic missionaries, *encomenderos* were expected to care for the spiritual well being of the Indians living and working on their lands.
EZLN	Ejército Zapatista de Liberación Nacional (Name of indigenous rights movement in Chiapas that has attracted worldwide attention in 1994).

Gabán	A Spanish term for overcoat. The word is used in Hueyapan, instead of the more familiar poncho, to refer to the blanket men wear to keep themselves warm in the chilly hours of the day.
Gachupín	Deprecating work for Spaniards. See p. 260, n. 23.
Hacendado	Owner of a *hacienda*. Unlike the *encomendero*, the *hacendado* purchased his land, either from the Mexican government or from a private individual.
Hacienda	A large rural estate or plantation.
Huaraches	Leather-thong sandals with rubber-tire soles, worn by men. The word is also spelled with a "g" (*guaraches*).
IEBM	Instituto de Educación Básica del Estado de Morelos.
Indio	Indian. In 1969–1970, this was the polite term to use when had deeply insulting connotations. In recent years, however, in particular since 1994 and the rise of indigenous rights movements in Mexico, Indians are assuming their identity with pride and are using this term to identify themselves.
Indígena	Indigenous person. In 1969–1970, this was the polite term to use when referring to an Indian. The term is still used widely.
Ixcactles	*Agave*-fiber sandals worn by women. The word comes from *Nahuatl*.
Jefa	Female form of jefe, meaning chief or leader. Maestro Rafael used the terms affectionately when referring to his mother, the matriarch of the family.
Jitomate	Red tomato in Mexican Spanish. The term comes from the *Nahuatl*.
Kalpull	Usually spelled calpulli, this Nahuatl term refers to the *Aztec* kinship and land tenure system.
Ley Indígena	Popular name for legislation passed in early 2001 to protect the cultural rights of Mexican Indians. The law was vigorously criticized for being too weak by indigenous rights activists in Mexico.
Licenciatura	Equivalent of a Bachelor's degree in the United States.
Mano (hand)	Heavy rolling pin made out of volcanic rock, used for grinding corn, *chiles*, tomatoes, and other foods on the *metate*.
Maestro(a)	Title used for a school teacher.
Maestría	Equivalent of a Master's degree in the United States.
Malinche	Also known as Doña Marina. Malinche was Cortés' mistress and interpreter. Mexicans who collaborate with Americans and Europeans are called Malinchistas. See p. 219, n. 24.
Maquila	A measure of corn kernels (about the size of a quart in Central Mexico).
Mayordomo	Sponsor of a religious fiesta.
Mestizaje	The term used to describe the process of constructing the hybrid racial and cultural identity of the *Mestizo*.

Mestizo	The term technically means hybrid or cross-breed. In post-revolutionary Mexico, the *Mestizo* represented the idealized Mexican—the racial and cultural descendant of two great civilizations (the Spanish and the Indian).
Metate	A heavy slab of volcanic rock used for grinding corn, *chiles,* tomatoes, garlic, and other spices and vegetables. The *mano* and *metate* date to prehispanic times. The word *metate* comes from the *Nahuatl.*
Misterio	Small image of a saint kept in the home of the *mayordomo.*
Mole	An elaborate sauce served over meat, fish, or sometimes only beans, made with *chiles* and, depending on the particular mole, a wide variety of spices and other ingredients. In Hueyapan the preferred variety of *mole* is called *mole* colorado.
Morral	In Central Mexico the term refers to an *agave*-fiber bag.
Municipio	Municipality. Hueyapan belongs to the Municipality of Tetela del Volcán.
Nahuatl	The language spoken by the Aztecs and by other peoples living in Central Mexico at the time of the Spanish conquest. *Nahuatl* remains one of the most widely spoken indigenous languages in Mexico in the early years of the twenty-first century.
Nixtamal	Stewed corn kernels—the first step in the preparation of corn for making *tortillas* and *tamales.*
PAN	Partido de Acción Nacional. The name of Mexico's main conservative political party whose candidate, Vicente Fox , became president of the nation in 2000, deposing the reigning party for the first time in over 70 years. The acronym mean bread.
Peso	Mexico's basic monetary unit. In 1969–1979, there were 12.5 *pesos* to the dollar. The currency rate changed in 1976.
Petate	Straw mat placed on the floor of a house or on the ground outside—used for sleeping or sitting. The word comes from *Nahuatl.*
PRD	El Partido Revolucionario Democrático. A national political party founded in the 1980s to challenge the hegemony of the *PRI* from the left. The founding leader of the *PRD* was Cuauhtémoc Cárdenas, the son of Mexico's legendary socialist-leaning president of the 1930s, Lázaro Cárdenas.
Presidente de Fiestas Patrias	*Mayordomo* of secular fiestas celebrating national holidays.
PRI	El Partido Revolucionario Institucional. The reigning political party of postrevolutionary Mexico that was deposed for the first time in 2000 by the conservative party *PAN.*
Pueblo	Village.
Pulque	Fermented juice of the *agave* plant. This beer-like drink dates back to prehispanic times. The word *pulque* comes from the *Nahuatl.*
Rancho	Hamlet. Hueyapan has five *barrios* and a few satellite *ranchos.*
Rebozo	Shawl worn by women.

Salsa	Hot sauce made traditionally with red or green tomatoes, *chiles*, and other spices.
Sombrero	Hat. The word was incorporated into Hueyapan *Nahuatl* as xonblelotle.
Tamales	Dumplings made out of corn and steamed in corn husks. On fiesta days in Hueyapan, plain *tamales* and *tamales* filled with fried bean paste were served with mole at the main meal of the day. For breakfast, *tamales* cooked with small bits of pork and *chile* sauce, were served with *atole*.
Tejocote	Fruit of the Mexican Hawthorn.
Temascal	Steam bath. This *adobe* steam bath (see p. 20) dates back to prehispanic times. The word comes from Nahuatl.
Tenate	Straw basket used to serve hot *tortillas*. Word comes from the *Nahuatl*.
Teotl	*Nahuatl* term for god or supreme being.
Tlatelolco	A sister city of Tenochtitlán in prehispanic times. In postrevolutionary Mexico, it became the site of the Plaza of the Three Cultures, where monuments symbolize the melding of indigenous and Spanish cultures, and where, in 1968, a bloody confrontation took place between the Mexican government and a strong political movement made up of students and workers.
Tomate	Green tomato, known as a tomatillo in Caribbean Spanish. The term comes from the *Nahuatl*.
Tomin	The term used in *Nahuatl* to refer to a *centavo*. *Tomin* was a monetary unit in the colonial period. The word comes from the Arabic thumin (see p. 205, n. 19).
Tonto	Fool or Foolish (see p. 204, n. 3).
Tortilla	A flat bread made traditionally out of corn.
Xale	Residue of fried pork and fat.
Xincueite	Traditional black wool skirt worn by women in Hueyapan. The word comes from the *Nahuatl*.
Zócalo	Town square.

NOTES

Preface

1. See notes in chapter nine.
2. I have, however, edited heavily for style and expanded the text slightly in chapters four and five. The footnotes included in the first edition have now become endnotes and those notes have increased in number, allowing me to update the text and/or comment briefly on issues I thought were important but did not develop in chapter nine. Finally, I have also updated the bibliography.
3. See Elena Poniatowska's *La Noche de Tlatelolco* for a moving account of this terrible event.

Introduction

1. Eric Hobsbawm and Terence Ranger's *Invention of Tradition* and Benedict Anderson's *Imagined Communities: Reflections on the Origin and Spread of Nationalism* had not yet been published. They both appeared in 1983. The work that influenced me in the late 1960s was Julian Pitt-Rivers' article, "Mestizo or Ladino."
2. After the massacre in 1968, student activists referred to Tlatelolco as the plaza of two and a half cultures. In 1985, a terrible earthquake destroyed parts of Mexico City and damaged many important buildings, including the office building on the Plaza of the Three Cultures. The archeological site and the church both survived, virtually unscathed.
3. In the first edition of the book, I frequently referred to the villagers as "Hueyapeños," as I heard virtually everyone do at the time. Since then, I have learned that some villagers consider the term deprecating. I have, therefore, dropped "Hueyapeño" from the text. When I discussed the matter at some length with Maribel Vargas in the spring of 2005, she said that when villagers met one another away from Hueyapan, in other towns or cities, they often referred to the *pueblo* as their home or "casa," in both Spanish and Nahuatl. "*Voy a la casa*," or "*mantiagan casa*" is the code way of saying, "I'm going to Hueyapan."
4. By "culture," I mean a "system of symbols," following in the tradition of Talcott Parsons, Clifford Geertz and David Schneider. See, Schneider, *American Kinship*, 1.

5. In Mexico today, in the early years of the twenty-first century, we find equivalents to the Black Power and Red Power movements among those identified as Indians. I discuss these changes in chapter nine.
6. Given how politicized the term has become, the 1975 definition given here would generally be dismissed as inadequate. At the time, however, it was perfectly acceptable.
7. As I note in the preface to this edition, I never lost touch with Hueyapan or the family. My last trip to Hueyapan was in June, 2001, six months before Doña Zeferina died. Since then, I have remained in regular phone and e-mail communication with Maribel Vargas and her family, by which I mean we hear from one another at least once a month. Maribel and I saw each other most recently in New York City in the spring of 2005, when she came for a brief visit, together with her partner Apolinar Osorio and their daughter Abril, to celebrate her MA graduation from the National Pedagogical University. Maribel wrote her Master's thesis on the work of the Hungarian philosopher Agnes Heller. She graduated with honors. See chapter nine.

Chapter One   Zeferina Barreto and Her Family (1969–1970)

When I was writing this chapter over 30 years ago, very few anthropologists were looking critically at ethnography as a "literary genre." Clifford Geertz, of course, was addressing the issue, as were some of his students, but the problem was not yet a matter of general concern. Although I adopted the ethnographic convention of writing in the present tense, I did not embrace the idea of a "timeless" ethnographic present. I used it instead to mark a particular moment in ethnographic time—the 12 months I spent in Mexico during the late 1960s and early 1970s. For further discussion about ethnography as a genre of writing, see chapter nine.

1. As Figure 1 indicates, when I lived in the house, the family had two bedrooms, a kitchen, and a storeroom off the kitchen. In the yard behind the house stood the family's outhouse. Although many families had electricity by then, they did not, for the most part, have running water or indoor plumbing. Doña Zeferina's family got running water in the early 1970s and began installing indoor plumbing in the mid-1980s. Over the years, the family has added three more bedrooms, an indoor toilet, a bathroom with a waterheater, a stall shower, and washing machine. Today, the kitchen still has the old *temascal* and hearth, but the family has added a gas stove and a refrigerator. Bedroom A has become the sitting room and guest bedroom. Furnished with a couch as well as a bed, the family uses the room to watch television and movies on a VCR. The outside wall of the house, facing Calle Morelos, is now made out of red brick and the new metal door, which has replaced the old wooden one, is located at the west end of the south wall. In the early 1970s, the village acquired a public telephone and by the late 1990s, many homes had their own private lines, including Doña Zeferina's family. After Doña Zeferina died, her surviving children, Angelina and Ernestino,

laid claim to their inheritance on Calle Morels, dividing up their mother's property and squeezing the now widowed Doña Juana into considerably smaller living quarters—a harsh thing to do, in the eyes of Doña Juana's children, given the fact that Doña Juana had cared for Doña Zeferina on a daily basis for nearly 50 years.

2. Doña Zeferina turns 65 in August, 1970.

3. Doña Zeferina had 2 more sons. One of them died, the other, Ernestino, lives in Cuernavaca. Ernestino left Hueyapan in the early 1950s to work in a textile factory in Cuernavaca.

4. Maestro Rafael died on October 2, 1991, just before his sixty-third birthday. Doctors attributed the cause of death to complications following an operation on his pancreas.

5. Doña Juana has had 11 healthy children, all of whom are still alive as this book goes to press. She lost one baby in childbirth. Today, she is a grandmother and a great grandmother. Except for having to watch what she eats—she was diagnosed with diabetes in the late 1990s—she is clearly enjoying this period of her life, assuming the authority she has earned with age. Doña Juana receives the respect and admiration of her children, who have faithfully stood by her, after Doña Zeferina died, and defended her interests as best they could against the claims of their uncle and aunt. Although Doña Juana remains quiet, she is no longer timid about voicing her opinions.

6. In the fall of 1970, Arturo passed the entrance examination for normal school in Tenería, Mexico and began preparing himself to follow in his father's footsteps and become a primary schoolteacher. As the book goes to press, Arturo is the father of four children and the grandfather of two. For many years, he has been living in Cuernavaca, where he is teaching primary school and working two shifts—one in the morning and the other in the afternoon. His schedule has made it difficult for him to complete his studies and earn a *licenciatura*, the equivalent of a BA, but he is trying to do so. After his father died, Arturo began writing poetry and songs, developing a local reputation as "the bard of Morelos." In 1999, he won a national competition sponsored by CONACULTA (Consejo Nacional para la Cultura y Artes) for an essay he wrote about Hueyapan, based on one of Doña Zeferina's favorite stories about a magical cave near the base of the volcano Popocatepetl. Finally, like his father, Arturo plays a role in politics and has recently become involved in the indigenous rights movement in the state of Morelos and nationally. Recognized as a leader for several years, he has been serving as secretary of the Consejo Autónomo Estatal de Pueblos Indígenas de Morelos, a position he continues to hold as this book goes to press. The Consejo is an NGO concerned with promoting the autonomy of indigenous communities in Morelos. He serves as well as vice president of Muosieual Sentlalistle Temoanchani, A.C. (The Gathering of Indigenous Peoples), a society dedicated to promoting the Nahuatl language.

7. Rosa attended secondary school in Tetela and preparatory school in Temoac, both neighboring towns of Hueyapan. She then left home and went to Oaxaca to the Escuela Normal Superior, where she received her *licenciatura* in Spanish literature. For years now she has been teaching secondary school in the town of Chalco, Mexico, where she has built two houses. She currently lives in the one

most recently constructed, together with her daughter Xanath and the child's father. When she gave birth, Rosa's younger sister Maribel encouraged her to give the baby girl the Totonac name, Xanath, which means flower of the vanilla bean. Tall and willowy, Xanath has demonstrated promise as a dancer and is studying to become a ballerina.

8. Raúl went to secondary school in Tetela and normal school in Cuautla, the second largest city in the state of Morelos. He then went to Celaya, Guanajuato to study at a branch of the Universidad Pedagógica Nacional and received a *licenciatura* in Pedagogy. Raúl married a young woman from Guanajuato and has remained in the area ever since, where he has been teaching primary school in the mornings and serving as director of a primary school in the afternoon. Over the years, he and his wife have had four children. As this book goes to press, he has two grandchildren as well.

9. Héctor went to secondary school in Zacualpan and preparatory school in Saltillo (state of Coahuila). He then remained in Saltillo to study for an advanced degree in agrarian engineering, but he never completed the program. Since then, he has been making a living painting houses. In 1998, Héctor settled down with a young woman from Hueyapan and two years later, he became the father of a little girl.

10. Maribel won a scholarship to attend secondary school at Palmiras, a highly regarded boarding school in Cuernavaca. Graduating in 1979, she continued her studies in Cuautla at the city's normal school. Afterwards, she went on to study at the Normal Superior in Querétero where she received her *licenciatura* in Spanish. In 1983 she began teaching primary school in Jilotepec, state of Mexico. Three years later, she accepted a new postion in the town of Tezoyuca, which is near the city of Texcoco. Then in 1994, Maribel settled down with Apolinar Osorio, who is also a school teacher, and they have one daughter. Since 1998, the couple has been living in Tezoyuca, most recently in a new house that they designed together and decorated with wood furniture made in Hueyapan. In addition to teaching primary school, Maribel has been training primary school teachers at a branch of the National Pedagogical University (Unidad UPN 153) in Ecatepec, about an hour away by car from Mexico City, while studying for her Master's degree at the main branch of the National Pedagogical University in Mexico City—she graduated with Honors in 2004. In 2000, Apolinar was elected secretary of the *ayundantaría* (of Tezoyuca), having been swept into office on the ticket of the left-leaning PRD (Partido Revolucionario Democrático), which won the elections that year in the village. The party was voted out in 2003.

11. Reyna went to secondary school in Tetela and normal school in Xochitepec (Morelos). She then continued her studies for a *licenciatura* in Education at the Cuautla branch of the National University of Pedagogy, specializing in early childhood education. After teaching kindergarten-age children for many years, in 2001, she was appointed director of a kindergarten in the village of Metepec, located in the municipality of Ocuituco, within easy commuting distance from Hueyapan. Reyna chose not to have a family of her own and has stayed at home with her mother. In recent years, she has been a real source of support to Doña Juana, sharing in the chores and keeping her mother company.

12. Angel went to secondary school in Hueyapan and preparatory school in Tetela. The family had wanted to send him to a military academy, but his grades were not competitive enough. In the end, he never finished his studies. Instead he went to work in Cuernavaca at the Burlington Textile Mills, where his uncle Ernestino had been employed since 1952. The factory went bankrupt in the late 1990s. Angel settled down with a woman from Hueyapan and has two children. He and his wife live in Cuernavaca, where he now works as a gardener.

When I lived in Hueyapan, Angel was the baby of the family and Doña Juana was expecting Salvador who was born just after I left. After Salvador, she gave birth to the following children, more or less at two-year intervals: Eugenio, Mario, Angélica, and Israel. Salvador and Angélica have followed in the family tradition and become schoolteachers—Salvador in Quintano Roo and Angélica in the state of Mexico. Salvador has two *licenciaturas*, in primary school education and in math. While studying in Quintano Roo, he settled down with a woman from the region. They have three children. Angélica has a *licenciatura* in the natural sciences from the Escuela Normal Superior of Cuautla. She teaches and lives with her partner and their son in Chalco, near her sister Rosa. Her companion is from Tetela del Volcán. Mario dropped out of school, but has managed to put enough money together to open a store in Hueyapan that sells panes of glass. He settled down with a woman from Hueyapan and they have one son. Israel never finished his studies either. He makes ends meet by taking odd jobs in Cuernavaca, where he settled down in 2004 with a woman who is also from Hueyapan. As this book goes to press, they still have no children. Of the younger set of children, Eugenio is the big success story: After finishing secondary school in Hueyapan, Eugenio went on to Chapingo, a very prestigious school in the state of Mexico, to study agrarian engineering. He is now married and working in Mochis, Sinaloa, affiliated with a sugar refinery, and is the father of two little girls. Encouraged by his sister Maribel, he and his wife, who is also from Hueyapan, have named their second daughter Yoalli, which means evening in Nahuatl.

13. In 1970, Angelina moved to Cuernavaca and eventually took Lilia with her. There she settled down with Ermeterio López, who was originally from Hueyapan and was working at the time at the Burlington Textile Mills with Angelina's older brother Ernestino. They had two boys and a girl, all of whom are now married. As this book goes to press, Angelina has five grandchildren.

14. After finishing primary school in Hueyapan, Lilia moved to Cuernavaca with her mother and went to a private secondary school there. She then went on to a state-run (as opposed to national) normal school. For years now, she has been teaching primary school and as this book goes to press she is working two shifts. Lilia married a talented young artist who worked for many years for Walt Disney, where he earned a comparatively good living. Presently, he is the head of illustration for a magazine published by the teachers' union in the state of Morelos. They have two children.

15. During the year I lived with the family, the sleeping arrangements were as follows (figure 1): in bedroom A, Maestro Rafael, Doña Juana, Reyna, and Angel shared a double bed and Rosa and Maribel the single bed. In bedroom B, Doña

Zeferina, Don José and Arturo slept in a double bed; Maestra Angelina and Lilia shared the single bed. Raúl and Héctor slept together in the storeroom off the kitchen on a narrow bed made out of wooden planks and cushioned by a thin straw mat (*petate*). I slept in bedroom A for most of my stay on an army cot that the family had purchased several years earlier for Arturo to use while he was studying in Yecapistla. At times, when there was company and they needed the cot, I shared Rosa's bed and Maribel joined the others in her parents' bed. In June 1970, Doña Zeferina bought a new double bed for Maestra Angelina and I then shared it with her and her daughter. Arturo inherited his aunt's single bed. With the exception of the bed in the storeroom, all the others were store-bought with headboards decorated with religious scenes.

16. There are 100 *centavos* in a *peso*. In 1969–1970, there were 12.5 *pesos* to one U.S. dollar.

17. The *comal*, traditionally, is made out of clay. Flat and round, it fits over the hearth and serves as a griddle for cooking *tortillas*. Because they break easily, Doña Juana prefers using a *comal* made out of thin metal.

18. The word is also spelled "*guarache.*"

19. Blessed by the Church, *comadres* (female) and *compadres* (male) enter into special relationships with one another after sponsoring important life-cycle rituals, such as the baptism of a neighbor's son, or the wedding of a daughter.

20. Cuautla is the second most important city in Morelos; Cuernavaca is the first. The Estrella–Roja bus line that provides service to Hueyapan departs from Cuautla. The city is about 50 kilometers away.

21. Tlacotepec is 11 kilometers away. It is the last village before Hueyapan on the Cuautla–Hueyapan bus route. Tlacotepec is a lowland village and the ascent from there to Hueyapan is quite arduous.

22. As the years went by, the social and economic differences between Maestra Angelina and Doña Juana became painfully obvious and played out in unfortunate ways within the family. With the benefit of hindsight, my passing remark about the nature of their friendship sounds naive, at best, and somewhat patronizing. When we look at their relationship today, it is hard to imagine that the scene described here ever took place. But it did, even if things were never as simple as I suggest in the text.

23. Hueyapan is divided into five *barrios*, each one named after a different saint: San Miguel, San Jacinto, San Andrés, San Bartolo (Bartolomé), and San Felipe. Following local custom, I frequently refer to San Miguel and San Jacinto as the Centro and to the other three as the outlying *barrios*. The market is located in the Centro, as is Doña Zeferina's home.

24. Tetela del Volcán is the municipal seat and is located on the other side of the Amatzinac gorge, about 12 km away—if you take the roads built for vehicles, but much closer if you follow the old foot path, known as *el camino real*, that dates to colonial times.

25. After the elections of 2000, in both Mexico and the United States, this joke takes on a new ironic twist.

26. Doña Zeferina's green tomatoes are not red tomatoes waiting to ripen. They are a different variety entirely, immediately recognizable by the thin leaf-like

membrane that envelopes the little green fruit. In Mexican Spanish, red tomatoes are called *jitomates* and green tomatoes *tomates*. In the Caribbean, the Spanish term for *tomates* is *tomatillos*.

27. Incorporated into postconquest Nahuatl, *madiotzin* is the Nahuatl form of the traditional Spanish greeting, *adiós*. The suffix *tzin* signals respect. Frequently, villagers, particularly the young, use the Spanish form of the greeting.

28. White linen pants and a shirt that poor rural peasants traditionally wear, be they Indians or Mestizos. The term is usually translated as "pajamas."

29. A long black wool skirt secured at the waist by an elaborately woven red wool belt. This is the traditional Indian skirt worn by Indian women in the region.

30. Only children's urine is used for medicinal purposes, because the urine of adults, Doña Zeferina explains, has too many impurities.

31. The *temascal* is an adobe steam bath built in the shape of a miniature igloo (figure 2). It is usually located in a family's kitchen, or just outside. In Doña Zeferina's home, it is in the kitchen. Doña Juana takes charge of preparing the bath. First, she lights a fire in the little chamber (A) about two or three hours before the bathing process begins and places fresh hay on the floor of chamber B to provide a comfortable surface for reclining bathers. Taking a bath in Doña Zeferina's *temascal* means taking a bath with the old woman, who installs herself in chamber B with the first bather and does not leave until after everyone has finished, enduring the intense heat for about two hours. In addition to Doña Zeferina, the bathers usually include Maestra Angelina, Doña Juana, and Don José. Occasionally, Rosa and the other girls enter the steam bath as well.

The bathers take off their clothes in the bedroom and wrap themselves up in blankets. Around their heads they tie cotton rags. Returning to the kitchen, they crouch down before the *temascal* and back in on all fours. Once inside chamber B, they remove their blankets and lie down. It is just about wide enough to accommodate two adults and long enough for people no taller than five feet to stretch out completely. Before the bathing begins, Doña Zeferina rubs her body and the body of the other bather with *medicina*, a boiled solution of children's urine, tobacco, and alcohol. This mixture cuts the oils on the bathers' skin and is supposed to cure aches and pains. Next, another female member of the household, who is waiting her turn, hands the bathers a bucket of cold water. The same person helps Doña Zeferina close off the entrance to the chamber with a straw mat. Doña Zeferina then splashes cold water against the wall that connects chamber B with chamber A, creating a lot of steam. As the hot vapor fills the enclosed area, Doña Zeferina and the other bather beat themselves vigorously with young branches of the *cebolleja* bush. If the chamber gets too hot, Doña Zeferina opens the door slightly, to let the bathers rest in cooler air. She then repeats the process, throwing more cold water against the heated wall, etc. After three or four rounds, Doña Zeferina asks for a bucket of warm water perfumed with sprigs of rosemary and gives it to the other bather. Scrubbing herself down with small porous stones and a little bar of soap, the bather rinses herself off with this aromatic warm water. When she has finished, the bather asks for her blanket, dries herself off in the *temascal* and then, wrapped up once again, crawls out of the chamber. Doña Zeferina washes herself only after the final bather completes her ablutions.

Large *petates* are spread out on the kitchen floor in front of the *temascal* so that the bather might lie down for a few minutes before getting dressed and enjoying a cup of herbal tea, after which she excuses herself and goes straight to bed.

32. The Nahuatl for *cebolleja* is *tonalogotl.*
33. The village got electricity in the early 1960s. See chapter three.

Chapter Two   The History of Doña Zeferina and Her Family

I was invited to republish a shortened version of the biographical sketch for: *Creating Spaces, Shaping Transitions: Women of the Mexican Countryside, 1850–1990*, Ed. Heather Fowler-Salamani and Mary Kay Vaughn. In the introduction, I added the following:

> The story I tell is one I heard many times in the intimacy of Doña Zeferina's home, usually in the evening as we sat around the hearth in the *adobe* brick kitchen, eating *tortillas* and beans, and drinking herbal tea. The children and I loved to listen to the old woman reminisce about her life or tell one of the many fairy tales she had committed to memory from a published collection of stories a schoolteacher had loaned her when she was still a young girl, during the Mexican Revolution. Sometimes I taped Doña Zeferina while she talked, but only rarely, for she was self-conscious when the machine was on. What follows here has been pieced together from copious notes taken over the many months I spent with Doña Zeferina and her family. Our close relationship has given me the courage to risk writing the story of this Indian woman in my own words, mostly, relying only occasionally on hers for descriptions of the most dramatic events in her life.
>
> I believe that my version of Doña Zeferina's story comes very close to the way she would have told it herself. Before publishing the Spanish translation of *Being Indian in Hueyapan*, I returned to the village with the manuscript in hand and read to Doña Zeferina what I had written about her, giving her the opportunity to correct any errors I might have made and to endorse or reject my interpretation of her life. After I finished, she gave me her blessings, only to regret having done so the following year when I returned to the village with copies of the book: now everybody would know the full story, she complained—as if they did not already! Much to my relief, Doña Zeferina soon began to take pleasure in the fact that she had become a bit of a "star" with tourists and anthropologists, who, after reading about her experiences, wanted to meet her. Outsiders visiting Hueyapan looked up the woman whose stories had given them a glimpse into the life of one individual in Morelos during the Mexican Revolution and the turbulent years that followed.
>
> Historians, anthropologists, and others have been debating the value of collecting oral histories for many years. In the late 1960s, when I recorded

Doña Zeferina's life story, I already had serious reservations myself, but I decided to proceed for two main reasons:

First, I solemnly believed, and continue to believe, that anthropologists must accept the challenge of demonstrating how their theoretical arguments relate to the data they collect by the ethnographic method and to the "every-dayness" of what the anthropologist observes in the field. While I firmly rejected the idea that one could generalize from the experiences of a single individual and her family, I wanted the reader to meet a few people in Hueyapan, at least through my eyes, before I provided other forms of documentation to analyze the Indian question in Mexico.

My second reason was simple: Doña Zeferina had a wonderful story to tell. She gave texture, not information, to the world I wanted to describe. In thinking about the problem of writing life histories, Ruth Behar puts it beautifully, paraphrasing Walter Benjamin. With her words, I rest my case:

"Information," in Benjamin's analysis, is a mode of communication linked to the development of the printing press and of capitalism; it presents itself as verifiable, it is "shot through with explanation," and it is disposable because it is forgettable. Storytelling, on the other hand, is "always the art of repeating stories," without explanation, combining the extraordinary and the ordinary; most importantly, it is grounded in a community of listeners on whom the story makes a claim to be remembered by virtue of its "chaste compactness" which inspires the listener, in turn, to become the teller of the story. ("Rage and Redemption: Reading the Life Story of a Mexican Market Woman," 227.)

1. As I mention in chapter one (note 6), Doña Zeferina's grandson Arturo Vargas won a prize from CONACULTA (Consejo Nacional para la Cultura y Artes) in 1999 for his interpretation of this story. See chapter nine as well.
2. Originally, there were no official street names in Hueyapan. People gave names to their houses instead and used these names as addresses. The house Don Manuel built was known as Hueyapalcalco (the big house constructed out of planks of wood). The original plot of land included the lots that belong today to Juan Maya Cortés (on the west side of Doña Zeferina's property) and to Reyes Maya Cortés, Don Juan's brother (on the east side).
3. John Womack, *Zapata and the Mexican Revolution*, 35–36.
4. See my article, "Pacts with the Devil: Stories Told by an Indian Woman from Mexico," for translations and analyses of some of Doña Zeferina's favorite fairytales.
5. Doña Zeferina and almost everybody else in Hueyapan addressed me as Maestra in recognition of the fact that I taught English in the school and served occasionally as a substitute teacher. By the end of the year, Doña Zeferina was introducing me to people as her American daughter, but she would still, out of habit, call me, Maestra.
6. Fried pieces of pork and pork rind.
7. "Baldy," or "*pelón*" was one of the derogatory terms used for federal soldiers during the Mexican Revolution.

8. Tallarín was a nickname given to various rebel leaders during the Cristero Rebellion (Jean Meyer, pers. comm.).
9. Julia did not want to work. She found a man instead and began almost immediately to have a family. She and her common-law husband, a migrant worker from Guerrero, had four children in 1970 and lived in one of the worst slums of Cuernavaca, just off the railroad tracks.
10. Doña Zeferina died in 2001. See chapter nine for an update on the family.

Chapter Three   The History of Hueyapan

For more information on the history of Hueyapan, particularly on the agrarian economy, see S. López M., "Hueyapan: Un pueblo de la tierra fría," *Los campesinos de la tierra de Zapata*, vol. 1: *Adaptación, cambio y rebelión*, ed. L. Helguera R., S. López M., and R. Ramírez M, 15–100.

1. Fray Diego Durán, *Historia de las Indias de Nueva España e islas de la Tierra Firme*, vol. 2, 21.
2. According to Marcelino Montero Baeza, Hueyapan's resident doctor and self-appointed historian, the first people to settle in Hueyapan were the Xicalancas. When the Xochimilcas arrived, which Dr. Marcelino places between 700 and 900, they mixed peacefully with the native population and shared their more sophisticated agricultural techniques with them, showing the villagers how to cultivate vegetables unknown to them before. Then in 1503, the Aztecs took the area by force. Obliged to pay tribute to Moctezuma II, the people of Hueyapan wove cloth out of maguey fibers on the backstrap loom, which they handed over to local warlords to transmit to the Aztec emperor (unpublished text prepared in 2001 for the August 4th fiesta celebration of Santo Domingo, village patron saint). As I note in chapter four, I found archeological evidence in Hueyapan that suggests the villagers were spinning cotton as well to pay tribute, no doubt, to the Aztecs (note 27.)
3. Durán, *Historia de las Indias*, vol. 2, 573.
4. In his famous account of the conquest of New Spain, Bernal Díaz identifies María de Estrada as the only Castilian woman to accompany the Spanish conquerors. Unfortunately, María de Estrada does not appear in the popular translation of Bernal Díaz's account, prepared by J.M. Cohen. The relevant passage occurs at the end of the chapter in which Bernal Díaz describes the flight of the Spaniards from Tenochtitlán (*la noche triste*). I quote from the 1956 translation by Albert Idell:

> "I have forgotten to write how glad we were to see that our Doña Marina, Cortés' Indian mistress, was still alive, and Doña Luisa, the daughter of Xicotenga, who escaped at the bridges with the help of some Tlaxcalans, and a woman named María de Estrada, who was the only Castilian woman in Mexico." (*Bernal Díaz Chronicles*, 270)

5. Durán, *Historia de las Indias*, vol. 2, 573.
6. Carlos Martínez-Marín, *Tetela del Volcán*, 28.

7. Peter Gerhard, "El señorío de Ocuituco," 112. Entirely missing from my account of the history of Hueyapan during early colonial times is any discussion of the creation of "*la república de los indios*," established by the Spanish Crown to manage indigenous affairs. For an excellent description of the political division of New Spain into a Republic of Indians and a Republic of Spaniards, and the impact this division had on the construction of the Indian, see Claudio Lomnitz, *Exits from the Labyrinth: Culture and Ideology in the Mexican National Space*, 262ff. The *encomienda* and *corregimiento* systems as well as the Catholic Church, all functioned within the two republics. In the República de los indios, indigenous communities had certain privileges and their own governmental structure, comprised of an internal political hierarchy with specific officers assigned to represent the concerns of their constituencies to the Spaniards.

8. Peter Gerhard, "El señorío de Ocuituco," 112. The *encomienda* belonged to a private person who received a land grant from the government and who, in return, paid taxes to the king of Spain. The *corregimiento*, in contrast, belonged to the government and was supervised by an appointed official of the king.

9. Peter Gerhard (pers. comm.)

10. Unlike the *encomienda*, which was a gift from the Crown to the conquerors of New Spain, the *hacienda* was a private tract of land, purchased from the king or from the previous landowner. Thanks to research conducted in the late 1990s by Dr. Marcelino, we now know that the inhabitants of Hueyapan received a land grant from the Crown in 1615. In 1831, the new government of an independent Mexico acknowledged the existence of this land grant. Some of the land "stolen" from Hueyapan by the Santa Clara Hacienda, in the story I tell here, may have included fields bequeathed to the village in 1615.

11. Maribel Vargas did some more research in the spring of 2005 on the landgrab by the Santa Clara Hacienda. From what she was able to ascertain, the land was probably stolen during the Porfiriato period, in the late 1800s. This makes a good deal of sense, given how many people still knew about the event in the late 1960s. According to the information provided to me by Maribel, the Santa Clara Hacienda traditionally participated in the celebration of Hueyapan's patron saint's day (August 4th). The landowners provided the *pueblo* with alcoholic beverages, for which they expected to be paid. Since the villagers had no money, the *hacendados* suggested that they pay with land. According to one version of the story, the number of hectars was then determined by the trick described in chapter three. Another version describes the landowners proposing that they take only as much land as the length of a bull. The *hacendados* then butchered a bull in such a way that the sinews of the animal extended over many kilometers. In both versions, the villagers lost virtually all of their land.

12. The Cuilotepec Hacienda also gained control of land that technically belonged to Hueyapan. These *hacendados* grabbed the woods north of the village. By the second half of the nineteenth century, the Cuilotepec Hacienda was cutting down the thick forests and selling the lumber to the federal government to use for railway ties (Montero, pers. comm.). In those years, Mexico was in the process of building a railroad across Mexico.

13. Carlos Martínez-Marín, *Tetela del Volcán*, 64.
14. Ibid., 65.
15. According to Marcelino Montero's research, the bell tower was finished in 1784.
16. A village becomes "secularized" when the Catholic Church replaces the religious orders (e.g., Augustinians, Dominicans, Franciscans, and Jesuits) with members of the "regular" clergy.
17. Marcelino Montero reports the following: Hueyapan did not play much of a role in the War of Independence (1810–1820). The villagers, however, had to defend themselves against bandits who were taking advantage of the unstable political situation in the area during those years of chaos, stealing food and clothing from defenseless peasants. To protect themselves, the villagers abandoned their homes and ran into the hills surrounding the *pueblo*. Near the end of the war, an unidentified epidemic ravaged the *pueblo*, causing the death of at least 900 villagers. According to an official document of the period that Marcelino Montero has found, a man by name Rafael de Prada was sent to Hueyapan to determine why the villagers had stopped paying their taxes. On June 5, 1819, he described the devastation.
18. Don Facundo was born in 1880 and died in 1973.
19. The *Zapatistas* were primarily local peasants, whose uniforms consisted of *calzones* and leather-thong sandals, the traditional dress of the rural poor, Indian, and Mestizo alike. As a way to insult the Zapatistas, the Federales called them *indios*, and many believed, incorrectly, that Zapata himself spoke Nahuatl.
20. At that time, Don Facundo told me, he was fighting under General Porfirio Cázares, who was from Jumiltepec, Morelos. Although this general is not mentioned in John Womack's comprehensive study of the Mexican Revolution in Morelos, *Zapata and the Mexican Revolution*, when I consulted the author he confirmed the identity of the general and gave me his full name: Porfirio Cázares Anzures. See also: Gildardo Magña, *Emiliano Zapata y el Agrarismo en México*, vol. 2, 131.
21. Victoriano Huerta was one of Francisco Madero's generals, until he betrayed the first president of the Mexican Revolution and had him killed. In 1913, Huerta became president himself for a year, but he too was ousted a year later by Venustiano Carranza. During the early days of the Revolution, General Huerta staged a devastating military campaign against the peasants of Morelos.
22. At the time I was writing the book in the early 1970s, there was no biography of Poncho Villa comparable to John Womack's *Zapata and the Mexican Revolution*. There was, however, John Reed's wonderful journalistic account *Insurgent Mexico*. Then in 1998, Friedrich Katz published his long awaited masterpiece, *The Life and Times of Pancho Villa*.
23. It is probably safe to say that Indians did not take part in the fighting as much as Mestizos did. Marginalized economically and linguistically, they trusted nobody and often tried to remain neutral.
24. John Womack, *Zapata and the Mexican Revolution*, 310–311.
25. See Womack's *Zapata and the Mexican Revolution* for details on Ayaquica.
26. Tlaltizapan, Morelos was Zapata's main headquarters during most of the Revolution.

27. The villagers told me that two members of their community had signed the Plan de Ayala, Captain Apolinar Adorno and Lieutenant Cipriano Sandóval. There are multiple copies of this historic document and the list of signatures are not always the same. I have seen two copies, dated November 25 and 28, 1911, but there are more. Apolinar Adorno's name appears on the latter. See: Gildardo Magña, *Emiliano Zapata y el Agrarismo en México*, vol. 2, 131.

28. According to Dr. Marcelino, in 1922, the agrarian reform returned to Hueyapan the wooded communal lands that they had lost to the Cuilotepec *Hacienda*. In 1929, they received *ejido* lands. Although Dr. Marcelino does not identify the source, these *ejidos* may represent the land taken from them by the Santa Clara Hacienda.

29. There are 100-liter measures of corn to a *carga*.

30. The situation began changing dramatically in the 1980s, when men started leaving home once again in considerable numbers, this time to seek work in the United States. Since most of these migrants were illegal then and are still illegal, I do not have the exact figures. From what people tell me, however, there was probably not a single household left in Hueyapan at the time this book went to press, that did not have (or did not recently have) a member of the family working in the United States. Although women continue to leave the village as well, Hueyapan has become increasingly feminized over the last 20 years, as mothers remain behind to raise the children of absent men, who support their families long distance, over the telegraph wires, but who rarely return to spend time with their families. According to the 2000 census, there are 3,048 females and 2,833 males. These numbers do not fully report the situation, since absent men still claim Hueyapan as their place of residence. See Fuente XII Censo General de Población y Vivienda, 2000, Resultados por localidad, INEGI.

31. Only the avocados and *tejocotes* are indigenous to Mexico. Spanish priests introduced the other fruits to the village during colonial times.

32. In the late 1960s, there were only two buses a day from Cuautla to Hueyapan; one left at 5:40 AM, the second at 11:30 AM. The last bus from Hueyapan back to Cuautla departed at 3:30 PM. Once the roads were paved in the 1980s, bus service increased and other forms of transportation became available as well. In addition to regular bus service to Tlacotepec and Tetela, people can now take collective taxis as well.

As the roads got better, commerce increased and families began purchasing trucks, relying less on public transportation of any kind. In 1971, only seven or eight families in Hueyapan had trucks, and these few individuals transported most of the villagers' produce to Mexico City. By the 1980s, however, virtually every villager who was growing a cash crop had a truck of his own. In addition to the varieties of fruits mentioned in the text, by the 1980s, villagers in Tetela and Hueyapan had begun to diversify and were growing flowers and raspberries for international markets.

In an attempt to create economic incentives in rural areas and slow down the massive migration to cities, the Mexican government encouraged local entrepreneurs, giving them subsidies to open up small factories in the countryside. In the early 1980s, a few families pooled resources to create small knitting factories that made sweaters and shawls, and woodworking shops. Although the knitting never really took off, Hueyapan today has a certain reputation for its furniture, built from wood cut down from communal lands belonging to the village. Finally, with the hope of expanding commerical opportunities in the village, during the 1990s, the government contributed funds to help the village rebuild the bridge at the entrance of town that stretches over the Amatzinac gorge.

33. In the late 1980s, the village paved over the plaza and moved the market out of the center of town to a lot located on Calle Morelos on the far side (east side) of Don Reyes' corn mill. See figure 1 in chapter one.

34. In the first edition of the book, I suggested that more villagers in the Centro had running water in 1971 than was probably the case. According to Marcelino Montero, many villagers had to wait until 1985.

Chapter Four   What It Means to Be Indian in Hueyapan (1969–1970)

Although I did not acknowledge it at the time I was writing chapter four, my thinking was influenced by Jean-Paul Sartre's *Anti-Semite and Jew*. Sartre's work has had a lasting impact on me and I read it for the first time in college in the 1960s, about five years before I went to Mexico.

1. When I talk about the villagers' perception of their Indian identity, I am talking about a time over 30 years ago. I firmly believe that much of my argument still holds today, but the villagers described their Indianness differently in 1969–1970 from the way they do in the early years of the twenty-first century. The differences, however, are sadly predictable. Let me not get ahead of the story. In this chapter, I describe the situation as I saw it several decades ago. To remind the reader of that fact, I use the past tense in the text.

2. See, for example: Bartolomé de las Casas, *The Devastation of the Indies*; Shelbourne F. Cook and Woodrow Borah, *The Aboriginal Population of Central Mexico on the Eve of the Spanish Conquest* and *Essays in Population History: Mexico and the Caribbean*; Judith Friedlander, "Malaria and Demography in the Lowlands of Mexico," Eric Wolf, *Sons of the Shaking Earth*, 195. For more general works on the impact of diseases on indigenous populations during colonial conquests, see Jared Diamond, *Guns, Germs and Steel: The Fates of Human Societies* and William McNeill, *Plagues and Peoples*.

3. Calling an Indian "foolish" (*tonto*) slipped into American popular culture as well. Consider, for example, the name given to the sidekick of the Lone Ranger, an icon of the American Western, (Tonto)!

4. In the 1960s, Elvira Hernández went to Harvard University to work with a linguist who was studying contemporary dialects of Nahuatl. She then went again in the early 1970s, this time to Indiana University, to work in the same capacity. A devout evangelical Christian, Elvira has a beautiful voice and enjoys singing religious hymns that have been translated into Nahuatl by missionaries of her church (Iglesia Cristiana Universal).

5. In 1970, the Mexican census identified Indians as Mexicans who spoke an indigenous language. In the 2000 census, a person could identify him or herself as Indian without speaking an indigenous language.

6. In 1969–1970, there were very few televisions in the village, but many homes had radios, beds, tables, and chairs. Most everybody also wore store-bought clothing.

7. Those who left home, and took up residence in a city, could hide the fact that they came from Hueyapan. In 1970, a young woman from the village got a job selling fast food in a "picnic" stand at the Chapultepec station of the urban underground in Mexico City. When I went looking for her, I discovered that she had told her fellow workers that she came from Cuautla.

8. As noted in chapter three, according to the village's local historian, the correct answer today would have been the Xicalancas, descendants of the Olmecs (Marcelino Montero, pers. comm.).

9. Apaches were routinely disparaged in the popular expression: "*Ay Chihuahua tantos apaches sin huaraches*" (Ay Chihuahua, so many barefoot Apaches)—a more polite substitution for any number of profanities that begin with "*chinga*" (fuck).

10. All this will change. By 2000, people freely volunteered that Indians represented a different race.

11. By the early years of the new millennium, television sets were common place throughout the village, the way radios were in the late 1960s.

12. "Poor Indian," of course. There was no such thing, in their eyes, as a "rich Indian."

13. It is now the only part of town that has a secondary school.

14. Today, the bus stops in the San Andrés Barrio as well.

15. Ironically, this had changed by the end of the twentieth century, when government programs began singling out indigenous villages for special development programs and attractive loan opportunities, encouraging women in particular to start local businesses. All of a sudden, communities in Morelos that never considered themselves Indian and whose inhabitants had not spoken indigenous languages for decades were registering as Indians and applying for special grants from the Fondo Estatal para Mujeres Indígenas de Morelos.

16. My argument here has caused controversy. Where some saw resistance on the part of the Indians, I saw a successful strategy, first introduced in early colonial times, of incorporating a few indigenous traditions into the culture of a decidedly non-Indian Mexico, emptying these vestiges of their original meaning and giving them new signification, to borrow a term from the structuralists. Although I did not know his work at the time, what I saw in Hueyapan resembled what Roland Barthes brilliantly described in his essays on French colonialism in *Mythologiques*.

17. According to Marcelino Montero Baeza, most villagers over the age of 40 in 2001 still spoke Nahuatl. Those between 25 and 40 understood the language, but did not speak it well. Those under 25 hardly understood it and could only say a few words. According to the 2000 census, 37% of the villagers (1885 out of 4972), who are over five years old spoke Nahuatl (Fuente XII Censo General de Población y Vivienda, 2000, Resultados por Localidad).

The Morelos branch of INI has actively been encouraging people in Hueyapan to preserve their language. With the support of governmental agencies, Marcelino Montero and a few other villagers have promoted the idea as well. Since 1998, they have been giving classes in Nahuatl and trying to organize annual celebrations of Nahuatl and other indigenous languages on August 4, the fiesta day of Santo Domingo, the patron saint of Hueyapan (Marcelino Montero and Elivira Hernandez, pers. comm.).

18. Every student of Spanish knows about the influence Arabic has had on Spanish and learns to recognize the provenance of words like *alcázar* (castle) or *ojalá* (may it come to pass). What intrigued me here was the fact that by studying Nahuatl, a linguist might identify long forgotten Arabic terms that have dropped out of contemporary Spanish.

19. In an old Arabic-French dictionary, compiled by Belkacem Ben Sedira (Algiers: Collection Jules Carbonal, 1956), we find the following: *thumin* (vulg.), "*petite pièce de monnaie valant 0.25f.*" According to *The Hans Wehr Dictionary of Modern Arabic* (ed. by J.M. Cowan), *thumin* comes from the root *tham*, which means "to assess/to estimate." In mainstream dialects of Arabic, "thamin" means costly, precious, valuable. I am grateful to Marnia Lazreg (Professor of Sociology at Hunter College) for her help in tracking down the term. In Hueyapan, the word is pronounced "*tomin*," but in other dialects of Nahuatl, it is pronounced "*tumin.*" (J. Melquiades Ruvalcaba, *Manual de Gramática Náhuatl*, 40).

20. *Aguacate* means avocado.

21. Nahuatl was the language of the Aztecs and became the *lingua franca* during early colonial times. When the Spaniards needed an indigenous term to identify something they had never seen before, they invariably adopted the word from Nahuatl.

22. Today, in the early years of the twenty-first century, as rural migrants have fanned out over many parts of the United States, you can hear people speaking Nahuatl and other indigenous languages in the subways of New York, undoubtedly for the same reasons you hear it in Mexico City.

23. George Foster, *Culture and Conquest: America's Spanish Heritage*, 101–102.

24. The archeologist Michael Smith uses my photo of Epifania Alonso weaving on the backstrap loom to suggest that prehispanic traditions continue in the present: *The Aztecs*, 289.

25. Jacques Soustelle, *The Daily Life of the Aztecs*, 132.

26. Junius Bird and Gordon Eckholm (pers. comm.).

27. It is interesting to note that in Mexico today Mayan Indians use the Nahuatl term *huipil* to refer to the dress their women wear.

28. See Jacques Soustelle, *The Daily Life of the Aztecs*, 132–138 for a longer discussion of clothing in prehispanic Mexico. Also, see Charles Gibson, *The Aztecs Under Spanish Rule: A History of the Indians of the Valley of Mexico, 1519–1810*, 336ff and George Valliant, *The Aztecs of Mexico*. Descriptions here rely heavily on the work of these three scholars.

29. *Gabán* (overcoat), *bufanda* (scarf), *rebozo* (shawl) are all Spanish words. *Xincueite* (skirt), *huipil* (blouse), and *ixcactles* (sandals) are derived from the Nahuatl. When I asked the weaver Epifania Alonso to give me the Nahuatl

name for *bufanda*, she only had the Spanish term. Recently, however, Maribel Vargas learned the Nahuatl word for the wool scarf from a niece of Doña Epifania who continues to weave: *quechquemelolle*.

30. Soustelle, *The Daily Life of the Aztecs*, 27.
31. For more on cooking in Hueyapan, see my article "The Aesthetics of Oppression." For a more general treatment of the subject, see, John C. Super, *Food, Conquest and Colonization in 16th-century Spanish America.*
32. To cure a bad cough, Doña Zeferina also recommended the old European technique of "cupping," which involved rubbing the patient's chest with alcohol, then lighting the alcohol with a match and quickly placing a cup over the flame, creating a vacuum that would, in theory, draw out the cough. For "sissies" like me, she recommended "*un Vics*" (a Vick's Vapor Rub).

    Since the late 1990s, "rustic" healing has had somewhat of a comeback. Influenced by tourism and government agencies, several women now sell indigenous creams for a variety of aches and pains that they produce in the village by mixing locally grown herbs and vaseline.
33. In sixteenth-century Europe and Mexico, people believed that shadows caused illness.
34. By 1969–1970, several hundred villagers had converted to one of several evangelical Protestant sects. In 2000, the census reported that 15% of the population no longer identified themselves as Catholic. Most of these residents probably belonged to evangelical churches (Fuente XII Censo General de Población y Vivienda 2000, Resultados por Localidad, INEGI).
35. Miguel Barrios, "Textos de Hueyapan, Morelos," 64–69.
36. Scholarship focused on the origins of the *mayordomo* system and the civil-religious hierarchy in Central America has created a great deal of controversy over the years. At the time I was writing *Being Indian in Hueyapan*, many anthropologists firmly maintained the prehispanic origins of the system. I did not. See my article "The Secularization of the Civil-Religious Hierarchy."
37. Describing the *chirimía* exactly as I experienced it, Luis Weckman observes that it is "a sort of rustic oboe with an intense, monotonous sound." *The Medieval Heritage of Mexico*, 551. The Mexican *chirimía* is a descendant of the Renaissance wind instrument, belonging to the oboe family, known in English as the shawm (*chaume* or *chalemie* in old French).

Chapter Five   Religion in Hueyapan

In the first section of this chapter, I add material that appeared in two of my articles published after 1975: "The Secularization of the Civil-Religious Hierarchy," and "Pacts with the Devil." The expanded section on the Moors and the Christians is based on research conducted specifically for this edition of the book.

1. As I reported in chapter four (note 34), according to the 2000 census, 15% of the population (769 people) over five years of age, claim to belong to a religion

other than Catholicism or claim no religion at all. Most of these people are probably evangelical Christians.

2. Carlos Martínez-Marín, *Tetela del Volcán*, 64.
3. Francisco del Paso y Troncoso, "Relación de Tetela y Ueyapan," 289.
4. Eugène Boban, *Documents pour servir à l'histoire du Mexique*, vol. 1, Plate No. 25.
5. Paso y Troncoso, *Papeles de Nueva España*, 284.
6. Unless otherwise noted, the description that follows draws heavily on the more complete French edition of Robert Ricard's classic work, *La Conquête Spirituelle du Mexique*, a study that remains invaluable to the present day. For the new edition of *Being Indian of Hueyapan*, I have also relied on D.A. Brading's *Mexican Phoenix: Our Lady of Guadalupe*, Jacques Lafaye, *Quetzalcoatl et Guadalupe*, Luis Weckmann, *The Medieval Heritage of Mexico*.
7. Robert Ricard, *La Conquête*, 338. I am also grateful to the late Victor Turner for having encouraged me to study the distribution in Mexico of the colonial settlements of the different monastic orders. More often than not, wherever the Dominicans built monasteries in the sixteenth century, we find dense concentrations of Indians today—most dramatically in Chiapas and Oaxaca, but also in villages, such as Hueyapan and Tepoztlán, in the state of Morelos.
8. For further details, see my article "The Secularization of the Cargo System: An Example from Postrevolutionary Mexico."
9. This pattern was practiced by Christians in Europe as they conquered and converted pagans across the continent, long before they came to the New World. The model was developed in 601 AD to train Roman missionaries setting out to convert the peoples of Britain. For an excellent description of these early methods of conversion, see The Venerable Bede, *History of the English Church and People*, 86–87; and Charles Gibson, *Spain in America*, 72–73.
10. Charles Gibson, "The Transformation of the Indian Community in New Spain, 1500–1810," 585 and *Spain in America*, 72–73; also Robert Ricard, *La Conquête*, 221.
11. Jacques Lafaye, *Quetzalcoatl et Guadalupe*, 287.
12. Ibid.
13. In addition to D.A. Brading and Jacques Lafaye, whose work I have already cited, see Eric Wolf's much earlier, pioneering article, "Virgin of Guadalupe: A Mexican National Symbol."
14. According to Maribel Vargas, the custom of dressing *de indito* has still not caught on.
15. *The Song of Fierabras* and *The Song of Roland* are part of a collection of medieval epics known as the Carolingian cycle. They both describe battles that took place in the last quarter of the eighth century AD, during the reign of Charlemagne. The more famous of the two describes the death of Roland at the hands of the Saracens (Moslems living in Spain). Roland was the Duke of Marches and Charlemagne's nephew. Although the plot revolves around a historic conflict between Christians and Moslems in the eighth century, the subject struck a contemporary chord during the time of the Crusades, when Christian Europe declared war on the Moslems. In 1095, Pope Urban II called upon Christians to rise up and free Palestine from the Moslems who were accused of desecrating

the Holy Land. Between 1096 and 1270, Europe's Christians conducted eight Crusades, murdering Jews and Moslems in Europe and the Middle East. *The Song of Roland* was written in the eleventh century, and the lesser known *Song of Fierabras* in the twelfth. The final Crusade—and inquisition—occurred in Spain in 1492, the same year that Columbus "discovered" America.

16. Ricard, *La Conquête*, 227–229.

17. Ibid., 224–225.

18. In 1970, I paid 1,000 *pesos* ($80.00) for the manuscript.

19. There are many versions of The Moors and the Christians and of other Dances of Conquest, some of which abandon medieval European themes and describe wars of conquest in the New World. There is also a sizable scholarly literature on the subject. Nobody to my knowledge, however, has yet done the kind of close reading of various versions of the text that I begin to do here. For excellent studies, see, for example (listed in chronological order): Luis Chávez-Orozco, "El Romance en México" (1930); Robert Ricard, "Contribution à l'étude des fêtes de moros y cristianos au Mexique" (1932); Arturo Warman Gryj, *La Danza de Moros y Cristianos, un estudio de aculturación* (1968); Matilde Montoya, *Estudio sobre el baile de la conquista* (1970); Fernando Horcasitas, *El Teatro náhuatl— épocas novohispánica y moderna* (1974); Gisela Beutler, "Algunas observaciones sobre los textos de Moros y Cristianos en México y Centroamérica"; Luis Weckmann, *The Medieval Heritage of México* (1992); Mery Blunno, Luis Miguel Morayta Mendoza, Ed., *Los doce pares de Francia, Historia para teatro campesino en tres noches* (1994).

20. When we compare the San Juan Amecac version to the twelfth-century epic, the overlap is striking. In both versions, we find Charlemagne and the following vassals: Roland (Roldán in Spanish), Naimon (Naymes), Olivier (Oliveros), the Duke of Burgandy (Borgoña), etc. Faithful to the anachronisms found in the original and in the sixteenth-century translation, the San Juan Amecac version introduces Richard the Lionheart (Ricarte), who was an historic hero at the time the twelfth-century epic was written, but not in the days of Charlemagne. In the Spanish translation of the French epic, chapter 48 is entitled, "Como Ricarte de Normandia llego al Exercito de Carlo Magno" (see full reference for editions of the Piamonte translation in bibliography).

On the side of the Moors, the text is also faithful to the original. The king of the Moors, Emir Balán, becomes Almirante Balán (*Emir* means commander in Arabic and was translated into Spanish as Admiral). The king has two children, a son Fierabras, who is known in the original French and later Spanish translations as a giant from Alexandria and a daughter Floripes. In all versions, Floripes converts to Christianity and marries the Duke of Burgandy. Fierabras, however, is diminished in the San Juan Amecac version and is no longer all-powerful. As for Balán, he becomes a more poignant symbol of Christian sacrifice in the Mexican version than he is in the European renditions. A popular figure in medieval folklore, Fierabas was

the greatest giant that ever walked the earth. For height of stature, breadth of shoulder and hardness of muscle he never had an equal. He possessed all Babylon, even to the Red Sea; was Seigneur of Russia, Lord of Cologne,

Master of Jerusalem and even of the Holy Sepulchre. He carried away the crown of thorns and the balsam which embalmed the body of Our Lord, one drop of which would cure any sickness or heal any wound in a moment. One of his chief exploits was to slay the fearful huge giant that guarded the bridge Mantible. His pride was laid low by Olivier, one of Charlemagne's paladins. The giant then became a child of God and ended his days in the odour of sanctity; meek as a lamb, and humble as a chidden slave. Sir Fierabras figures in several medieval romances and is an allegory of Sin overcome by the Cross. (E. Cobban Brewer, LLI, *The Dictionary of Phrase and Fable*, 458)

The Song of Fierabras was translated into Spanish in a prose version by Nicolás de Piamante in 1525 and the character himself figures in the works of two major Spanish writers in the seventeenth century: Cervantes' novel *Don Quixote de la Mancha* (completed in 1615) and Calderón de la Barca's play, *La Puente de Mantible* (1630).

21. A reference, no doubt, to the fact that the Moslems had conquered Constantinople in 1453, presenting a new threat to the Christian world, just 40 years before the Spanish expelled the Moors from Spain and "discovered" America.

22. We know from *The Song of Roland* that Olivier is Roland's close companion and friend.

23. The Philippines were a Spanish colony from 1527 until 1896, at which time the Filipinos rose up and rebelled. Two years later, the United States won the Spanish-American War and took control of the islands. Still too weak to defend themselves against colonial powers, the Philippines became a protectorate of the United States. I have yet to determine when the Filipinos were added to this and perhaps other Spanish versions of the twelfth-century French epic.

24. Clearly, this is a later addition to the text. Don Estanislao said his family inherited the script in 1845, but Alexander Graham Bell only invented the telephone in 1876. When I saw the play performed in Hueyapan, there was still not a single phone in the village or in San Juan Amecac.

25. The Bridge of Mantible exists in all the versions of the epic and, is, as I have already noted, the title of a play by Calderón de la Barca.

26. Trying to be as dismissive as possible, Don Delfino likened Protestants in Hueyapan to the Aztecs and Moors, adding insult to injury by referring to them disdainfully as "*los hermanos*" (brothers), the term of greeting evangelical Protestants used among themselves. Nothing could offend a villager more than to associate him or her with the Aztecs and Moors.

27. I am grateful to French medieval scholars Evelyn Birge Vitz and Francesca Sautman and Spanish medieval scholar Marithelma Costa for guiding me to the texts in the original French and the translations/interpretations in Spanish, beginning in the sixteenth century. There are still many questions left unanswered, in particular about the curious ending of the San Juan Amecac version of the play. I hope to continue doing research on the fascinating history of the play, from its original twelfth-century version to its contemporary form. Let me share what I have found so far about the changes taking place over the centuries in the critical baptismal scene.

The story of Balán's apparent willingness at first to convert to Christianity and then his sudden change of heart dates back to the twelfth-century French epic. In the original, however, his last minute reversal has nothing to do with a priest's cruel demand that he renounce his soldiers, as it does in the San Juan Amecac version. Balán simply gets angry and refuses to abandon "Mahomet." Defying the Christians, he spits into the baptismal font. As I have already noted, the epic was translated into Spanish by Nicolás de Piamonte in 1525. I have studied an eighteenth-century copy of that original translation: *Historia del Emperador Carlo Magno en la qual se trata de las grandes proefas, y hazañas de los Doze Pares de Francia: y de como fueron vendidos por el traydor de Ganalon, y de la cruda batalla que huvo Oliveros, con Fierabras, Rey de Alexandria, hijo del Almirante Balàn* (Barcelona: 1732). The relevant scene occurs in Chapter LVII, which is entitled, "Como el Almirante por ruegos, ni por amenazas nunca quiso ser Christiano y como Floripes fuè bautizada, y casada con Gui de Borgoña, y fueron coronados Reyes de toda aquella tierra." In the previous chapter, Almirante almost dies at the hands of the Christians, as he does in the San Juan Amecac version, but in this earlier version, he does not have the privilege of testing his prowess against Charlemagne alone. Here, he fights the regular soldiers who, instead of killing Balán on the spot, take Almirante prisoner and deliver him to Charlemagne. The emperor receives the Moor kindly, and tries to persuade him to convert to Christianity. Almirante refuses. Then, Fierabras appears, goes down on his knees, and tries to convince his father to listen to reason. At first, it seems that Fierabras has succeeded in persuading Balán: Almirante, we are told, does not want to die. But during the ceremony, the Moor changes his mind as he did in the original French epic, attacks the priest violently and defies the church with the same sacriligious gesture of spitting into the baptismal font (I have faithfully copied the text, spelling errors and all):

> Y el Almirante huvo miedo de morir, y dixo que le plazia: y Carlo Magno, y todos sus Cavalleros, huvieron gran plazer dello, y fueron aparejadas las cosas para ello necessarias, y muy cumplidamente, y con mucha honra. Y estando el Almirante cabe la pila donde avia de ser bautizado, le dixo un Arçobispo: Sr. Almirante, negays de puro coraçon todos vuestros Idolos, que tanto tiempo vos han traìdo engañando, y creys en nuestro Redemptor Iesu-Christo, el qual naciò de la Virgen Santa Maria Señora nuestra, siendo Virgen antes del parto, y en el parto y despues del parto? Entonces el Almirante Balàn temblando como azogado de grande enojo, y la cara encendida, como desesperado dixo, que no: y escupiò en la pila en menospreciò del Santo Bautsimo, y alço la mono, y diò al Arçobispo en la cara, y le hizo saltàr la sangre por la boca, y por las narizes; y le tomò por los cabellos, y le ahogára en la pila, sino se lo quitàran, y desto fueron todos maravillados; y si no fuera por Fierabràs le matàran subitamente. Viendo esto el Emperador Carlo Magno, mandò llàmar à Fierabràs, y dixo: Fierabràs, bien visteys lo que hizo vuestro padre, y no fuè tan liviano, su yerro, que no mereciesse cruel muerte por ello, mas por vuestro amor, no se le ha hecho mal alguno. (175–176)

Fierabras tries again to persuade his father to convert but does not succeed. Finally, Floripes tells Charlemagne that he is wasting his time. Her father will never convert. They should give up and get on with it. Charlemagne listens to Floripes and has the Moor killed.

In the *romance* version composed by Juan José López in the eighteenth century, the story evolves little. Balán remains brutal and obstinate.

The *romance* is divided into eight sections or *relaciones*, taking the Carolingian epic up through the death of Roland at Ronceveaux ("al campo de Ronce Valles"). The sixth *relación* is entitled "en que prosiguen los valerosos hechos de Fierabras y Carlo Magno, para ganar la puente Mantible." In this section, we find the same story of Balán first agreeing and then refusing to convert to Christianity. The scene is brutal. Balán violently hits the archbishop during the baptismal ceremony, but he does not spit into the baptismal font. (The following text comes from an undated manuscript preserved at the Hispanic Society of America that has been attributed to Juan José López, entitled *Historia de Oliveros, Fierabras y Carlomagno* (I have faithfully copied the text, spelling errors and all):

> Vino a la noche Floripes,
> y Fierabras con muy tiernos
> suspiros le suplicaban,
> que cree en Dios eterno,
> y el traidor de Almirante
> los engaño, asi diciendo:
> que queria ser cristiano;
> y quedararon muy contentos,
> y á otro dia de mañana,
> prevenidos los peltrechos,
> á la Iglesia lo llevaron
> entre muchos caballeros.
> Vino el Señor Arzobispo,
> dandole buenos consejos;
> y en fado de escucharlo,
> levantó el brazo soberbio,
> y á el Arzobispo en la cara
> le dió un bofeton tan recio,
> que le ha bañada en sangre,
> y lo asió por los cabellos
> para meterlo en la pila
> y Fierabras viendo esto,
> llegó, y le dijo á su padre
> con muy doloridos ecos,
> dulce padre de mi vida,
> deja esos ídolos fieros,
> recibe el Santo Bautismo,
> y tendrás parte en el cielo.
> Respondió muy enojado:
> en valde es cansaros, necio,

que mas quería morir,
que no olvidar los preceptos
de su profeta Mahoma,
que son muy santos y buenos
pero viendo Fierabras,
que se hallaba tan protervo,
mandó luego á los peones,
que al campo lo saquen fieros,
y allí le diesen la muerte,
pues que no tiene remedio (3, col. 2 and 4, col.1).

Here, finally, is the baptismal scence in the San Juan Amecac text that offers a more sympathetic portrait of the Moor than does the Piamonte translation or López *romance*. Unlike the European versions, the Moor is prepared to renounce his religion and land, but when asked to renounce his soldiers, he draws the line. He remains faithful to the men who gave their lives for him. Although he threatens to cut the priest up into little pieces, the Moor lets the "*capellán*" (chaplain) escape. In the other versions, Balán lashes out before giving the priest the chance to get away. As students of Spanish will note, the San Juan Amecac text has loosely preserved the style of the Juan José López version. Again, I have faithfully copied the text, spelling errors and all. The only editorial changes I have made are in the use of question marks:

CAPELLAN:
Oh muy digno carlo magno
he venido en el momento
Cual es el turco que dices
que desea el sacramento
CARLOS:
Señor: el rey almirante
aqui lo teneis delante
de su ley ya renuncio
quiere resibir la fe
el poderoso almirante
ya el bautismo lo pido
Conque ya se convencio
CAPELLAN:
Almirante rey de turquia
¿Como estas como te va?
¿quieres resibir la fe?
y del corazon te renacio ya
ya te nace el ser Cristiano
¿con toda tu voluntad
vas a renunciar las pompas del ynfernal Zatanas?
ALMIRANTE:
voy a renunciar muy pronto
muy pronto renunciare

CAPELLAN:
Pues quiero que tu me digas
que si crees en esta cruz
en donde murio el salvador
Nuestro Cordero Jesus
ALMIRANTE:
Sí Creo
CAPELLAN:
¿Crees que jesucristo
rezibio muerte y
pacion por salvar alos hombres pecadores?
ALMIRANTE:
Sí Creo
CAPELLAN:
¿Crees en la encarnacion
ylas tres divinas personas?
ALMIRANTE
Sí Creo
CAPELLAN:
¿Crees en los misterios santos
que resa la religion
El que pide Misericordia
Encuentra su Salvacion?
ALMIRANTE:
Sí Creo
CAPELLAN:
Pues dime si ya renunicas
Del ynfernal Zatanas
ALMIRANTE:
Renuncio de Zatanas
que el me tenia engañado
y por eso gran señor
yo lo tengo detestado
CAPELLON:
¿Ya renuncias de tus siestas ?
el que vivias engañodo?
ALMIRANTE:
Ya he renunciado mil veces
y Mil Veces renunciaré
CAPELLAN:
¿Qué Renuncies de la espada
Lo primero que has de hacer?
ALMIRANTE:
De la espada ya renuncio
Hoy mil pedasos lo hare.

¿Para qué quiero la espada
si Cristiano moriré?
CAPELLAN:
¿Ya rrenuncias de alcoran
al que tanto tu querias?
ALMIRANTE:
Sí de alcorán yo rrenuncio
no lo quisiera ni Ver
Ese alcoran fue un traidor
No me supo defender
CAPELLAN:
¿Renuncias de tu corona
Por ser corona africana
para que tu alma se salve
y adores la fe cristiana?
ALMIRANTE:
La corona me la quito
¿pero mi palabra qué ago?
Prometi por mi corona
el morir por mis soldados
CAPELLAN:
Ah tambien de tus soldados
Renuncias estan condenados
ALMIRANTE:
Que rrenuncio de mis soldados
mas que nunca me bautize
Eso sino lo hede hacer
con qué ellos por mi murieron
y yo hede rretroceder
yo me promiti Vengar
la Sangre de mis soldados
y esto lo hede ejecutar
aunqué sea despedasado
diran qué se me ha olvidado
ver ami jente tirada
a ellos les di mi palabra
y todo el publico lo oyo
me diran qué no es honor
que soy Rey y no lo cumplo
que ya con nada me asusto
cierto es que los que muerieron
todos de mi nada oyeron
pero el publico lo hoyo
y no bautizo no
mejor quitame la vida
que diria mi comitiva

si de la tumba se levantaran
me dijeran Almirante
¿adonde esta tu palabra?
¿adonde esta lo prometido?
¿donde esta tu adverza suerte
no nos dijistes amigo
decias qué tu por nosotros
rrecibirias fiera muerte?
¿qué rrespondería à todos?
¿qué Caracter qué Verguenza?
morir es mi rrecompensa
Renuncie de africa toda
de la espada y la corona
Pero de mis soldados
retirate sacerdote
hántes que te haga pedasos (260–262 of unpublished manuscript)

28. Maybe as many as five families owned television sets in 1969. I only knew of two households. Even fewer of them had gas stoves.
29. Protestants only participated as godparents in secular ceremonies like school graduations.
30. By the 1990s, Protestants had a strong enough following in Hueyapan for one evangelical group to establish a foothold in the Centro. The Israëlitas have recently built a church in the San Miguel Barrio on Calle Morelos, across the street from Doña Zeferina's home.
31. Miguel Barrios, "Textos de Hueyapan, Morelos," 53–75.

Chapter Six The Role of the State in Postrevolutionary Mexico: A New Period of "Evangelization" in Hueyapan

The original title of this chapter was, "Postrevolutionary Agencies: A New Period of Evangelization in Hueyapan."

1. The historical background provided here on the Cultural Missions came from a pamphlet distributed by the Department of Cultural Missions in 1970.
2. In other parts of Mexico, INI centers performed the same functions. As I discuss in chapter nine, by the mid-1970s, the number of INI centers had increased and taken over many of these functions. Then, when Fox became president, Congress absorbed INI into a new Commission to address issues of development in indigenous areas (see chapter nine).
3. In the historical fact sheet about Hueyapan that he prepared for the village in the early years of the new millennium, Marcelino Montero Baeza notes bitterly that the Cultural Missions sent schoolteachers to the *pueblo* who did not speak Nahuatl and who aggressively did away with the bilingual system of instruction that he claimed was still in place at the time. Dr. Marcelino may have been speaking about a program introduced by "cultural extremists" that existed briefly in the 1950s and that I describe in chapter seven.

4. The problem of confusing the Cultural Missions with religious sects was widespread. When I visited the Mexico City office of the Cultural Missions, one of the first things they told me was that they had nothing to do with any religion.

5. By the 1980s, a group of men from the San Andrés Barrio had a small furniture factory that produced handsome, rustic-looking pieces. The furniture was very popular among the more affluent members of the community, particularly with those, like Maribel Vargas, who had moved away and wanted to carry a bit of Hueyapan with them. The artisans used wood from the surrounding area, cutting down trees on the village's communal land.

6. The *hibachi* soon gave way to the gas range. As I explain in chapter one (note 1), by the 1980s, many families had gas ranges and refrigerators as well.

7. That said, there have been other attempts to modernize the technology and produce cheaper goods that are woven with store-bought wool. As I mention in chapter three (note 36), in the early 1980s, a few villagers created a small knitting factory as well to produce sweaters on machines. Once again, the project failed.

8. By the 1980s, Hueyapan had a regular doctor assigned to the village, diminishing the role of Doña Modesta and other healers in the village (see chapter nine for an update on Doña Modesta). As this new edition goes to press, Marcelino Montero Baeza is the current doctor and he doubles as the village's local historian. A native of the *pueblo*, Dr. Marcelino is one of the most active members of a new cultural revival group in Hueyapan (Grupo Cultural Náhuatl).

9. Pablo Castellanos, *Horizontes de la música precortesiana*, 83.

10. Although *tamales* are indigenous—at least the plain *tamales* and probably the bean—they are prepared on fiesta days and all fiestas (including birthdays and weddings) are sponsored either by the Church or the State.

11. Miguel Barrios, "Textos de Hueyapan, Morelos," 53–75.

12. Although Maestro Cecilio did not explain it in any detail, the pranksters, dressed up in "funny" red costumes, portrayed the wicked Jews who were supposed to be the enemies of Jesus. Jews also accompanied Jesus to his death during the dramatic procession of the Crucifixion on Good Friday.

13. In the 1980s, Maestro Rafael produced a historical/ethnographic essay about Hueyapan, basing much of the text, without attribution, on passages taken word-for-word from the Spanish translation of *Being Indian in Hueyapan*. Amused by the irony of the situation, I never questioned Maestro Rafael about what he had done. By the late 1990s, Dr. Marcelino had established his own team of researchers and was producing studies that went beyond the research I had done for my book. Both of these ethnohistorical works present the village's Indian identity in a positive light, reflecting the changes in discourse that have taken place on the Indian question in recent years. See chapter nine.

14. For an excellent analysis of the role Justo Sierra played during the dictatorship of Porfirio Diaz, see Josefina Vázquez de Knauth, *Nacionalismo y educación en México*, 81ff.

15. Ibid., 133.

16. Finally, in the mid-1980s, the villagers decided to fix up the plaza, turning it into a *zócalo* once again.

17. When I first came to Hueyapan, only the school in the Centro went up to the sixth grade. Then, in the 1980s, the Centro opened up its own secondary school as well.

18. In 1959, the Mexican government established La Comisión Nacional de los Libros de Textos Gratuitos de Educación Pública and in 1960, the Comisión produced a set of textbooks for all six grades of primary school. In 1969–1970, Hueyapan's school was still using the 1960 edition. My descriptions and occasional quotes come from this edition. In 1973, a new set of textbooks replaced the ones that were being used when I lived in Hueyapan, and they corrected many of the objectionable features I describe here. The new series made a special effort to strike a balance between urban and rural Mexico, presenting the countryside in a more favorable light than the previous textbooks did.

19. It is interesting to note that in the late 1960s/early 1970s, the TV had not yet made its appearance in the textbooks distributed by the national school system.

20. The Tlaxcalans and Cholulans tried at first to defend themselves against the Spaniards. After losing many warriors, they joined the conquerors and helped them defeat the Aztecs. According to Bernal Díaz, Cortés' mistress and translator was an Indian princess whose father had died when she was a child and whose mother and new husband sold the little girl into slavery. By the time the Spanish arrived, she was fully grown and was presented to Cortés as a peace offering. Gifted in languages, she quickly learned Spanish and became the conqueror's interpreter. See Bernal Díaz, J. M. Cohen trans:, *The Conquest of New Spain*, 85–87.

21. That, of course, changed after 1994 when Subcomandante Marcos and the EZLN turned Zapata into a major national hero. Since then, one hears a great deal more about the importance of April 10, 1919 in the history of Mexico.

22. I have borrowed the idea of the "deep myth of culture" from Victor Turner, *Dramas, Fields and Metaphors*, 122ff.

23. According to Maribel Vargas, even today, in the early years of the twenty-first century, schoolteachers still ignore the role played by the villagers themselves in the struggle for land and liberty. She would be surprised to hear that the names of the villagers who signed the Plan de Ayala (Captain Apolinar Adorno and Cipriano Sandóval) were ever mentioned in school-sponsored celebrations. See: chapter three, note 27.

24. In 1975, Rivera Crespo made good use of Hueyapan's indigenous credentials when the UN chose Mexico City as the site for holding its first international conference on the status of women. See chapter nine.

25. According to Classical Nahuatl scholars, "Nonantzin" was composed after the Spanish conquest and could not, therefore, have been written by Netzahualcoyotl, who died nearly a hundred years before the fall of Tenochtitlán. Although there is no evidence to support it, many people continue to consider Netzahualcoyotl the author of the poem. Over the years, "Nonantzin" has been translated into modern dialects of Nahuatl throughout Morelos and, no doubt, throughout other states as well. See Birgitta, Leander, *La poesía náhuatl: Función y carácter*, 50.

Chapter Seven   Cultural Extremists

1. Josefina Vázquez de Knauth, *Nacionalismo y educación en México*, 219.
2. Ibid. The debate about Cuauhtémoc's remains was still a hot issue in 1969–1970, and was the subject of an article in the English language newspaper, *The News*, Mexico City, May 8, 1970.
3. Alfonso Caso, quoted in S. Moiron A., "Indigenismo de escaparte," *El Día*, Mexico City, December 2, 1969, 9.
4. Ibid.
5. Gonzalo Aguirre Beltrán, "Indigenismo y Mestizaje," 44.
6. A good example of this is the Caste War in the Yucatán that took place in the middle of the nineteenth century. See Nelson Reed, *The Caste War of Yucatán*. There were, of course, many Indian uprisings in the early colonial period, and occasional uprisings later on, but the later ones usually involved non-Indians in significant ways, like the one in the Yucatan and the most recent uprising in Chiapas (1994).
7. In recent years, the ideas, once identified exclusively with cultural extremists, have made their way into the ideologies of a number of different groups, ranging from indigenous rights activists to members of INI. See chapter nine.
8. Frank Tannenbaum, "Agrarismo, indianismo y nacionalismo," 420–421.
9. By the 1990s, the center of gravity had switched back to Maya-speaking regions of Mexico, like Chiapas, and to Oaxaca, where there are large concentrations of speakers of Zapotec and Mixtec.
10. Although I did not think of it then, Juan Luna Cárdenas sounds a great deal like Don Ramón Carrasco in D.H. Lawrence's *The Plumed Serpent*. The novel was published in English in 1926 and came out in Spanish translation in 1940 (*La Serpiente emplumada*). It would not surprise me to learn that Juan Luna Cárdenas had read *La Serpiente emplumada* or that D.H. Lawrence had met the likes of Juan Luna Cárdenas.
11. See María del Carmen Nieva's *Mexikayotl*, the book published by Rodolfo Nieva's sister. The volume includes a photo of Lic. Rodolfo with Eulalia Guzmán and another one with Miguel Alemán, who was president of Mexico from 1946–1952. The caption accompanying the first photo identifies Eulalia Guzmán the "notable investigator of anthropology," congratulating Lic. Rodolfo on his work. The caption accompanying the second announces that Lic. Rodolfo has just made Miguel Alemán an honorary member of the Movimiento.
12. "Nahuatl Language Gaining in Mexico," *The New York Times*, June 14, 1964. The Movimiento used the name *Izkalotl* for their newspaper as well.
13. In addition to Cuauhtémoc, the group counted among its members one Tlacaelel, one Tetlazohtlani, one Kuamatzin, and one Xochitl. Xochitl was the name of the daughter of Maestra María del Carmen's maid. The others were adult men: Tlacaelel was a small-time entrepreneur (he owned a factory); Tetlazohtlani wrote for the Movimiento's newspaper; and Kuamatzin was a schoolteacher. After the Mexican Revolution, it became fashionable in middle-class circles to give children Nahuatl names. President Cárdenas, for example, named a son

Cuauhtémoc. In the late 1980s, Cuauhtémoc Cárdenas broke away from the PRI and founded a new political party, the PRD (Partido Revolucionario Democrático) in an effort to end the hegemony of the one-party system.

14. María del Carmen Nieva, *Mexikayotl*, 35–36.

15. Maestra María del Carmen explained to me that Nahuatl place names still exist in areas well beyond the borders of present-day Mexico. Nicaragua, for example, means "near the water," and Michigan means "where there are fish" (pers. comm.).

16. *Teotl* means god in Nahuatl. For further discussion of the Maya epoch, see María del Carmen Nieva, 37–38.

17. Ibid., 148.

18. Ibid.

19. Ibid., 71.

20. Ibid., 22–23. María del Carmen Nieva does not provide the reader with any references to confirm her assertion that there was a ruler of Anauak who stood above the emperor Moctezuma.

21. Ibid., 148–149.

22. The quotes come from three issues of the Movimiento's newspaper *Izkalotl* (Mexico City): December 1968, March, 1969, December 1969.

23. *Gachupín* is the Spanish rendition of the Nahuatl word *catzopin*; *cac* means sandal or shoe and *tzopin* means, in this context, to kick. Nahuatl-speaking Indians called the Spanish *catzopin*, because they kicked the Indians with the spurs of their boots.

24. A great deal has been written about the custom of identifying Malinche as the quintessential symbol of a Mexican traitor. Perhaps, the most famous essay on the subject is by Octavio Paz, published in his frequently cited collection of writings on Mexico, *The Labyrinth of Solitude*, 65–88. In defense of Malinche, feminists have recently made her the symbol of the oppression of women in Mexico. Both Mexican and Chicana feminists have criticized their men for having turned the tragedy of an enslaved Indian princess into the story of a traitor. The name Malinche is the corrupted form of the Nahuatl Malintzin, which in turn is the Nahuatl pronunciation in the reverential form of the baptized name Marina— the Aztecs could not pronounce "r," so "Marina" became "Malina" and "Malina" became "Malintzin" in the reverential form. As Angel María Garibay reports, some people believe that the name Malinche has Nahuatl, not Spanish, roots and comes from Malinalli, which means "from where the king comes." But this is less likely, because the reverential form of Malinalli would have been Malinaltzin, not Malintzin. See: Angel María Garibay, *Llave del Náhuatl*, 305.

25. For well-known studies of the role disease played in world history, see William McNeill, *Plagues and Peoples* and Jared Diamond, *Guns, Germs and Steel: The Fates of Human Societies*. For demographic studies of colonial Mexico, see works by demographers Shelbourne F. Cook and Woodrow Borah, *The Aboriginal Population of Central Mexico on the Eve of the Spanish Conquest* and *Essays in Population History: Mexico and the Caribbean*. For a study of the impact of malaria on indigenous Mexico during colonial times, see Judith Friedlander, "Malaria and Demography in the Lowland of Mexico: An Ethnohistorical Approach."

26. *Izkalotl*, Mexico City, December 1969.

27. After María del Carmen Nieva, *Mexikayotl*, 225.

28. After the illustrations included in the program by the Grupo Mexicano de Belleza at El Teatro del Bosque, October 21, 1969.

29. Milpa Alta, on the outskirts of Mexico City, was a major center of cultural extremist activity. To read a sympathetic description of the community's cultural extremists, see Rodolfo Van Zantwijk, "Supervivencias intelectuales de la cultura náhuatl en el municipio de Milpa Alta, D.F."

30. If the date is accurate, he could not have been at INI, which was only established in 1948.

31. *Petl* is not a word in Nahuatl.

32. Juan Luna had been establishing schools in indigenous villages for decades. In the early 1970s, the linguist Karen Dakin told me that Juan Luna had opened up a school in Tepoztlán in the 1930s. Eight students took classes there and five of them went on to study in Mexico City. The academy closed after a short period of time (pers. comm.).

    Although I did not mention it in the first edition of this book, it was common knowledge in Hueyapan that Juan Luna Cárdenas had a child with Don Eliseo's daughter. They called the boy *Huitzi* in Nahuatl, after the Aztec god Huitzilopochtli, but he preferred his Spanish name Rey (King), an understandable reaction of any child who wanted to fit in, but all the more so in his case, because other children in the village used to tease the boy mercilessly, changing the pronunciation of his Nahuatl name slightly to produce a vulgarity (Elvira Hernández, pers. comm.). By the time I got to Hueyapan, Rey was about 12 years old and a bit of a troublemaker. One of his favorite pranks was to race into town on the back of a donkey.

33. As I explain in greater detail in chapter nine, since the late 1990s, Marcelino Montero and others in town have started a new campaign in Hueyapan with the hope of persuading parents to send their children to an after-school program to learn Nahuatl.

34. Miguel León-Portilla, "El canto de Oztocohcoyohco," 62.

35. Miguel Barrios, "Textos de Hueyapan, Morelos," 53–75.

36. For example, the word for wind in the Hueyapan dialect of Nahuatl is pronounced *yiyigatl*, not *ehecatl*, the classical form reproduced in the prayer Lino Balderas gave to León-Portilla.

    A committed speaker of Nahuatl and a seasoned instructor of the language, Elvira Hernández was my Nahuatl teacher. Before she married, she accepted two invitations to go to the United States to serve as a Nahuatl informant, once to Harvard University to work with the linguist Marlys McClaran in the mid-1960s and again in 1970, to Indiana University to work with the linguist Joseph Campbell (not to be confused with the scholar of primitive myths). As an evangelical Christian, with a superb singing voice, she taught me many of the songs I learned in Hueyapan, from her repertoire of religious hymns and secular pieces. In the late 1990s, when Dr. Marcelino and others in the village began their local campaign to preserve Nahuatl in the village, they asked Elvira Hernández to play a major role in the revival.

37. Juan Dubernard went on to publish works of his own, for example: *Apuntes para la historia de Tepoztlán*.

38. Thanks to Juan Dubernard, some of Doña Epifania's woven garments became part of a permanent ethnographic exhibit in Cuernavaca, located in Cortés' Palace.
39. In 1977 workers at the Cuernavaca branch of the Burlington Textile Mills went on strike for several months. After things settled down, the workers gained little and Juan Dubernard lost his job. His courtly manner of running the business had a prerevolutionary feel about it. He could not adjust, or so it seemed, to the changes taking place in the Mexican economy or to the rising militancy of the work force.

Chapter Eight   The Anthropologist and the Indians

1. Guillermo Bonfil and Arturo Warman had already identified Hueyapan as an interesting place to send students. When I came to Mexico in 1969, Bonfil recommended the village to me. A Mexican student (Luis Biruecos) had done some preliminary work there, before going off to Michigan State University to do his PhD, but he subsequently abandoned the idea of using the *pueblo* for further research. By the early 1970s, Arturo Warman had begun an extensive regional study of the state of Morelos with the help of MA students based at the Centro de Investigaciones Superiores of the Instituto Nacional de Antropología e Historia and the Universidad Iberro-Americana. In addition to publishing a number of books under his own name (for example, *We Came to Object: The Peasants of Morelos and the National State*), he arranged to publish the work of his students in several volumes, subsidized by the Instituto Nacional de Antropología e Historia, under the general series title, *Los campesinos de la tierra de Zapata*. The first volume, *Adaptación, cambio y rebelión*, includes an article on Hueyapan: S. Lopez M., "Hueyapan, un pueblo de la tierra fría, 15–100."
   Although Warman had made a name for himself as a spokesman for the peasants of Morelos, in the eyes of many, he abandoned that legacy in the final years of his short life. In 1992, he played a critical role in dismantling the *ejido* system of Mexico (Article 27 of the Constituion), while serving as secretary of the Agrarian Reform under President Carlos Salinas.
2. As we see in chapter nine, a great deal would change, as Mexican anthropologists of the generation of 1968 came of age.
3. See, for example, Anselmo Marino Flores, "Indian Population and its Identification." In chapter nine, I provide a more contemporary set of references, including reflections on the situation in Mexico since the Zapatista uprising in 1994.
4. Eric Wolf, *Sons of the Shaking Earth*; Rodolfo Stavenhagen, *Clases, colonialismo y aculturación*; and Arturo Warman et al., *De eso que llaman antropología mexicana*. By the late 1980s, Stavenhagen had swung over even more to the culture camp. See bibliography.
5. See, for example, George Foster, *Culture and Conquest: America's Spanish Heritage* and Charles Gibson, *The Aztecs under Spanish Rule*.
6. Pedro Carrasco, "Tarascan Folk Religion, Christian or Pagan?" 6.
7. See, for example, Thomas Weaver, ed., *To See Ourselves: Anthropology and Modern Social Issues*.

8. As I say in the preface, I went on to work with Jewish intellectuals in France of the generation of 1968 (See *Vilna on the Seine: Jewish Intellectuals in France Since 1968*). Although I have no regrets about having broadened my research interests, the defense I give for why I left Mexico is not a satisfactory explanation. In the end, I agree with Clifford Geertz when he says that the "malaise" expressed by anthropologists of my generation was rather "self-serving" (see chapter nine).

Chapter Nine   Being Indian Revisited

1. I thank Claudio Lomnitz for having introduced me to this corollary: *Deep Mexico/Silent Mexico: An Anthropology of Nationalism*, 260.
2. A new paragraph was added to Article 4 of the Mexican Constitution, affirming Mexico's earlier endorsement of the United Nations' International Labor Organization (ILO) Convention 169. This frequently quoted Convention protects the cultural rights of indigenous peoples living within sovereign states.
3. For an excellent summary, see Courtney Jung, "Indigenous Identity."
4. Clifford Geertz, *Available Light*, 93. While I was studying at Chicago, members of the full-time tenured faculty who belonged to the post–World War II generation included Bernard Cohn, Lloyd Fallers, Paul Friedrich, Clifford Geertz, Robert McCormick Adams, McKim Marriott, Manning Nash, David Schneider, Raymond Smith, Victor Turner, and Nur Yalman. The "senior statesmen" included Fred Eggan, Milton Singer, and Sol Tax.
5. See, for example, Oscar Lewis' *Pedro Martínez.*
6. As I make clear in the acknowledgments to the first edition of this book, I was also deeply influenced by the late Victor Turner. Before going to the field, I participated in his seminar "Myth and Ritual," one of the great events in Chicago in those years, that he taught with Terrence Turner. I then had the very special privilege of seeing Vic on a weekly basis during my first few months in Mexico. While I was exploring the possibility of expanding my project beyond the Movimiento, Vic and Edie Turner were in Mexico City to encourage me to take the plunge. As luck would have it, Vic was doing research then on Catholic pilgrimages in Mexico and had decided to make the Distrito Federal his base of operations. In early October, the Turners invited me to join them on a one-day excursion to see colonial churches in the state of Morelos. Hueyapan's church was part of their itinerary.

   I was also influenced by several other anthropologists during my years in Chicago: Julian Pitt-Rivers, who introduced me to the idea of the "phony folk"; Robert McCormick Adams, who helped me tie my archeological interests to the ethnographic problem I was trying to address; Eva Hunt, who guided me through the vast ethnographic literature on Mexico; and Bernard Cohn, who helped me to see, along with Paul Friedrich, the importance of doing historical research for ethnographers.
7. Let me repeat in this context what I say in the acknowledgments to the first edition. Before turning to social and cultural anthropology in the late 1960s, I expected to become an archeologist. In 1961, while I was still in high school, I started working as a student volunteer, at the American Museum of Natural

History, for Junius Bird, Curator of South American Archeology. After spending an inspirational summer between my junior and senior year, I kept coming back, using every free moment I had during my college years and the early years of graduate school. After Chicago, I returned to the Museum as an Ogden Mills Fellow, before beginning to teach at SUNY Purchase. Thanks to Junius Bird and his assistant Milica Dimitrijevic Skinner, I became interested in indigenous textiles woven on the backstrap loom.

8. I had not yet discovered Roland Barthes, whose *Mythologiques* might have given me the vocabulary I was looking for. Although it was published in France in 1957, it did not become popular in the United States until the mid-1970s. As I have already noted, neither Eric Hobsbawm and Terrence Ranger's *Invention of Tradition* nor Benedict Anderson's *Imagined Communities* had yet been published. Their works too would have helped. In addition to Paul Friedrich, the person who influenced me the most in my thinking on the question of invented traditions was Julian Pitt-Rivers, who was way ahead of his time in the way he thought about constructed identities.

9. Geertz, *Available Light*, 94–95.

10. Ibid., 95–96.

11. Rodolfo Stavenhagen, for example, wrote a particularly scathing review of *Being Indian in Hueyapan* in *Nexos* (September 1978). Irritated, apparently, by the attention the Spanish edition of my book had received in the Mexican press, Stavenhagen went for the jugular, dismissing my work as another one of those MA or PhD theses that American universities were mass producing at the time. He criticized me in particular for my methodology, which he characterized—to my shock and disappointment—as if I had done nothing more than ask the villagers how they felt about an insulting epithet:

> In Chapter 4, J. Friedlander discusses what it means to be Indian in Hueyapan. How does she proceed? By simply asking the people what it feels like to be "Indian." Since the word "indio," as it is used by Mestizos, has negative and disparaging connotations, the villagers answer defensively and negatively, to such a degree that the author does not dare to address the issue during her first and longer period of fieldwork. What a strange way to analyze the ethnic identity of a social group that is historically discriminated against and abused! It would be like . . . reducing the identity of Blacks in the U.S. to their reaction to the aggressive and discriminatory word "nigger." (Trans. by J. Friedlander)

12. Claudio Lomnitz identifies the years between the 1970s and the 1990s as the period in Mexican anthropology when colleagues attempted "to move from an anthropology dedicated to the study of 'Indians' to an anthropology devoted to the study of social class" (*Deep Mexico/Silent Mexico*, 231). But those "devoted to the study of class" did not accept my idea that what we called culture was yet another marker of social class. Perhaps, I sounded too much like Oscar Lewis, even though I had rejected his infamous thesis about the "culture of poverty."

13. See Eric Hobsbawm, "Farewell to the Classic Labour Movement," 69–74 and the final chapters of *Age of Extremes*; also Judith Friedlander, *Vilna on the Seine*.

14. Emiko Saldívar, *Everyday Practices of Indigenismo.*
15. See, for example, De la Peña's article, "Territorio y ciudadanía étnica en la nación globalizada."
16. Claudio Lomnitz, *Exits from the Labyrinth* and *Deep Mexico/Silent Mexico;* Deborah Poole, "An Image of 'Our Indian': Type Photographs and Racial Sentiments in Oaxaca, 1920–1940."
17. Claudio Lomnitz, *Exits from the Labyrinth,* 275–276.
18. Ibid., 276.
19. Ibid., 275–277.
20. See, for example, Donna Lee Van Cott, *The Friendly Liquidation of the Past: The Politics of Diversity in Latin America* and her edited collection, *Indigenous Peoples and Democracy in Latin America;* Charles Hale, "Does Multiculturalism Menace? Governance, Cultural Rights and the Politics of Identity in Guatemala," and "Rethinking Indigenous Politics in the Era of the 'Indio Permitido' "; Claudio Lomnitz, *Exits from the Labyrinth* and *Deep Mexico, Silent Mexico;* Courtney Jung, "The Politics of Indigenous Identity: Neoliberalism, Cultural Rights and the Mexican Zapatistas"; Carmen Martínez Novo, *Who Defines Indigenous? Identities, Development, Intellectuals, and the State in Northern Mexico;* Guillermo de la Peña, "Nationals and Foreigners in the History of Mexican Anthropology"; Emiko Saldívar, *Everyday Practices of Indigenismo;* Saúl Velasco Cruz, *El Movimiento indígena y la autonomía en México.*
21. According to Marcelino Montero Baeza, Fray Diego Durán even lived in Hueyapan, something I did not know when I was first writing the book (Montero, "Hueyapan," unpublished paper, 2001).
22. Cited in Claudio Lomnitz, *Deep Mexico/Silent Mexico,* 245.
23. Claudio Lomnitz, Ibid., 249–250.
24. Ibid., 245.
25. Unless otherwise indicated, this section relies on arguments I made in "The National Indigenist Institute of Mexico Reinvents the Indian."
26. Manuel Gamio, *Opiniones y juicios sobre La población de Teotihuacán,* vol. 2, 51.
27. Cited in Christian Deverre and Raul Reissner, "Les Figures de l'indien-problème de l'indigénisme Mexicain," 155.
28. As I mention in chapter seven, Carmen Nieva's book *Mexikayotl,* (published in 1969), has a picture of Miguel Alemán, probably taken in the early 1960s. We see him receiving a plaque from Rodolfo Nieva in recognition of the fact that the former president of Mexico has become an honorary member of the Movimiento. In that same chapter, I quote Caso at length, in an interview he gave in the very same year *Mexikayotl* was published, in which he vigorously attacks the cultural extremists and defends the policy of Official Indigenismo.
29. In those years, Arturo Warman and his team of researchers were fanning out all over the state of Morelos, concentrating their efforts in Mestizo peasant towns. By the mid-1970s, Warman's students had succeeded in publishing a three-volume series on *Los campesinos de la tierra de Zapata,* that included an article about Hueyapan in volume 1 (S. M. López, "Hueyapan un pueblo de la tierra fría"). During the same period, Guillermo de la Peña settled down in the Mestizo town of Tlayacapan, Morelos, having joined a team of church activisits

and anthropologists who were collaborating with the inspirational Jesuit priest Claude Fauvier. De la Peña's research resulted in the publication of *A Legacy of Promises: Agriculture, Politics and Ritual in the Morelos Highlands.*

Among its many claims to fame, Tlayacapan enjoyed the special distinction in 1969 of having served as the backdrop for the final shootout scene in *Butch Cassidy and the Sun Dance Kid,* Robert Redford and Paul Newman's prize-winning film that was shot in Mexico, even though the story took place in Bolivia. This was also the time when John Womack's celebrated book on Zapata was published, which provided a magnificent portrait of the revolutionary from Morelos, the great symbol of the *campesino* in Mexico (*Zapata and the Mexican Revolution*).

Urban Anthropology in Mexico took off after the publication of Oscar Lewis's *Five Families* and his more controversial work *Children of Sanchez.* By the late 1960s, Angel Palerm's student Larissa Lomnitz was doing research in a Mexico City slum. Her book came out a few years later, first in Spanish, then in English, and it has since become a classic of its own (*Networks and Marginality: Life in a Mexican Shantytowns*).

30. Most famously, *De eso que llaman antropología mexicana.*
31. Elena Poniatowska, *La Noche de Tlatelolco.*
32. As we saw in chapters two, three, and four, agrarian rebels were organized in rural areas before the urban disturbances in the late 1960s and early 1970s. In this period, however, the two groups started working together.
33. The main tribunal took place in Brussels in 1976 and I organized a second one in New York. See Judith Friedlander, "Tribunal on Crimes Against women: An Overview."
34. I describe this encounter in the epilogue of the French edition to the book *L'Indien des autres.*
35. See chapter six.
36. On June 30, 2006, "a judge ordered the arrest of Luis Echeverría on genocide charges in connection with his role during the massacre of student protesters" (James C. McKinley Jr., "Mexico Charges Ex-President in '68 Massacre of Students," *The New York Times,* July 1, 2006, A3). Echeverría was charged with having orchestrated the government's terrifying response to students and workers in Tlatelolco while he was serving as minister of the interior under President Díaz Ordaz. He was also accused of staging a crackdown in 1971 during his own term as president of Mexico. Then on July 8, 2006, a federal judge threw the charges out of court, ruling that the "statute of limitations had expired" (*The New York Times,* July 9, 2006, A6). This was not the first time that prosecutors had tried to bring Echeverría trial (see Enrique Krauze, Op-Ed Page, *The New York Times,* August 10, 2004).
37. Edited by Arturo Warman, Guillermo Bonfil, Margarita Nolasco, Mercedes Olivera, and Enrique Valencia.
38. The name was taken from the Spanish translation of the title of an American Western: "The Magnificent Seven" (1960). The film is an American remake of Kurosawa's classic, "The Seven Samurai." In the U.S. version, Yul Brenner recruits six tough guys to defend a group of Mexican peasants from bandits. Although there is some discussion about whether there were really seven *magníficos* in 1970, most people agree that the cast of anthropologists included the five contributors to *De eso que llaman antropología mexicana.*

39. Claudio Lomnitz, *Deep Mexico/Silent Mexico*, 261.

40. Ibid., 261.

41. Courtney Jung, "The Politics of Indigenous Identity," 44.

42. Donna Lee Van Cott, cited in Saúl Velasco, *El Movimiento indígena y la autonomía en México*, 122.

43. Saúl Velasco, *El movimiento indígena*, 122 (trans. J. Friedlander).

44. See contributions to these deliberations by Claude Lévi-Strauss, in 1952 and again in 1971. The evolution of Lévi-Strauss' thought on the subject is entirely relevant to the discussion here. In Mexico, most recently, as I have already noted, Rodolfo Stavenhagen spent three years in Paris working for UNESCO (1979–1982). Then in 2001, he was named Special Reporter on Human Rights for Indigenous Peoples at the United Nations.

45. There were exceptions, of course, especially later on. In the 1990s, for example, Luis Vázquez Léon did me the honor of choosing a title for his book that alluded to the Spanish title of mine: *Ser Indio Otra Vez: La purepechización de los tarascos serranos*.

46. This point would be elaborated upon by Bonfil in his later writings. See, for example, Guillermo Bonfil, ed. *Utopía y Revolución: El pensamiento político contemporaneo de los indios en América Latina* and *México profundo: Una civilización negada.*

47. José López Portillo, *Quetzalcoatl.*

48. See Saúl Velasco's *El Movimiento indígena y la autonomía en México*, 126, and Jonathan Fox's *The Politics of Food in Mexico: State Power and Social Mobilization.* For an excellent analysis of the history of INI, see Emiko Saldivar's *Everday Practices of Indigenismo*, her doctoral dissertation (New School for Social Research) that is coming out in Spanish (see bibliography).

49. In Hueyapan and Tetela during these years, a few enterprising people started growing flowers on a massive scale for international markets. They also opened up small knitting factories to produce machine-made sweaters. The knitting factories did not last.

50. Deverre and Reissner, "Les Figures de l'indien-problème de l'indigénisme mexicain, 166.

51. The series of films was called "El México Indígena." I described the tenth film in the series (at the time there were already 28) that featured the Pame Indians of Santa María Acapulco (San Luís Potosí). At the end of the documentary, which is very weak on ethnographic detail, we see a local schoolteacher organizing the community to demand its indigenous rights.

52. Luz María Valdés, *Los indios mexicanos en los censos del año 2000*, 7–8.

53. Data from INEGI.

54. Saúl Velasco, *El Movimiento indígena y la autonomía en México* (reference found only in doctoral dissertation version of manuscript—UNAM—119, 122). See also Rodolfo Stavenhagen, "Reflexiones sobre demografía étnica."

55. Guillermo Bonfil, translated by Judith Friedlander, quoted in Saúl Velasco, *El Movimiento indígena y la autonomía en México*, 84–85.

56. Luis González, *Obras Completas, El indio en la era liberal*, vol. 5, 167–168 (cited in ibid., 85).

57. Cited in Ibid.

58. Ibid.

59. In 2001, 11 villages in the state of Morelos, all identified as indigenous, received funding, including Hueyapan. Of those, only Hueyapan had a sizable population of speakers of an indigenous language. According to a chart prepared by INI, based on the national census of 1990, 43% of Hueyapan's population spoke Nahuatl in 1990 (out of an overall population of 5,566 people). Of the ten remaining communities, only San José de los Laurelos (Municipio de Tlayacapan) could claim that a significant percentage of its population spoke an indigenous tongue (Nahuatl)—12% of the 1,008 residents living in this small *pueblo.*

60. I am grateful to Saúl Velasco for having collected all these data (96ff). He also reproduced a chart (57) published by Ann Helwege in "Poverty in Latin America: Back to the Abyss?" that compared the percentages of Indians and non-Indians who were below the poverty line in four Latin American countries (based on the 1990 census of each country):

Country	Indians	Non-Indians
Bolivia	64.3	48.1
Guatemala	86.6	53.9
Mexico	80.6	17.9
Peru	79.0	49.7

The good news is that the percentage of non-Indians in Mexico living in poverty is considerably lower than it is in the other countries. The bad news is that the percentage of Indians is extremely high.

61. Emiko Saldívar, *Everyday Practices of Indigenismo,* 75.

62. Ibid., 76.

63. Guillermo Bonfil, cited in Ibid., "Por etnodesarrollo se entiende el ejercicio de la capacidad social de un pueblo para construir su futuro, aprovechando para ello las enseñanzas de su experiencia histórica y los recursos reales y potenciales de su cultura, de acuerdo con un proyecto que se defina según sus propios valores y aspiraciones."

64. Ibid., 32.

65. Ibid., 32.

66. Ibid., 79–80. Warman's document is called, "Políticas y Tareas Indigenistas:1989–1994."

67. Ibid., 81.

68. Warman defended the government's radical decision in the left-wing press: Arturo Warman, "La reforma al artículo 27 constitucional," *La Jornada,* March 8, 1994 (Special Section—"Perfil"), 2–4.

69. Claudio Lomnitz, *Deep Mexico/Silent Mexico,* 260–261.

70. In addition to Charles Taylor, the thinkers most frequently cited are: Franz Fanon, Will Kymlicka and Alain Tourraine.

71. Sympathetic to those who stopped reading Anthropology in Mexico, Claudio Lomnitz described the crisis in 1992 in the following way:

The problems came on two sides. On the one hand, anthropologists began to pay a high price for ignoring all knowledge that had not been generated through anthropological fieldwork. Writers began discrediting the importance of fieldwork by charging that anthropologists were only rediscovering the obvious, while sociologists complained that anthropological information was not adequately linked to what was going on at "higer levels" of the system and therefore was not "representative" of anything. On the other hand, anthropological case studies began piling up, but no new theoretical understanding seemed to be emerging. Anthropology was providing plenty of food for thought, but anthropologists were not being trained to do the thinking. As consciousness of these problems spread, the promise of deriving important political conclusions from anthropology diminished, and anthropology's own (partly misplaced) claim to holism was corroded. Anthropology in Mexico is today unsure of its place and of the place of its analyses in national politics. (*Exits from the Labyrinth*, 256–257)

72. The eventual signing of the San Andrés Accords is a long and complicated story. Suffice it to say that the final document did not have the enthusiastic support of any faction of the Indigenous Rights Movement.

73. The coverage of the Indigenous Rights Movement in Spanish and English is enormous. Let me suggest the following representative authors/editors, some of whom have already been cited and whose works are all included in the bibliography. Selections of works by some of the major voices in the movement have been collected in English in Tom Hayden's reader. I list their names here and indicate that they are included in the reader: Eduardo Galeano (see Tom Hayden), Aldolfo Gilly (see Tom Hayden), Alma Guillermo Prieto (see Tom Hayden), Tom Hayden, Courtney Jung, Carlos Monsiváis (see Tom Hayden), June Nash, Octavio Paz (see Tom Hayden), Elena Poniatwoska (see Tom Hayden), Judith Adler Hellman, Saúl Velasco Cruz, Kay Warren, John Womack. The publishing house, ERA in Mexico, has also collected important documents over the years in a series called EZLN. It begins in 1994 with writings by some of the same people found in the Tom Hayden reader.

74. See, for example, Carmen Martínez, "The 'Culture' of Exclusion."

75. It is entirely likely that households have included absent members of their families who are working illegally in the United States.

76. The last cleanup was in 2003.

77. In 1990, 43% of the villagers still spoke Nahuatl. In 2000, the percentage was 37.

78. Why women and not men? Perhaps, in part, because the women are staying home, while the men seek work in the United States. But that clearly is not the only reason. Since 1975, when the United Nations began focusing on the social and economic needs of women, development programs around the world have been investing modestly in women.

79. These books include two works edited by Marcelino Montero Baeza and other members of the Grupo Cultural Náhuatl: a small grammar book for learning Nahuatl and a bilingual collection of poems and short works of fiction by children living in Hueyapan. The remaining three volumes include collections of contemporary poems and short works of fiction by adults raised in Hueyapan

and in neighboring villages. Two of the collections have pieces by Arturo Vargas Espinoza, Maestro Rafael's oldest son—his version of his grandmother's stories that we all used to enjoy listening to, as we sat in the kitchen at the end of a long day, sipping herbal tea and enjoying a light supper of reheated *tortillas* and beans.

80. According to Maribel Vargas, two groups in Hueyapan were competing with one another for control of the August 4th fiesta in 2004—Dr. Marcelino's Nahuatl Culture Group and those identified with Jaime Pérez, who was the municipal officer in charge of education. Don Jaime prevailed and persuaded Hueyapan's *ayudante* to invite a band from the village of Tlayacapan to come to the village to perform. Called La Banda de Viento, they were simply terrific. Complicating matters more, Maribel continued, Dr. Marcelino is really too busy these days, given his obligations as the village's doctor, to maintain the same high level of cultural activity as he did before in the early years of his practice. As a result, fewer children are studying Nahuatl these days, but informal instruction continues.

81. Multiculturalism has served the interests of liberal democracies for decades, as any student of East and Central Europe knows. The experience of minorities in that part of the world offers a fascinating comparison and a cautionary tale. Hannah Arendt's brilliant analysis of the nation-state in *Origins of Totalitarianism* is critical to this discussion. See also Judith Friedlander, *Vilna on the Seine*, chapter three. Closer to Mexico (Guatemala), see the work of Charles Hale, "Does Multiculturalims Menace?" and "Rethinking Indigenous Politics in the Era of the 'Indio Permitido,' " and James McKinley, Jr., "Where Poverty Drove Zapatistas, the Living is No Easier," *The New York Times*, September 11, 2005, Section 1, 12.

82. Born in 1929 into a Jewish family, Agnes Heller survived World War II in Nazi-occupied Budapest. As a young woman studying in Communist Hungary, she worked closely for many years with the Marxist critic Georg Lukács. When she later joined the Hungarian uprising in 1956, she sacrificed her academic career at home, but not her influence as a philosopher. Despite efforts to silence her, she continued to write and her manuscripts were successfully smuggled out of the country and eventually published in many languages. Finally, in the 1970s, she left Hungary for Australia and accepted a position at the University of Melbourne, together with her husband, the philosopher Ferenc Feher. In the 1980s, the couple came to the New School. As this book goes to press, Agnes Heller divides her time between Budapest, where she returned a hero after 1989, and New York.

83. Maribel Vargas Espinosa, *La formación de profesores en servicio desde la pedagogía de lo cotidiano. El caso de la UPN Ecatepec.*

84. The paper was translated into Spanish by the sociologist Jorge Capetillo, a sociology student from Mexico who was finishing his PhD at the New School in 2000. The Mexican philosopher Carlos Pereda read the translation in Mexico City and Jorge Capetillo read it in Ecatepec. Two articles about the event appeared in the progressive newspaper *La Jornada* (May 30, and June 6, 2000), the latter by a young philosophy student, Pablo Rodriguez, who interviewed Agnes Heller. In the weeks preceding the conference, Luis Eduardo Primero Rivas published a book that was highly critical of the recent work of Agnes Heller: *¿Cuál Agnes Heller? Introducción a la obra de la filósofa húngara.*

Bibliography

Aguirre Beltrán, Gonzalo. "Indigenismo y Mestizaje." *Cuadernos americanos*. 78 (July–August, 1956):35–51.

Anderson, Benedict. *Imagined Communities*. London: Verso, 1983.

Arendt, Hannah. *Origins of Totalitarianism*. New York: Harcourt Brace, 1951.

Barrios, Miguel. "Textos de Hueyapan, Morelos." *Tlalocan*. 3.1 (1949):53–75.

Barthes, Roland. *Mythologiques*. Paris: Le Seuil, 1957.

Bede, The Venerable. *History of the English Church and People*. Trans. Leo Shirley Price. London: Penguin, 1968.

Behar, Ruth. "Rage and Redemption: Reading the Life Story of a Mexican Market Woman." *Feminist Studies*. 16.2 (1990): 223–258.

Bennett, William and Junius Bird. *Andean Culture History*. New York: American Museum of Natural History Handbook Series, 16, 1960.

Beutler, Gisela. "Algunas observaciones sobre los textos de 'Moros y Cristianos' en México y Centroamérica." *Actas del VIII Congreso de la Asociación Internacional de Hispanistas*. Ed. A. David Kossoff, José Amore y Vázquez, Ruth Kossoff and Geoffrey W. Ribbons. Centro Virtual Cervantes (1983):221–233.

Blunno, Mery and Luis Miguel Morayta Mendoza. Eds. *Los doce pares de Francia. Historia para teatro campesino en tres noches*. Mexico City: Miguel Angel Porrúa & el Gobierno del Estado de Morelos, 1994.

Boban, Eugène. *Documents pour servir à l'histoire du Mexique*, vol. 1. Paris: Ernst Leroux, 1891.

Bonfil, Guillermo. Ed. *Utopía y Revolución: El pensamiento político contemporaneo de los indios en América Latina*. Mexico City: Editorial Nueva Imagen, 1981.

———. *México profundo: Una civilización negada*. Mexico City: CONACULTA and Grijalbo, 1990.

Brading, D.A. *Mexican Phoenix: Our Lady of Guadalupe: Image and Tradition Across Five Centuries*. Cambridge: Cambridge University Press, 2001.

Brewer, LLI, E. Cobban. *The Dictionary of Phrase and Fable*. New York: Averel Books, 1978, 1870.

Carrasco, Pedro. "Tarrascan Folk Religion, Christian or Pagan?" *The Social Anthropology of Latin America: Essays in Honor of Ralph Beals*. Ed. William Goldschmidt and Harold Hoijer. Los Angeles: University of California Press, 1970, 3–15.

Caso, Alfonso. *Métodos y resultados de la política indigenista en México*. Mem. 6 Mexico City: Instituto Nacional Indigenista, 1954.

Castellanos, Pablo. *Horizontes de la música precortesiana*. Mexico City: Fondo de Cultura Económica, 1970.

Chávez-Orozco, Luis. "El Romance en México." *Contemporáneos.* 8 (April–June, 1930):253–267.

Cook, Shelbourne F. and Woodrow Borah. *The Aboriginal Population of Central Mexico on the Eve of the Spanish Conquest.* Berkeley: Iberro-Americana, 45 (1963).

―――. *Essays in Population History: Mexico and the Caribbean,* 2 vols. Berkeley: University of California Press, 1971, 1974.

De las Casas, Bartolomé. *The Devastation of the Indies.* Trans. Herma Briffault. Baltimore: Johns Hopkins University Press, 1992.

De la Peña, Guillermo. *A Legacy of Promises: Agriculture, Politics and Ritual in the Morelos Highlands.* Austin: University of Texas Press, 1981.

―――. "Nationals and Foreigners in the History of Mexican Anthropology." *The Conditions of Reciprocal Understanding.* Ed. James Fernandez and Milton Singer. Chicago: University of Chicago Center for International Studies, 1995, 276–303.

―――. "Territorio y ciudadanía étnica en la nación globalizada." *Descatos: Revista de Antropologia Social,* 1 (1999):13–27.

Deverre, Christian and Raul Reissner. "Les Figures de l'indien-problème de l'indigéisme mexicain." *Cahiers Internationaux de Sociologie.* 68 (1980):149–166.

Diamond, Jared. *Guns, Germs and Steel: The Fates of Human Societies.* New York: W.W. Norton, 1999.

Díaz del Castillo, Bernal. *The Bernal Díaz Chronicles.* Trans. and ed. Albert Idell. Garden City: Double Day, 1956.

―――. *The Conquest of New Spain.* Trans. and intro. J.M. Cohen. London: Penguin, 1963.

Díaz-Polanco, Héctor. *La Rebelión Zapatista y la Autonomía.* Mexico City: Ediciones siglo veinte y uno, 1997.

Dubernard, Juan. *Apuntes para la historia de Tepoztlán.* Cuernavaca: No Imprint, 1983.

Durán, Fray Diego. *Historia de las Indias de Nueva España e islas de la Tierra Firme,* 2 vols. Ed. Angel María Garibay K. Mexico City: Porrua, 1967.

Firth, Raymond. *We, The Tikopia.* Boston: Beacon Press, 1965.

Florescano, Enrique. *Etnia, Estado y Nación: Ensayo sobe las identidades colectivos en México.* Mexico City: Nuevo Siglo Aguilar, 1996.

Foster, George. *Culture and Conquest: America's Spanish Heritage.* New York: Viking Fund Publication in Anthropology, 27 (1960).

Fox, Jonathan. *The Politics of Food in Mexico: State Power and Social Mobilization.* Ithaca: Cornell University Press, 1993.

Friedlander, Judith. "Malaria and Demography in the Lowlands of Mexico." *Forms of Symbolic Action.* Ed. Robert Spencer. Proceedings of the 1969 Annual Meetings of the American Ethnologicial Society, 217–233.

―――. *Being Indian in Hueyapan: A Study of Forced Identity in Contemporary Mexico.* New York: St. Martin's Press, 1975.

―――. *Ser Indio en Hueyapan.* Trans. Celia H. Paschero. Mexico City: El Fondo de Cultura Económica, 1977.

―――. *L'Indien des autres.* Trans. Aline and Isabelle Vellay. Paris: Payot, 1979.

―――. "Tribunal on Crimes Against Women: An Overview." *Heresies: A Feminist Publication of Art and Politics.* 6 (Summer, 1978):38, 40–43.

―――. "The Aesthetics of Oppression." *Heresies: A Feminist Publication of Art and Politics.* 4 (Winter, 1978):1–9.

Friedlander, Judith. "The Secularization of the Cargo System: An Example from Post-revolutionary Mexico." *Latin American Research Review.* 16.2 (1981):132–143.

―――. "The National Indigenist Institute of Mexico Reinvents the Indian." *American Ethnologist.* 13.2 (May, 1986):363–367.

―――. "Pacts with the Devil: Stories Told by an Indian Woman from Mexico." *New York Folklore.* 16.1–2 (1990):25–42.

―――. *Vilna on the Seine: Jewish Intellectuals in France since 1968.* New Haven: Yale University Press, 1990.

―――. "Doña Zeferina Barreto: Biographical Sketch of an Indian Woman from the State of Morelos." *Creating Spaces, Shaping Transitions: Women of the Mexican Countryside, 1850–1990.* Ed. Heather Fowler-Salamani and Mary Kay Vaughn. Tuscon: University of Arizona Press, 1994, 125–137.

Friedrich, Paul. *Agrarian Revolt in a Mexican Village* Englewood Cliffs: Prentice Hall, 1970.

Gamio, Manuel. *Opiniones y juicios sobre la obra La Población del Valle de Teotihuacán,* 2 vols. Mexico City: Secretaría de Agricultura y Fomento, 1924.

Garibay K., Angel. *Llave del Náhuatl.* Mexico City: Editorial Porrúa, 1961.

Geertz, Clifford. *Available Light: Anthropological Reflections on Philosophical Topics.* Princeton: Princeton University Press, 2000.

Gerhard, Peter. "El Señorío de Ocuituco." *Tlalocan.* 6.2 (1970):97–114.

Gibson, Charles. "The Transformation of the Indian Community in New Spain, 1500–1810." *Journal of World History.* 1 (1954):581–607.

―――. *The Aztecs Under Spanish Rule: A History of the Indians of the Valley of Mexico, 1519–1810.* Stanford: Stanford University Press, 1964.

―――. *Spain in America.* New York: Harper Torchbooks, 1966.

González, Luis. *Obras completas: El indio en la era liberal,* vol. 5. Mexico City: Editorial Clio, 1996.

Hale, Charles. "Does Multiculturalism Menace? Governance, Cultural Rights and the Politics of Identity in Guatemala." *Journal of Latin American Studies.* 34 (2002):485–524.

―――. "Rethinking Indigenous Politics in the Era of 'Indio Permitido'." *NACLA.* 38.1 (2004):16–20.

Hayden, Tom. Ed. *The Zapatista Reader.* New York: Thunder's Mouth Press/Nation Books, 2002.

Helguera R., L. S. López M. R. Ramírez M. Ed. *Los campesinos de la tierra de Zapata,* 2 vols. Mexico City: SEP/INAH, 1974, 1977.

Heller, Agnes. *Everyday Life.* London: Routledge, 1984.

Hellman, Judith Adler. "Chiapas real y virtual: el realismo mágico y la izquierda." *Este País.* 100 (July 1999): 23–38. "Real and Virtual Chiapas: Magic Realism and the Left." *Socialist Register* (2000):161–186.

Helwege, Ann. "Poverty in Latin America: Back to the Abyss?" *Journal of Interamerican Studies and World Affairs.* 37.3 (Autumn 1995), 99–123.

Hobsbawm, Eric. "Farewell to the Classic Labour Movement?" *The New Left Review.* 173 (1989):69–74.

Hobsbawm, Eric. *The Age of Extremes: A History of the World, 1914–1991.* New York: Pantheon, 1994.

Hobsbawm, Eric and Terrence Ranger. *The Invention of Tradition.* Cambridge: Cambridge University Press, 1983.

Horcasitas. *El Teatro náhuatl—épocas novohispánica y moderna,* part 1. Mexico City: UNAM, 1974.

Jung, Courtney. "The Politics of Indigenous Idenitity: Neoliberalism, Cultural Rights and the Mexican Zapatistas." *Social Research.* 70.2 (Summer, 2003):433–462.

Katz, Friedrich. *The Life and Times of Pancho Villa.* Palo Alto: Stanford University Press, 1998.

Lafaye, Jacques. *Quetzalcoatl et Guadalupe. La formation de la conscience nationale au Mexique (1531–1813).* Paris: Editions Gallimard, 1974.

Lawrence, D.H. *The Plumed Serpent.* New York: Alfred Knopf, 1926.

———. *Le Serpiente emplumada.* Trans. Carmen Gallardo de Mesa. Buenos Aires: Editorical Losada, 1940.

Leander, Birgitta. *La poesía náhuatl. Función y carácter.* Göteborg, Sweden: Etnografiska, 1971.

León-Portilla, Miguel. "El canto de Oztocohcoyohco." *Tlalocan.* 4.1 (1962):62–63.

Lévi-Strauss, Claude. "Race and History." *Structural Anthropology,* vol. 2. Trans. Monique Layton. New York: Basic Books, 1976, 323–362.

———. "Race and Culture." *The View from Afar.* Trans. J. Neugnschol and P. Hoss. New York: Basic Books, 1985, 3–24.

Lewis, Oscar. *Five Families.* New York: Vintage Books, 1959.

———. *Children of Sánchez.* New York: Basic Books, 1964.

———. *Pedro Martínez.* New York: Random House, 1964.

Lomnitz, Claudio. *Exits from the Labyrinth: Culture and Ideology in the Mexican National Space.* Berkeley: University of California Press, 1992.

———. *Deep Mexico/Silent Mexico: An Anthropology of Nationalism.* Minneapolis: University of Minnesota Press, 2001.

Lomnitz, Larissa. *Networks and Marginality: Life in a Mexican Shantytown.* Trans. Cinna Lomnitz. New York: Academic Press, 1975.

López, Juan José. *Historia de Oliveros, Fierabras y Carlomagno* (undated manuscript attributed to Juan José López). Located at Hispanic Society of America.

López Méndez, Sinecio. "Hueyapan: un pueblo de la tierra fría." *Los campesinos de la tierra de Zapata,* vol. I: *Adaptacíon, cambio y rebellión.* Ed. L. Helguera R., S. López M. and R. Ramírez M. Mexico City: SEP/INAH, 1974, 15–100.

López Portillo, José. *Quetzalcoatl.* Mexico City: Librería Manuel Porrúa, S.A., 1965.

Magaña, Gildardo. *Emiliano Zapata y el Agrarismo en México,* 5 vols. Mexico City: Institute of Nacional de Estudios Historicos de la Revolución Mexicana, 1985.

Marino Flores, Anselmo. "Indian Population and its Identification." *Handbook of Middle American Indians,* vol. 6. Austin: University of Texas Press, 1967, 12–25.

Martínez-Marín, Carlos. *Tetela del Volcán.* Mexico City: UNAM Instituto de Investigaciones Históricas, 1968.

Martínez Novo, Carmen. "The 'Culture' of Exclusion: Representations of Indigenous Women Street Vendors in Tijuana, Mexico." *Bulletin of Latin American Research.* 22.3 (July, 2003):249–268.

————. *Who Defines Indigenous? Identities, Development, Intellectuals and the State in Northern Mexico.* New Brunswick: Rutgers University Press, 2005.

McNeill, William. *Plagues and Peoples.* Garden City: Doubleday, 1976.

Melquiades Ruvalcaba, J. *Manual de Gramática Náhuatl.* Guadalajara: No imprint, 1968.

Montero Baeza, Marcelino, Salustia Lara de la Cruz, Delia Ramírez Castellanos, Eustacia Saavedra Barranco, Roselio Torres Moreno. *Ejercicio para el apredizaje de la lengua náhuatl de Hueyapan.* Cuernavaca: Impresos Júpiter, 2000.

————. *Había una vez/Oyiya sepa.* Cuernavaca: CONACULTA, 2000.

Montoya, Matilde. *Estudio sobre el baile de la conquista.* Guatemala City: Editorial Universitaria, 1970.

Nash, June. *Mayan Visions: The Quest for Autonomy in an Age of Globalization.* New York: Routledge, 2001.

Nieva, María del Carmen. *Mexikayotl.* Mexico City: Editorial Orion, 1969.

Paso y Troncoso, Francisco del. "Relación de Tetela y Ueyapan." *Papeles de Nueva España,* Segunda Serie, Geografía y Estadística, vol. 6. Madrid: Manuscritos de la Real Academia de la Historia de Madrid y del Archivo de Indias en Sevilla, Años 1570–1582, 1905, 283–290.

Paz, Octavio. *The Labyrinth of Solitude.* Trans. O.P. Lysander Kemp. New York: Grove Press, 1961.

Piamonte, Nicolás de. *Historia del Emperador Carlo Magno en la qual se trata de las grandes proefas, y hazañas de los Doze Pares de Francia: y de como fueron vendidos por el traydor de Ganalon, y de la cruda batalla que huvo Oliveros, con Fierabras, Rey de Alexandria, hijo del Almirante Balàn.* Translation of the twelfth-century French Epic. Barcelona: No imprint, 1738 [1525]. In modern orthography: *Historia del Emperador Carlo-Magno o los doce pares de Francia.* México: Exlibro Español, 1963.

Pitt-Rivers, Julian. "Mestizo or Ladino." *Race.* 10.4 (1969):463–477.

Poniatowska, Elena. *La Noche de Tlatelolco.* Mexico City: Era, 1971.

Poole, Deborah. "An Image of 'Our Indian': Type Photographs and Racial Sentiments in Oaxaca, 1920–1940." *Hispanic American Research Review.* 84.1 (2004):37–82.

Primero Rivas, Luis Eduardo. *¿Cuál Agnes Heller? Introducción a la obra de la filósofa húngara.* Tlalnepantla: Primero Editores, 2000.

Reed, John. *Insurgent Mexico.* New York: Simon and Shuster, 1969.

Reed, Nelson. *The Caste War of Yucatan.* Stanford: Stanford University Press, 1964.

Rendón, Estanislao. *La Historia de Carlos Magno y el Almirante Balán qué compone los dose pares de Francia.* Unpublished manuscript based on Juan José López's *Historia de Oliveros, Fierabras y Carlomagno.*

Ricard, Robert. "Contribution à l'étude des fêtes de moros y cristianos au Mexique." *Journal de la Société des Américainistes de Paris.* 24 (1932):51–84.

————. *La "Conquête spirituelle" du Mexique.* Paris: Travaux et Mémoires de l'Institut de l'Ethnologie, University of Paris, vol. 10, 1933.

————. *The Spiritual Conquest of Mexico.* Trans. Lesley Bryd Simpson. Berkeley: University of California Press, 1966.

Saldívar Tanaka, Emiko. *Everyday Practices of Indigenismo: An Institutional Analysis of Mexico's Instituto Nacional Indigenista.* Doctoral Dissertation in Sociology. New

School for Social Research, 2002. In Spanish: *Prácticas cotidianas del Indigenismo: Una etnografía de Estado*. Mexico City: UIA, forthcoming.

Sartre, Jean-Paul. *Anti-Semite and Jew*. Trans. George J. Becker. New York: Schocken, 1948.

Schneider, David. *American Kinship*. Englewood Cliffs: Prentice Hall, 1968.

Sierra, Justo. *Mexico: Its Social Evolution*, 3 vols. Mexico City: J. Ballescá & Co., 1900.

Siméon, Rémi. *Dictionnaire de la langue Nahuatl ou Mexicaine*. Graz: Akademische Druck-U. Verlagsanstalt, 1962.

Smith, Michael. *The Aztecs*. Oxford: Blackwell, 2003.

Soustelle, Jacques. *The Daily Life of the Aztecs*. Trans. J.O'Brian. Stanford: Stanford University Press, 1970.

Stavenhagen, Rodolfo. *Clases, colonialismo y aculturación*. Cuadernos del Seminario de Integración Social Guatemalteca, no 19, 1968.

———. "De indios y antropólogos." *Nexos*. 1.9 (September 1978):30.

———. "Reflexiones sobre demografía étnica." *¿Existe demografía étnica?* Ed. Ricardo Pozas. Mexico City: UNAM, 1986.

———. *Derecho indígena y derechos humanos en América Latina*. Mexico City: Instituto Interamericano de Herechos Humanos IIDH and El Col/egio de México, 1988.

———. "Derechos indígenas y derechos culturales de los pueblos indígenas. *Lo propio y lo ajeno. Interculturalidad y sociedad multicultural*. Mexico: Plaza y Valdés, 1996.

———. "El sistema internacional de los derechos indígenas." *Autonomías étnicas y estados nacionales*. Ed. Miguel A. Bartolomé and Alicia M. Barabas. Mexico City: CONACULTA and INAH, 1998.

———. *Derechos humanos de los pueblos indígenas*. Mexico City: Comisión Nacional de Derechos Humanos, 2000.

Super, John. *Food, Conquest and Colonization in 16th-Century Spanish America*. Albuquerque: University of New Mexico Press, 1988.

Swadesh, Mauricio and M. Sancho. *Los mil elementos del Mexicano Clásico*. Mexico City. Instituto de Investigaciones Históricas de la UNAM, 1966.

Tannenbaum, Frank. "Agrarismo, indianismo y nacionalismo." *Hispanic American Historical Review*. 23 (1943):394–423.

Turner, Victor. *Dramas, Fields and Metaphors*. Ithaca: Cornell University Press, 1974.

Tylor, Edward B. *Anahuac, or Mexico and the Mexicans, Ancient and Modern*. London: Longman, Green, Longman and Roberts, 1861.

Valdés, Luz María. *Los Indios mexicanos en los censos del año 2000*. Mexico City: Instituto de Investigaciones Jurídicas de la UNAM, 2004.

Valliant, George. *The Aztecs of Mexico*. New York: Doubleday, 1944.

Van Cott, Donna Lee. "Indigenous Peoples and Democracy: Issues for Policymakers." *Indigenous Peoples and Democracy: in Latin America*. New York: St. Martin's Press, 1994.

———. *The Friendly Liquidation of the Past: The Politics of Diversity in Latin America*. Pittsburgh: University of Pittsburgh Press, 2000.

Van Zantwijk, Rodolfo. "Supervivencias intelectuales de la cultura náhuatl en el municipio de Milpa Alta, D.F." *América Indígena*. 18 (1958):119–129.

Vargas Espinosa, Maribel. *La formación de profesores en servicio desde la pedagogía de lo cotidiano. El caso de la UPN Ecatepec.* Mexico City: Primero Editores, 2005.

Vargas Espinoza, Arturo. "Tepeteuializtli" ("La Pelea de las montañas"). *¿Ustedes que saben? Testimonios y relatos nahuas.* Serie 2. Ed. Norma Zamarrón de León. Cuernavaca: CONACULTA, 2004, 19–22, 34–47.

———. "Tzintlan Popokatepetl" ("Junto a la montaña humeante"). *Aquí se trae la palabra: Poemas de escritores nahuas de Hueyapan.* Serie 1. Ed. Norma Zamarrón de León. Cuernavaca: CONACULTA, 2004, 16–17, 32–33.

Vásquez de Knauth, Josefina. *Nacionalismo y educación en México.* Mexico City: Centro de Estudios Históricos, El Colegio de México, Nueva Serie 9, 1970.

Vázquez León, Luis. *Ser indio otra vez: la purepechización de los tarascos serranos.* Mexico City: CONACULTA, 1992.

Velasco Cruz, Saúl. *El movimiento indígena y la autonomía en México.* Mexico City: Universidad Autónoma de México and Universidad Pedgógica Nacional, 2003.

Warman, Arturo Gryj. *La Danza de Moros y Cristianos, un estudio de aculturación.* Mexico City: Escuela Nacional de Antropología y Historia, 1968.

———. *We Come to Object: The Peasants of Morelos and the National State.* Baltimore: Johns Hopkins University Press, 1976.

Warman, Arturo, Guillermo Bonfil, Margarita Nolasco, Mercedes Olivera, and Enrique Valencia. Eds. *De eso que llaman antropología mexicana.* Mexico City: Editorial Nuestro Tiempo, 1970.

Warren, Kay. *Indigenous Movements and their Critics: Pan-Maya Activism in Guatemala.* Princeton: Princeton University Press, 1998.

Weaver, Thomas, Ed. *To See Ourselves: Anthropology and Modern Social Issues.* Glenview: Scott, Foresman, 1973.

Weckmann, Luis. *The Medieval Heritage of Mexico.* Trans. Frances M. López-Morillas. New York: Fordham University Press, 1992.

Wolf, Eric. "Virgin of Guadalupe: A Mexican National Symbol." *Journal of American Folklore.* 71 (1958):34–39.

———. *Sons of the Shaking Earth.* Chicago:University of Chicago Press, 1959.

Womack, John. *Zapata and the Mexican Revolution.* New York: Knopf, 1970.

———. Ed. *Rebellion in Chiapas: An Historical Reader.* New York: The New Press, 1999.

Zamarrón de León, Norma. Ed. *Aquí se trae la palabra: Poemas de escritores nahuas de Hueyapan.* Serie Palabras Infinitas. Cuernavaca: CONACULTA, 2004.

———. Ed. *Nuevo Canto Florido de Morelos: Reunión de relatos y poemas en lengua náhuatl.* Serie Palabras Infinitas. 3. Cuernavaca: CONACULTA, 2004.

———. Ed. *¿Ustedes que saben? Testimonios y relatos nahuas.* Serie Palabras Infinitas. Serie 2. Cuernavaca: CONACULTA, 2004.

INDEX

CPSIA information can be obtained
at www.ICGtesting.com
Printed in the USA
LVHW080152300722
724710LV00020B/1382